TAMING THE CRIMINAL

PATTERSON SMITH REPRINT SERIES IN
CRIMINOLOGY, LAW ENFORCEMENT, AND SOCIAL PROBLEMS

A listing of publications in the SERIES *will be found at rear of volume*

ADJUTANT DIRECTOR DELIERNEUX AND THE AUTHOR
AT MERXPLAS

PUBLICATION No. 71: PATTERSON SMITH REPRINT SERIES IN
CRIMINOLOGY, LAW ENFORCEMENT, AND SOCIAL PROBLEMS

TAMING THE CRIMINAL

Adventures In Penology

BY

JOHN LEWIS GILLIN, Ph.D.

Professor of Sociology in the University of Wisconsin

ILLUSTRATED

Montclair, New Jersey

PATTERSON SMITH

1969

SBN 87585-071-5

Library of Congress Catalog Card Number: 69-14927

PREFACE

CRIME is often said to be an adventure. No less so, although in another sense, are new ways of dealing with criminals an adventure. Experiments in dealing with law-breakers in the same sense as life itself are adventures. He who tries new ways with the criminal is an adventurer into the unknown.

The writer spent the year 1927–1928 visiting various countries around the world. He gave particular attention to the prison systems of these countries. His special quest was unusual methods in handling prisoners. He hoped that he might discover in these far countries new methods developed from original starting points free from the hampering leading-strings of older models, or fresh departures from old models, which would have the value of new inventions in penology. In spite of rather close reading of available material from all parts of the world, he was astonished at two conditions which revealed themselves as he travelled and studied: (1) how the world round the prison systems have been influenced by English and American precedents, and (2) how many adventures have actually been made by other peoples on the basis of the old models. Some of these experiments seemed significant enough to bear reporting to the English-reading public. There is all too little in English print about them. Some of them are original attempts to solve the problem of handling those who, "in the clutch of circumstance," have fallen into the hands of the law.

While the writer examined the penal and correctional systems of many countries, only those of Japan, the Philippine Islands, Ceylon, India, Switzerland, Belgium, England, and some of the Southern United States seemed to provide suggestions of great originality and value. Here and there some man or group of men have ventured an uncharted sea. Their experiments have all the venturesomeness of those hardy explorers who devised methods of conquering stubborn Nature and wresting from her her age-long secrets. They have plunged into the vast wildernesses of human nature and of social organization and have ventured on novel courses of handling criminals. They are adventurers in the true sense of the word.

The Social Science Research Council of the United States made possible this study. That organization should have credit for the faith it showed in this attempt of the writer to study, firsthand, these little-known experiments, especially in the Orient. That organization is not responsible for what the author reports. Neither are the many prison officials who gave ungrudgingly of their time and energy to enable a foreigner to see their institutions and to learn about their ideals and methods. Both, however, deserve this acknowledgment of deep indebtedness. Everywhere the greatest courtesy was extended. While perhaps this study cannot be described as "social research" in the strict sense of the term, it may be called an investigation which makes available knowledge not accessible to those who read English only.

For centuries organized society has been struggling with the problem of the control of the criminal. Only recently has it attempted to understand him. Hitherto, for the most part, it has not appreciated that he is a product of society's failure to help him during his formative years to organize his life in accordance with the standards of conduct approved by the group. To his despairing cry, "Thou hast made me what I am. Do with me as thou wilt," society has responded only with punishment or death. In words and action, society has said, "Thou hast a free will. Thou hast chosen to transgress. Suffer the consequences." Here and there in the last hundred years certain leaders have said, "No matter what the explanation of the criminal's act, most of them will go out of prison into society. Should not prison attempt to prepare them to be better citizens than before? Therefore we should attempt to re-train the criminal." That was an adventure in penology. Prison officials and law-makers have often forgotten the high spirit of that adventure; most people have never even glimpsed it. To them it is the idle dream of some sentimentalist. Here and there, however, it has been written into the penal law. Around the world the light has spread. In attempting to realize the dream of making bad men good, leaders in different lands have tried various methods. The following chapters describe some of these new adventures.

CONTENTS

ILLUSTRATIONS

TAMING THE CRIMINAL

TAMING THE CRIMINAL

CHAPTER I

JAPANESE PENAL INSTITUTIONS

WE were drinking tea in her cozy living-room. The hostess, Miss Caroline MacDonald, is the head of a social settlement in a part of Tokyo, Japan, where many poor people live. "Miss MacDonald," I said, "I wish to visit some of the prisons and other penal and correctional institutions of Japan. Do you know how I can get access to them?"

"Very easily," she said, "I know the Minister of Justice; many of the discharged prisoners are put on parole to me, and I shall be glad to go with you and see the minister and get passes for you." Naturally, I was delighted.

"When can we go?" I asked. She replied, "I will make arrangements this afternoon and will let you know. In the meantime," she said, "I wish to show you the original manuscript of a very interesting book written by a prisoner who was executed in one of our prisons. I have published this as a book and have called it 'A Gentleman in Prison'." My mind recalled the book. I had read it before I had left the United States. I remembered it as a very vivid description of life in one of the Japanese prisons. She brought out the old manuscript printed with a brush by this Japanese prisoner.

The next evening, in a rain and fog, Miss MacDonald and I went in a taxi to call on the Minister of Justice, Mr. Motoji. The passes were easily procured, but in the course of the conversation a hitch developed. Since most of the Japanese prison wardens cannot talk English, I needed an interpreter. Miss MacDonald asked for a pass for herself as my interpreter. The Minister of Justice reminded her that women were not allowed in Japanese prisons for men. She cannily replied, "But I am

1

not going as a woman. I am going as this gentleman's interpreter."

Laughingly he replied, "You American women always know how to get what you want." He issued the pass.

The next day, armed with these passes, Miss MacDonald and I proceeded to Kosugae Prison. This is the old Japanese prison which was shaken down by the earthquake and from which not a prisoner tried to escape because of respect for the warden then in charge, Mr. Arima. Mr. Arima had been transferred to the other large prison in Tokyo which was visited a day or two later. Mr. K. Ono was then the governor or warden at Kosugae Prison.

We were presented to a stout Japanese gentleman, who, after the usual formalities, took us about the prison.

Perhaps a word ought to be said about the usual formalities in Japan which precede any piece of important business. It was a cold, chilly day. There was no heat in the prison for the prisoners. In the warden's office there was only a brazier with sand in it in which were a few pieces of glowing charcoal. Over this brazier a person warms his hands, which is supposed to be the only part of his body which gets cold. One of the prison attendants was at once sent for tea. Soon steaming cups of tea, unsweetened and without any cream or lemon, appeared. Two cups of this hot tea were drunk as Miss MacDonald explained to the warden my purpose in visiting the prison. No matter how cold it is when one calls upon an official, he must remove his overcoat and his hat. In this respect, ladies have the advantage.

These formalities completed, Warden Ono kindly piloted us about the prison. At the time I visited it most of the work was that of reconstruction. Great cell houses were being built, shops were being constructed, and various other buildings were under way. Mr. Ono explained that the entire prison had to be rebuilt. However, in addition to these construction activities, certain temporary shops were occupied and different articles were being made by the prisoners, chiefly by hand.

In this prison there were 1087 inmates. The year previous

at the same time there were 1126. 350 of these men were in for theft, 357 for robbery, 249 for homicide, 73 for incendiarism, 14 for obscenity and adultery, a few were in for fraud, counterfeiting coins, counterfeiting documents, injuries, and disturbance. 110 of these men were in for life, 97 for terms of over fifteen years, 611 for terms of under fifteen years, 235 under ten years, 21 under five years, 10 under three years, and 3 under one year. Moreover, 384 of them were first offenders, 703 repeaters. Of the repeaters, 93 had been convicted a second time, 80 three times, 86 four times, 313 five times, and 184 ten times.

Moreover, the ages of these men are very much higher than they are in the United States. Only 2 were under twenty years of age, 23 were twenty-three years of age or under, 154 were over twenty-three, 331 were over thirty, 337 over forty, 191 over fifty, 46 over sixty, and 3 past seventy. 37 of them were in solitary confinement, 8 were alone at night, 1011 lived together, and 31 of them were in a small ward. 1068 of these men were at work.

I talked with the chaplain, a Buddhist priest, about some of these men. All of you who have read Lafcadio Hearn's books on Japan will remember the self-control which he describes as characteristic of the Japanese people. Anyone who has been in Japan will recognize the truth of that statement. The only brawlers I saw in Japan were drunken men.

Against this background of self-control, of courtesy, of affability among the people and the natural beauty of Japan stands out the grim tragedy of these lives. From the above statement it will be seen that they commit much the same crimes as are committed in our country.

As we went about this prison guided by the warden we saw these little Japanese working as we would see Americans in this country. However, the aspect was entirely different except for the closely cropped heads. The clothing of most of these men was of a red color; since they have no fire in the building they wear thickly padded clothing. Upon the front of each was a cloth insignia signifying the crime for which he was committed, the time which he had to serve, whether he was a first offender or a repeater, and various other matters regarding his status, especially as to whether he was under punishment or had made progress in prison life.

In conversation with the warden and the Buddhist chaplain, the stories of some of these men came out in brief outline. Of the two hundred and forty-nine murderers, as with us, some had killed out of passion. Here was one, a youth in whose eyes gleamed a sullen fire, who had murdered his mistress because he thought her unfaithful to him. Yonder was a man, with the insignia on his breast of good conduct over many years, who had killed his wife because she had been discourteous to his old mother. Many of them were guilty of murder because their intended victims of robbery had resisted, and here were others who in a drinking bout had fallen upon their fellows and done them to death.

In the afternoon we went to visit the other prison which was not so completely ruined by the earthquake and at the head of which is this old man who for fifty years has been in the prison service, Mr. Arima. Most of the Japanese officials are either Buddhists or Shintoists. Mr. Arima is a Christian. He is a typical Japanese gentleman now nearing seventy years of age. A gray mustache adorns his upper lip; his high cheekbones stand out beneath his glowing black eyes. He received us with all the courtesy of which the Japanese are capable; in meeting Miss MacDonald, he greeted her as an old friend. Here, also, after the usual formalities, he took us about the prison so we might see the ordinary routine of a prison where the usual activities were in operation. Here were the same red clothing, the same insignia. However, we had a chance to see some of the men who are in confinement. When men are first brought in, they are usually put in solitary confinement, not as we think of the term, in a dark cell, but in a small room by themselves, where they are given some work to do, perhaps something to read, and the prison officials visit them often in order to ascertain as much as possible about them and their attitude toward life. Mr. Arima said his purpose in having these men put apart was in order to understand them better so as to know how to deal with them. About the shops we went, the officials and prisoners everywhere giving the utmost respect to this man who was over them. This is the man who was in charge of Kosugae Prison when it was shaken down by the earthquake. It was at night, and many of the men were killed and others were injured, yet not a man attempted to escape. Why? Mr. Arima had treated them in such a way that they felt that, if they tried to escape, he, himself, would suffer the consequence. Yet for weeks in broken parts of the buildings and in tents these men lived without any guards other than their own officers, not one trying to escape because of their respect for this grand old man.

I asked Mr. Arima how he accounted for such control over his men. He replied, "You perhaps know that I am a Christian. I see in every man potentialities for good, and I try to treat him not as a prisoner but as a man. If he has grievances I listen to them; if possible I correct them. I try to be friends to these men; I try to show them the error of their ways if they have not already seen it; I try to help them to go out of the prison to lead an honest life."

I asked him, "Do you preach to them the Christian religion?"

After this had been interpreted to him, with a slow, hesitant manner he said, "No, I try to live it." The solemn benignity of his bearing, his sense of justice, his endeavor to understand, his efforts to help the men, both in the prison and when they go out, through these fifty years have wrought results testified to by the men who write back to him and consult him upon important matters in their life's affairs. Miss MacDonald says that she very rarely has trouble with men from his institution. They come to her, but they come because they know she is a friend to help them. She testifies that in Mr. Arima she always finds a sympathetic and helpful attitude toward the men discharged from this institution. He is one of the highest types of prison officials I have seen anywhere in the world. In spite of the fact that we could not converse directly, but only through an interpreter, I could see the wisdom characteristic of his dealing with the officers and men as we went about. When he stopped to speak to a man his attitude was not condescending but that of a friend, yet over all was the dignified Japanese bearing and the spirit of a fine character that made its impression upon these men.

JAPAN'S PRISON SYSTEM[1]

FOR sixty years Japan has been going to school to the Western world. In nothing is this more apparent than in her prison system. Under the leadership of her great Meiji Emperor and his advisers commission after commission was sent to Europe and America to study Western ways of doing things. They came back and the government put into operation what they had learned. The prison law is dated the 27th day of the third month of the 41st year of Meiji. Japan has followed the English system rather than the American, although certain features of the American system have been adopted.

In the Japanese system there are four kinds of prisons: (1) The prison for penal servitude; (2) the prison for imprisonment; (3) the house of detention; and (4) the prison for confinement. The first is for those who under the law are sentenced to penal servitude, much as in the English system. The second is for those guilty of less serious offenses who are sentenced to imprisonment. The third is for still less serious offenders who are sentenced under the law to detention. The fourth is intended for the confinement of accused persons awaiting trial, and for those under sentence of death. Also in the fourth may be confined temporarily those sentenced to any of the first three kinds of prisons. In a "house of custody" attached to a police station, persons sentenced to penal servitude or imprisonment may not be kept more than a month.

For youthful offenders under eighteen years of age special institutions are provided, if they have been sentenced to penal

[1] The substance of this part of the chapter was published in *Social Forces*, Vol. VII, No. 2, December, 1928.

servitude for two months or more, or in case such special
institutions have not yet been built, they must be confined
in a special part of another prison carefully separated from
older criminals. In such institutions or special departments
they may be kept until they are twenty years old, or for the
remainder of their sentences, if the sentences expire only three
months after they have arrived at the age of twenty. Exceptions to the application of this rule may be made in case it
seems necessary to do so, "having regard to the state, or the
mental and physical development of the offenders."

In every prison there must be provision for the separate
confinement of male and female offenders. Moreover, in
case that one of each of the four classes of prisons is located
in the same precinct, they must be separate institutions.

Visitation of the prisons must be provided by the Minister
of Justice. Judges and public procurators, or what we call
public prosecutors, may visit any of the prisons. Other persons who desire to visit the prisons for scientific purposes must
get special permission to do so from the Minister of Justice.
Only males may visit the male departments and only females the female departments of prisons, except by special
permission of the Minister of Justice. Exception is seldom
made, it was told me, when I successfully applied to have Miss
MacDonald go with me as my official interpreter. No minor
is permitted to visit a prison. In these matters Japan, like
England and France, has discarded Jeremy Bentham's theory
of the exemplarity of punishment. She has followed the
United States in the separate treatment of the young offenders
and has carried further the principle of classification to be
found in Europe.

Provision is made for complaints by prisoners against any
prison official. If these are sealed, no prison official may
open them but must forward them to the Minister of Justice.
In case the prisoner complains to an inspector, no prison official
may be present.

The head of the prison is called, as in England, a governor.
He must provide once or more a week a certain time when

prisoners may see him about prison treatment or about his own personal affairs. Records of these interviews must be kept by the governor of the prison. He has control of all the guards and others who have immediate charge of the prisoners. Upon him, as with us, depends the character of the prison.

The law provides that "a house of work" shall be attached to every prison. In spite of the quaintness of the language the meaning is clear to anyone who visits the prisons, that provision must be made for workshops in which the men may be employed. I found these in every prison I visited, except in those which had been shaken down by the earthquake, where the prisoners were engaged in rebuilding, and even here workshops were a part of the plant under construction.

None of these provisions applies to the military or naval prisons. They are governed under different statutes.

ADMISSION OF PRISONERS

The documents usually accompanying the prisoner when he arrives at a prison in the United States are provided for in the prison law of Japan. The person of the incoming prisoner may be examined by the governor of the prison, and the prison physician must examine him to determine whether he have any contagious disease. When in connection with the prison there is an isolation ward or hospital, the infected prisoner must be kept there until he recovers. If there is none, he may be removed to such an institution outside the prison. The governor may have a photograph taken of the prisoner. Since, however, the police are supposed to have a record of all identifying data, this is not often required. There are detailed provisions regarding the records to be kept at the prison concerning each prisoner. I saw these in a number of institutions. They are rather more detailed than those kept in most of our American prisons.

There is one rather peculiar provision concerning women prisoners. If the woman has a child, it may live with her until it is a year old if no other method of caring for it can be found. Then it must be given into the care of the civil authorities in the place where the prison is located. I am told that usually a proper guardian can be found for it outside the prison. The same rule applies to a child born in a prison. Care is taken that a woman warden examine and bathe a woman prisoner. This may seem strange when one remembers that in many parts of Japan men and women bathe together, and even in such cities as Tokio and Kyoto, the public bath houses, while having separate sides for the two sexes, are so arranged that a person entering may see into either side. Evidently this rule is intended to prevent abuse in the prison.

While nothing is said in the printed laws or in the published regulations about separate provisions for the sexes, I learned that in actual practice the two sexes are confined in different parts of the same prison. However, Japan has not gone as far in provisions for the care of women delinquents as has the United States or the European nations. Possibly the explanation is that there are very few Japanese women criminals.

CLASSIFICATION OF PRISONERS

Japan has attempted to carry out a very refined classification of prisoners.

A prisoner committed for the first time may be kept in solitary confinement for three days. During those three days a study shall be made of him on the basis of which he shall be classified according to character, physical and mental condition. During those three days the prison record of the man must be made up. Moreover, any prisoner may be sent into solitary confinement, except such as are deemed unfit for such treatment by reason of their physical or mental condition. Whether they shall be placed in solitary confinement depends upon the judgment of the prison governor. Evidently this is suggested by the English practice of "probationary" solitary confinement on commitment.

The law very definitely states that "In any case of associate confinement, different prisoners shall be kept in different cells, being clearly distinguished from each other according to their nature, with due attention to the nature of crimes, personal character, number of convictions, and age." As already noticed, all youths under eighteen years sentenced to penal servitude of two months or more, must be kept in a special institution or in a part of the prison definitely set apart for them. Others under eighteen must be kept in separate cells carefully separated from any of the same age or upwards. The prison regulations have ordered this matter of solitary confinement in greater detail. The order of preference in sending different classes to solitary confinement, or what we should historically consider "separate confinement" is as follows: (1) Any prisoners sentenced to two months or less; (2) any prisoners under the age of twenty-five; (3) first offenders; (4) those who have not yet served the first two months of their sentences. It is also provided that separate confinement should be given those who while under sentence are standing trial for another offence, or for an offence committed during imprisonment, if the cells can be found, and if it is not injurious to his healt , mental or physical. Particular attention is given either in the law or in the regulations that two prisoners who have been convicted of a joint crime should not be allowed to associate in prison, either in the cells or outside. While the law allows the congregation of prisoners of all classes for purposes of medical examinations or religious services, it urges that different times be used for different classes, and provides for box seats for each man in the assembly halls as in France, so that communication between men sitting side by side is difficult. Provision is made that if it is impossible to keep the classes named apart during the day in workshop or congregate cell, solitary cells for them should, if possible, be provided for night. Thus, Japan has tried to apply separate confinement to prevent corruption in accordance with the ancient Pennsylvania system, but modified by the more recent experience of England and France. More rigorously than in England Japan applies the "separate system" for these classes.

Save in exceptional cases, no prisoner can be kept in separate confinement more than two years at a time. In the exceptional cases, extension is for only six months at a time. If the prisoner is under eighteen years of age he cannot be kept in separate confinement without interruption more than six months. Any man in separate confinement must be examined every thirty days by the governor and medical officer, and by other prison officials at frequent intervals during the day. No man can be sent to separate confinement if it appears to be injurious to mental or bodily health.

In actual practice Japan is making strenuous efforts to carry out the separate confinement plan. In the new prison being built in Tokyo on the ruins of the old one destroyed by the earthquake even in the assembly hall two separate divisions are provided opening upon the same stage. But the dividing wall effectually cuts off from view the prisoners on the other side of the partition. In the law as well as in actual practice she has a great many congregate cells for three or more prisoners. She has not been able to build fast enough to carry out this plan of classification perfectly. However, the prison officials to whom I talked think it works very well.

She has built a large number of different institutions in the endeavor to provide the classifications contemplated in her law. For example the prison at Odawara is for first offenders from eighteen to twenty-three years of age. The two in Tokyo are intended for different classes of prisoners. So, scattered over the Empire are various classes of institutions intended to carry out treatment by classes of prisoners. In spite of a hundred years of experiment in the classification of delinquents it is still a moot question whether classification is worth all the money it costs to carry it out properly. One wonders whether better returns for the money would not be obtained by putting in superior officers and teachers of prisoners. However, something can be said for the scheme. Its value must wait upon careful study of the results.

DISCIPLINE

What the Japanese law describes as "Defence and Protection" pertains to measures to be taken to control unruly prisoners. The law tries to prevent the physical abuse of prisoners by officers by providing that "a sword or firearm which the prison officer carries with him under Law, Ordinance, or Order may be used against any prisoner" only in four sets of circumstances: (1) When a prisoner is dangerously committing or threatening to commit bodily violence; (2) when a prisoner carrying an offensive instrument sufficient to commit a dangerous act, does not comply with a direction to give it up; (3) when any prisoners are gathering together and raising a disturbance with intent to escape; and (4) when a prisoner who has attempted to run away from prison is attempting to escape arrest, or to run away without submitting to a quieting order.   In spite of the quaint language of the English translation, it is apparent that the Japanese have tried to prevent those abuses which have been revealed in American and English prisons.   The regulations in the matter provide for the use of certain restraints which are not now used in the best American prisons.   Five kinds of restraint are permitted under these regulations: (1) strait-jacket; (2) fetters; (3) handcuffs; (4) chains; and (5) ropes. None of these may be used without express order of the prison governor.   The strait-jacket must not be used in escorting prisoners, and can only be applied to those who threaten to commit violence.   It must not be used for more than six hours at a time.   I saw no prisoners wearing the waistcoat, and was assured by the prison officials that it is seldom used. The fetters, *i.e.*, anklets fastened together with a short chain, I saw frequently enough to show that in some prisons they are used rather freely.   The regulations provide that they are to be used only for the prisoners who try to commit violence or to escape.   A chain to which two iron balls are attached is run through the fetters and then wound around the waist and locked under the girdle.   This is a medieval device which is generally condemned in Western countries.   The handcuffs and ropes are to be used for prisoners under escort or threatening to escape or commit suicide or violence.   The chain is used to tie two prisoners together by binding it around the waist of each and locking it under the girdle and is used only for prisoners working outside the prison and then only in case of necessity. However, in one of the prisons I saw a number of prisoners inside the prison chained together, but not to anything like the extent I observed in the Chinese prison in the International Concession in Shanghai, China. Fetters, as well as the strait-jacket, are not to be used in escorting prisoners. And in case a gun or sword has been used against a prisoner it must at once be reported to the Minister of Justice. One wonders that these measures condemned by experience in America are still retained in use in progressive Japan. However, they are in general use in the Orient.

A very interesting provision in the law relates to measures to be taken in case of "a calamity suddenly caused by nature or casualty." This law is framed in view of Japan's frequent earthquakes. In such an event the prisoners may be transferred to another prison, or in case that is impossible, they may be set free with the express understanding that they are to appear within twenty-four hours at a police station and give themselves up. In case they do not surrender themselves, they are subject to severe punishment. Any prisoners who help the officers in case of such calamity are entitled to the same pecuniary rewards as those who have been injured or fallen sick while at work in prison industry. My visit was early enough after the great earthquake of 1924 to enable me to ascertain how this provision worked. Interestingly the walls of one of the Tokyo prisons were almost entirely destroyed, and the cell houses were disrupted, many prisoners perishing in the catastrophe. At the head of this prison was Mr. Arima, whom I have described above. As soon as possible after the quake, the chief of staff of the army sent a regiment of soldiers to surround this prison and guard the prisoners. The prison governor tried to get the officer in charge of the regiment to withdraw the troops, assuring him that if they were withdrawn, his prisoners would not escape, but the officer replied that he had been sent by the chief of staff and could not withdraw without his express command. Fire and smoke prevented direct approach from the prison to the army headquarters. The warden went far around until he was finally able to reach the army official and repeated his request to him that he withdraw the troops, saying that, unless they were withdrawn, he could not be responsible for the results, but promising to be responsible with his life for every one of his prisoners, if the troops were withdrawn. After some argument the army officer acceded to his request and withdrew the troops. Although months passed with the prisoners camped on the ruins of their prison, not a man escaped. At Yokohama, where the prison walls and cells were destroyed, only 14 of the 500 men who were released under the terms of this law did not give themselves up.

One wonders whether, with such an attitude toward law, the present stringent measures described above are necessary in Japan.

PRISON LABOR IN JAPAN

Japan's penal law provides for industrial work for the prisoners. In imposing industrial work on prisoners, consideration is given to the sanitary condition and the general economy of the prison. Also regard must be had for the length of penalty imposed, the health, ability, former occupation, and the future prospects. These general statements of the law are amplified by the prison regulations. In imposing industrial work upon prisoners under eighteen years of age the proper education of the prisoners must be kept in mind in addition to the above named considerations, an enlightened provision in full accord with Japan's emphasis upon education. Prisoners are not allowed to work on government holidays and the thirty-first day of December and the first two days of January; these are the Japanese New Year days. Any prisoner whose father or mother has died shall not work for three days.

The working hours, the kind of work each prisoner shall do is determined by the governor with the consent of the Minister of Justice. The stint to be required of each prisoner is the standard amount in free life, or may be a modification of this amount according to the capacity of the prisoners, or as fixed by the Minister of Justice. This amount may be varied in

Front View

Hospital

Building for Epileptic Patients

Interior View,
Separate Cells

Mr. Shirosuke Arima,
Governor

KOSUGE PRISON, TOKIO

Factory Building

Interior View, Factory

Spinning and Washing Shop

KOSUGE PRISON, TOKIO

the case of decrepit, unsound, or disabled persons, and for persons under eighteen years of age. However, a person who has finished his stint for the day must work on during the fixed working hours, a provision, one would think, not calculated to the development of all one's powers. When a prisoner has once chosen a particular kind of work, which he may do within limits, he may not change that work without good reason.

While all the income from the work of the prisoners goes into the national treasury, provision is made that under administrative order prisoners may receive a reward or *pécule*, as the French call it, according to ability and good conduct. Here we have a kind of wage for prisoners.

Contract work in the prisons is allowed with the consent of the Minister of Justice. No prisoner is allowed to work outside the prison except those who have spent three months of their sentence in the prison. Prisoners with a six months' sentence are not allowed to work outside. Those under eighteen are also exempt from these requirements.

In calculating the prisoner's wage, consideration is given to the amount he has produced, his conduct in the prison, and from that amount is deducted the value of any damage he may have caused to tools, goods, and materials from malice or wilful neglect. For the following persons such reward shall not be calculated and given: (1) Inmates who have not finished the first five months of their imprisonment since the second month of their committal; (2) persons who are in the month of their release; (3) inmates who have bad conduct records and a poor industrial record. For those who have been at work less than fifteen days no reward is computed. Those prisoners who are engaged in kitchen work or other domestic work in the prison, or who are engaged in other services necessary to the economical administration of the prison, and who may not be allowed the usual holidays and cessation from work for other reasons stated above, may be given an amount in excess of that allowed other prisoners.

The prison may impose conditions as to the way in which money is spent by the prisoners. In general, however, the wage earned is not supposed to be given the prisoner until he is released from prison. But, in case of those prisoners who are entitled to ten yen a month or more, and if the money is needed to support father, mother, wife, or child, or to compensate the sufferer for his crime, or to purchase books or other necessary articles, one-third of the amount may be given him while in confinement. Even the entire wage may be delivered him in case of especially urgent circumstances. Even an accused person awaiting trial in the prison may earn a wage and be given it under the same circumstances as a prisoner. In case the address of an escaped convict is not known for six months after his release any money coming to him under this scheme is cancelled back into the treasury.

Another interesting feature of the prison law of Japan is the provision that any prisoner who has been injured or has fallen sick while at work, and has died in consequence or has become unable to carry on any business, may be entitled to a pecuniary reward according to the circumstances of the case. Such money reward shall be granted to the prisoner at the time of his discharge from prison, or, in the case of his death, to his father, mother, wife, or child.

MORAL INSTRUCTION AND EDUCATION OF PRISONERS

All prisoners under eighteen years of age must be, and any others may be, given an education in prison. Even accused awaiting trial may, if they apply for it, be given the usual educational privileges. Those under eighteen must be given education in morals, reading, arithmetic, writing, or other necessary subjects in accordance with the primary school course of the Japanese school system not exceeding four hours per day. For those who have finished the primary school course, and for those in the same subjects as those who have graduated from the primary school, supplementary education shall be given for any term not exceeding two hours per day.

Moral instruction is to be given on Sundays or holidays or at other times at the discretion of the prison governor. This moral instruction is to be given to accused persons and prisoners in solitary confinement or in the infirmary. In the Japanese prisons any one who has received information of the death of father or mother is taken to solitary confinement, and must there be given instruction every day. If he requests it, a service must be held in behalf of his deceased parent. Instruction is to be given to those persons who have had relations with a deceased prisoner, the instruction taking place in front of the coffin.

When amnesty has been pronounced, as is often the case when a member of the royal family dies, when a man is discharged on trial, when provisional release is granted, or when a statement of a reward to a prisoner is made, instruction is to be given after calling together the whole or a part of the prisoners in the institution at the place where the ceremony is held.

Prisoners are to be permitted to read, look at maps or pictures, unless it is injurious to the good order of the prison. However, where prisoners are taken to associate confinement, not more than three volumes at a time, plus a dictionary, are allowed. But newspapers or writings concerning current topics are forbidden. Prisoners in solitary confinement may or may not, in the judgment of the prison authorities, be given ink, pen, and paper purchased at their own expense.

In accordance with these provisions, I saw a number of the Japanese prison classes being held in not only the primary subjects but also in subjects of practical value in preparing them for a trade. Buddhist chaplains are to be found in the prisons whose business it is to give moral instruction both by services and by private conference. Once Christian ministers were permitted to be prison chaplains, but recently only Buddhists have been permitted as regular chaplains, although Christian ministers are allowed to go into the prison at the request of prisoners to confer with Christians.

FOOD, CLOTHING, AND BEDDING

The prison law of Japan provides that "prisoners under sentence shall be furnished with some fixed prison garments and bedclothes; but any prisoners who have been sentenced to detention may be allowed to wear their own dress, and other prisoners may be allowed to wear undergarments at their own expense." Accused persons in prison and all other prisoners, except those described above—that is, those sentenced to "a house of work"—must provide garments and bedding at their own expense. If they are unable to do so, the prison is to lend them these necessary articles.

The regulations which have been made in applying this law go into great detail. The list shows that the articles to be supplied are the bare necessities. It is interesting to note, however, that among them is a toothbrush for each prisoner, and toothpaste or common salt. In addition to the ordinary garments there must be provided for those engaged in work a set of working garments. The governor with the permission of the Minister of Justice may extend the list of miscellaneous articles furnished to the prisoners according to the necessities of the case.

One who visits the Japanese prisons notes the dark red garments worn by most prisoners and the blue ones worn by others. The regulations explain these variations. They prescribe that the garments worn by prisoners under sentence are to be dark red. The blue ones are those lent to indigent prisoners, those supplied to persons sentenced to a workhouse, and the garments for prisoners under eighteen years of age.

The garments and bedclothes furnished by the prisoners themselves are limited to those fitted to the season and which do not interfere with the health and order of the prison. Moreover, the governor of the prison is given authority to regulate the kind and number of garments which a prisoner may furnish himself. Those furnished by the prisoners must be kept mended and washed by the prisoners at their own expense.

As I observed the garments and bedding, it seemed to me that the quantity and quality were adequate. The thickly padded cloaks and the quilts look awkward, but since no heat is supplied in Japanese prisons, such garments are necessary in winter to prevent suffering.

As to food, the law requires that "A necessary quantity of food and water shall be allotted to each prisoner, taking into consideration his constitution, health, age, and the kind of work he is doing." Persons awaiting trial are allowed to provide food for themselves.

The kind and quantity of food set down in the regulations are of interest. Each prisoner is allowed for each meal about a pint of "meshi," or main part of the meal. This is made up of two-fifths cleaned rice of an inferior quality and of three-fifths barley. For a side dish the governor may spend not more than five sen (*i.e.* 2½ cents) per day for each prisoner. The governor may change both the kind and quantity of provisions in special circumstances, such as difference in local conditions, health considerations, or fluctuations of price, with the consent of the Minister of Justice. The usual drink is hot water, which in special circumstances may be changed by the governor to tea or wheat water. No alcoholic drink or tobacco is allowed.

While this seems like a very meager ration, it is, in fact, about what the ordinary Japanese coolie requires, except that the latter often has tea. I noticed that in some of the institutions I visited the governor modified this ration by giving certain prisoners working at hard manual labor a small piece of fish in addition. That the ordinary ration is too little and too monotonous is contended by many people with whom I talked. I saw the meal of my ricksha man one day at Nara. It was merely a bowl of rice with a small fish on top. However, he topped it off with about half a pint of *sake,* or, as he called it for my benefit, sweet wine. That his ordinary meal did not satisfy that particular coolie was evidenced by the fact that he ate what was left of my meal, which was at least twice as much as he had had of his own. When I asked some of the prison authorities about this meager ration, they said that they would not dare to give more, else many people outside would want to get into prison in order to get more and better food. As I remember, I have heard something like that among us about people breaking into prison in order to get a house over their heads, food, moving pictures, baths, etc.   It has a strangely familiar sound.   It may be true in a country with such a low food standard for the coolie class.

Authority is given the governor to control the sale of goods to those within the prison.   The prison doctor is required to examine all provisions bought by the prisoners.   All food "self-bought," as the regulations style that provided by the prisoners themselves, must be eaten in the usual place by those who live in dormitories.   Those in solitary confinement, of course, eat it in their cells.

HEALTH AND MEDICAL TREATMENT

As one goes into the prisons of Japan he notices the closely clipped heads of the inmates.   The prison law provides for that.   Accused persons need not have their heads clipped, unless it is necessary for the health and cleanliness of the institution.   Sentenced prisoners must be shaved at least every ten days.   Prisoners must keep their own cells and dormitories clean.

Exercise is provided for all classes of prisoners.   The prisoners are exercised in the open air at least thirty minutes, except in rainy weather and under exceptional circumstances.   This period may be extended to an hour.   Gymnastic exercises may be used instead of just walking about in a circle.   In the case of working prisoners, daily exercise of the artificial variety is not required in some prisons.

According to the regulations, baths must be taken once or more every five days during the months from June to September, and once in seven days the rest of the year.   The governor may require a bath oftener according to the kind of work in which the prisoner is engaged.   I was interested to see the provisions for bathing in the new prison being built on the ruins of the one in Tokyo shaken down by the earthquake. In this prison, in the solitary cells, each had its own bathtub and its own toilet.   The associate cells have adjoining them a sufficient number of bathtubs to take adequate care of their inmates.   One familiar with the outbursts of certain people in this country against the "luxuries" provided by some of our states in the prisons, may imagine that an outcry will be made in Japan against these comfortable provisions. However, in Japan, the hot bath is looked upon as a necessity. In Japan the bathtubs are of a somewhat different form from ours. They are shaped very much like a half barrel. Instead of sitting down in them or reclining, therefore, it is necessary to squat down in them. Moreover, since the Japanese have very little heat in their houses, the hot bath in winter time is a means of getting warm. Therefore it is probable that the provisions for bathing are such commonplace matters in Japan that no outcry against these provisions on the ground of luxury will be made. Some of the old prisons, however, have very inadequate provisions for bathing and toilets. The bucket system and even the open latrine are still to be seen in some of them.

There is a surgeon provided in each prison, and some kind of infirmary in most. The law and the regulations are very strict about disease. The whole matter is complicated by the attempted classification and separation of the various classes in the prisons. Thus, it is provided that a man in solitary confinement shall be treated in his cell, unless it is necessary to take him to the infirmary, when he must, if possible, be confined in a solitary cell in the infirmary. Moreover, any person under eighteen needing medical treatment, whether in solitary confinement or not, must be kept separate from others and must have separate hours for treatment. Obviously this rule complicates matters for the prison authorities.

Anyone under eighteen in solitary confinement must be examined by the doctor once in every thirty days. Others, excepting those sentenced to associate confinement for more than a year, who must be examined once every six months, must be inspected at least once every three months. Strict provisions for isolation of contagious patients are laid down both in the law and in the regulations. They are to be isolated for a week if they come from a place in which there is contagious disease. They may be inoculated against such diseases. Insane persons and even sick persons for whom there is inadequate provision for treatment in the prison may be temporarily removed to a hospital. A prison officer is to make an inspection of the hospital every day. In the case of women in child-bed, the governor may employ a midwife, and a female prisoner two months before the birth of her child and one month after is to be treated as a sick patient.

My observations led me to the conclusion that while there is not the necessity for as large hospital facilities in Japanese prisons where they have so many in solitary confinement, the facilities are rather more limited than in the United States, and are poor in comparison with those of Bilibid Prison in the Philippines.   In the new prison being built in Tokyo, provision is much more adequate.

INTERVIEWS AND LETTER-WRITING

Visitors are allowed access to all prisoners above fourteen years of age.   Such visitors usually are relatives, but others may be allowed if the circumstances demand it.   These visits are permitted only during the business hours of the prison. Except in case the visitor is a lawyer, the interview may not last more than thirty minutes.   Visits are allowed to criminals sentenced to detention once a day, for those under sentence of imprisonment once a month, and for those sentenced to penal servitude once in two months.   That is, the more serious the offense the less frequent the visits.   The governor may relax these limits, if he thinks it necessary.   All interviews must be held in the reception-room, unless the prisoner is ill. The visit must be in the presence of a prison officer, and no foreign language may be used except by permission of the governor.

Except by permission of the governor a prisoner sentenced to detention may send or receive one letter every ten days, a prisoner under sentence of imprisonment one each month, and for the one sentenced to penal servitude one in two months. Careful regulations are made to provide against the sending or receipt of information detrimental to the order of the prison. The letters not permitted to be sent after censoring are to be kept and given to the prisoner on discharge. Postage and paper must be furnished by the prisoner, if he is able, except in case of a reply to a court or other official. All letters except those of immediate necessity must be written on Sunday, a holiday, or within recess time.

Here we see the restrictive measures so familiar to us in the prisons of the United States. Men are limited in trying to keep up social connections outside. However, a wise governor may allow more visits and more letters, if he desires.

DISPOSITION OF THE PERSONAL PROPERTY OF PRISONERS

Much the same regulations apply here as with us regarding the custody of the personal effects which the prisoner brings with him to the prison. They are kept for him, if they are not dangerous, and are delivered to him at his liberation, or to his heirs or successors in the event of death. In case no one claims them, or if he escapes and his address is not known after a year, they are confiscated by the state.

REWARDS AND DISCIPLINARY PUNISHMENTS

The Japanese prison law and regulations attempt, like most Western prisons, to secure obedience by rewards and punishments. Treatment and privileges are to be dependent on conduct.

Rewards are of two kinds, badges and privileges. There are three "badges of reward." Each of the badges is a piece of white linen 2⅖ inches long by 1⅕ inch wide sewed on the left sleeve between shoulder and elbow. Some privileges depend on the number of these badges a prisoner wears. "The rewarding treatment" or privileges are: (1) increasing the number of interviews and letters mentioned above; (2) permission to buy his own shirts; (3) permission to change his work; (4) increase of his prison wage by two-tenths for each badge; (5) supplying certain provisions and beverages; and (6) increase of the supply of side dishes mentioned above in the discussion of the food. This side dish he gets as many times per week as he has arm badges. Moreover, for certain special services he is rewarded by the gift of "prize money" of fifty sen (25 cents) or less.   These special services are as follows: (1) for giving private information of a prisoner about to run away; (2) for saving another's life, or for arresting prisoners on the point of escape; (3) for rendering service in connection with a calamity caused by nature or casualty, or in the case of the prevalence of contagious disease.   Japan does by regulation what we do in the United States by the secret disposition of the warden—bribe a prisoner to betray his fellows.

Disciplinary punishments are almost exact copies of those found in the prisons of the United States—deprivation of privileges, reduction of grade (in Japan the taking away of the badges), forfeit of his earnings, shutting up in solitary confinement, deprivation of food, except for accused persons and those below eighteen years of age, by one-half or one-third, and deprivation of exercise.   Japan as well as most of our prisons has the dark cell.   However, the regulations require frequent examination by the prison physician, for those in confinement as well as those in dark cells.   Nothing new is to be found in Japan's law or regulations on prison discipline. She does not use the stripes, but she has badges of distinction. She does not confine on bread and water, but she reduces the food.

LIBERATION

In Japan there are three methods of release from prison: (1) pardon (either absolute or conditional); (2) expiration of sentence; (3) "provisional release," or what we call parole.

Nothing needs to be said about pardon further than a reference to the custom of the Emperor proclaiming amnesty for a certain number of prisoners on his accession to the throne, or on the death of a member of the imperial family.   The release must be within twenty-four hours after the proclamation of release, in some cases within ten hours after the receipt of the order.

On expiration of sentence a prisoner must be released before six o'clock of the day after the expiration of sentence. If he has money the prisoner must provide himself with civilian clothes and transportation to the place to which he wishes to go. If he is without funds the prison supplies both. In any case, if the prisoner has been removed from one prison to another farther from home, the difference in the price of the transportation charges must be paid by the prison.

The following provisions are made for those who are provisionally released, or let out on parole: (1) He must take employment and engage in some lawful occupation with good conduct; (2) he must submit to the supervision of the police in the place to which he goes, although the police may entrust his supervision to some other authority on obtaining permission from the prison; (3) in case he wishes to remove his residence or travel for ten days or more, he must get permission from his supervisor. The Minister of Justice alone may grant him permission to leave the country. When he is granted provisional liberation he must be given a ticket-of-leave.

Any prisoner entitled to release from prison, but who is undergoing medical treatment on account of severe illness, may, on application, be permitted to remain.

Japan tries in her regulations to prepare the prisoner for release. For three days or less before release he is to be taken to solitary confinement, and instructed by the governor. The governor may, if he thinks it necessary, give an opinion concerning the prisoner's character and behavior, and suggestions concerning his guidance to the police officer to whose jurisdiction he is going, or to the person who will have him under custody.

Here is nothing new except that there is the suggestion of some measures of after-care for the released prisoner. In actual practice a number of the prison governors have tried on their own initiative to organize workshops and dormitories to which released prisoners may go until they find employment. I found these in operation at Odawara and at one of the prisons in Tokyo. They may exist elsewhere in Japan. They are not provided by the law or the prison regulations.

DEATH

On the death of a prisoner a record must be made of how he came to his death. If by natural causes, the cause of death, dates, etc., must be entered in the mortuary roll of the prison. If by suicide, notice must be given the police and an inspection made, and the facts recorded. If the corpse is not claimed within twenty-four hours, except in cases where the prisoner has expressed himself against it, it may be delivered to a medical school for dissection. In case the body is not claimed, or is not desired for dissection purposes, it is to be buried and a marker placed above the grave.

CONCLUSION

As one studies the outward appearance of the Japanese prisons and their working, he finds little that is new. Evidently the Japanese have borrowed most of their prison ideas from the British and the French. The attempt to segregate classes of prisoners according to age, class of crime, number of offense, the practice of solitary confinement for certain classes, not as punishment but for the prisoner's good, the disciplinary punishments, the rewards, the money permitted to be earned, the classification according to conduct—all these remind one of the British experiments. Many of these things were tried out in American prisons long ago, and their value proven dubious. Even in the attempt to introduce the scientific study of juvenile offenders by psychology and psychiatry, as yet in its infancy there, the Japanese have merely followed slowly in the wake of experiments in the United States and Germany. On the whole, one must conclude that Japan has something to teach us in the care with which she selects her prison wardens, the training of prison officials, and the unification of the whole treatment of offenders within the Empire. In this last she has followed in the wake of England. But it must be admitted that she has followed there to her great advantage. She has by unification of her system been able to segregate in different institutions some of the different classes named above. If classification is important, then she has learned

that lesson. But what if classification should be proved
to be a chimera? It is a very live question whether
classification should be on the basis of age, nature of crime
committed, number or offense, or on a character study of each
prisoner. Before that kind of classification can be attempted
much wider application of the methods of science in diagnosis
of the criminal must be made. It has been made neither in
Japan nor in any other country for any considerable class of
offenders, although a beginning has been made notably in
Belgium, in England, in some of the juvenile courts in the
United States, and New York has written into law, although
feebly, and has in no adequate way tried to carry it out, the
study and classification of all her offenders in the new building at Sing Sing. I had hoped that in this country, far removed from the traditions and iron-like customs of prison
practice of America and England, something new in the
treatment of offenders might be found. Had she invented
such a departure from colossal failure in prison practice as
is to be found in the Iwahig Penal Colony in the Philippines,
Japan would deserve the gratitude of the civilized world.
She is still clinging to the old belief that to confine a man in
solitude will somehow work a transformation in his character,
the old belief that the early reformers in Pennsylvania tried and
found a failure. She is still pursuing the dream that by keeping young prisoners apart from older ones, first offenders from
repeaters, she will somehow prevent contamination. How one
longs for radical experiment in this field as in the various fields
of business and science! No, the past dogs our foot-steps in
prison work and holds us bound to ineffectiveness. Japan has
in one prison warden I discovered provided a lesson, which she
evidently has not herself learned. One of her wardens has
been in that service for thirty-seven years. His prisoners love
him enough that when an earthquake shakes down the walls of
their prison house, they refuse to run away lest he suffer for
their deed. His prison is a model of industry and order. His
men come out, many of them, with a new view on life and firm
determination to be good citizens. All this without the aid

which science would bring him. But he has the rare quality of moving and managing men by drawing out in them the best. He is a "dangerous man!" He has been transferred "for the good of the service," I suppose, from that prison to another. Perhaps in order that he may show other wardens how it is done.

However, Japan has made certain advances in prison work which deserve the careful consideration of some American states. She has provided special institutions for her juveniles. I visited one of her institutions for boys. It is as fine an institution as I have seen anywhere. Education and trade training are stressed. A kindly attitude is shown by those in charge. Land is cultivated about the institution, thus providing the boys education in a practical field. She has an institution devoted to the special study by every means known to Western science of those delinquent boys who are suspected of being abnormal mentally. This institution separates those found to be of normal intelligence from the others and sends them to the institution mentioned above. The defectives are kept at the institution where they are studied, and are given special educational and psychiatric treatment.

Moreover, some of the wardens are trying out interesting experiments. At Odawara the warden had persuaded the Bureau of Fisheries to co-operate in providing a ship to which selected young prisoners from his institution were sent to be trained in deep sea fishing. He was very enthusiastic about the plan. Several of the wardens have tried out experiments in aftercare. One had interested certain private individuals to provide funds. Houses were hired in the town where the institution is located. Equipment was provided whereby the discharged man could earn his living and where he could live until he could find regular employment. The warden himself took a personal interest in this experiment. When he went with me to visit the houses it was apparent that he had more than an official interest in the men living and working there. Furthermore, the Minister of Justice and some of the wardens are deeply interested in certain private institutions which look after discharged prisoners. Miss Caroline MacDonald has now what we should call a social settlement in Tokyo. She has done a great work with discharged prisoners and their families. Because of her interest in them she has the admiration of the Minister of Justice and of the prison governors who have known of her work.

In Japan, as in America, too often politics dictate the appointment of prison wardens and officials. Yet there is one striking difference between the situation in the United States and in Japan. The homogeneous character of the population, together with the lively sense of moral unity through the person of the Mikado and the intense consciousness of kind among the Japanese people even across class lines, produce a submission to authority, a regard for the rights of others which make the treatment of the criminal there entirely different. The comparative docility of prisoners in Japan is striking to an American. They will put up with treatment which would cause prison riots in America. Moreover, the attitudes of the officers are moulded by that same sense of ethnic and spiritual unity. These prisoners, to them, are not social enemies; they are naughty children. Hence, a dignity sits upon these older prison governors; a docility possesses the prisoners—both puzzling to an American.

Moreover, the Japanese, through the Japanese Prison Association, have inaugurated one thing strangely lacking in most other countries. They train their prison officials. This association, organized in 1888, is "a corporate and judicial body." It has an endowment of about $100,000 and a membership of 12,000 divided into four classes. The honorary class composed of fifty persons is selected on the basis of learning, high repute, or distinguished services to the association. The other three classes—supporting, sustaining, and ordinary, as in American organizations—are composed of persons according to the amounts they contribute yearly to the association. The majority of the ordinary members are prison officials, only about twenty per cent being outsiders. Since there are about 11,000 ordinary members, it is apparent that only about 2200 outsiders belong to this class. It is probable that the 950 who compose the three higher classes are mostly non-official citizens.

The association is closely connected with the prison administration, not only through the ordinary memberships. The Minister of Justice is president, the Under-secretary of Justice is vice-president, and the chairman is director of the Prison Administration Bureau of the Department of Justice. The directors and superintendents are chosen by the president from among the personnel of the Prison Administration Bureau and from the prison governors. There are also three executive secretaries and a number of clerks in charge of affairs.

The chief functions of this association are: (1) conducting a training school for prison officials; (2) censoring educational materials, and (3) operating a kind of pension system for prison officials. A word should be said about each.

Two training courses are carried on, one for the higher prison officials, two months in length each year, and the other for the lower orders of officials, continuing for six months annually. In that for higher officials only chief warders of higher rank are trained. In the school for the lower prison officials are received chief warders of lower rank, jailers, and women jailers. The selection in both cases seems to be determined by examination. But whether those showing little knowledge of the theory and practice or those showing much knowledge are chosen, the literature on the subject leaves us uninformed. The common course was inaugurated in 1908, and in 1925 had graduated about 2000.

Moreover, some of the prison physicians are required to attend a two months' course of instruction in medical work for prisoners.

The subjects covered in the curricula for these three courses of prison officials are as follows:

1. The higher officials are given courses in penal politics; prison systems; prison industries; prison hygiene; welfare work; criminal procedure; comparative prison laws; prison architecture; criminal sociology; psychology of labor; factory management; efficiency; industries in general; financial law; psychopathology; social work; prin-

ciples of moral (religious) instruction; theories on purchase and sale.

2. Courses in the common school for prison officials are European and American prison systems and their histories; criminal law: general treatise; criminal law: special parts; criminal procedure; parole system; criminal psychology; ethics; principles of jurisprudence; juvenile law and discharged prisoners' aid in general; the finger-print system; history and practice of prison administration; general sociology.

3. The courses offered the prison physicians are internal medicine; surgery; ophthalmology; otorhinolaryngology; dermatology; venereal disease; psychology; bacteriology and serum therapy; labor hygiene.

In addition to these formal courses in any Japanese prison, officials are required to practice *judo* (jujitsu) and *kendo* (fencing). The association also publishes two journals, a monthly, *The Kei Sei* (Penal Administration) and a fortnightly journal, *The Hito* (Manhood), the latter of which it is hoped to make a weekly or possibly an alternate daily. Also scientific lectures are given monthly in the central building of the association to its members. The association also publishes information concerning prison administration, compiles prison laws and regulations, publishes books and collects books, pictures, instruments, and models bearing on prisons and their conduct, for the benefit of its members. The association also endeavors to develop preventive measures against crime.

This association offers scholarships for students of criminal science to enable them to pursue their studies in prison administration, criminal sociology, criminal psychology, etc. It also makes use of the moving picture as an aid to the mental and moral culture of the inmates of prisons. It has a squad which travels from prison to prison throughout Japan and shows pictures of an educational value.

The association also has a Board of Censors to select materials for prisoners. The chief materials censored are moving picture films, phonograph records, and reading matter. The object of this material which is given to the prisoners is to foster the virtues of self-restraint and diligence and to develop their personalities.

Another important function of the association is to provide relief measures for needy prison officials. Those who fall ill or are injured or killed on duty, who die from natural causes, or retire after a long service are given a sum of money in recognition of their services. Usually in no case is this sum more than $500. In addition the association has organized a Mutual Relief Association among the prison officials. The members pay monthly one per cent of their wages. Death, retirement, owing to injuries received or serious illness contracted while on duty, illness of fifteen days or more, death from natural causes, illness other than that contracted on duty if the member has to be absent for more than thirty days in succession, or any other disaster, are some of the things for which assistance is given. The amount given depends upon the monthly salary received. In case of death in pursuit of his duties, a man's family is given an amount not less than six months' and not more than two years' salary.

Here Japan has made an important contribution to penological practice. While many countries have pensions for policemen, very few have for prison officials. Moreover, in the conduct of training schools for prison officials, Japan probably leads the world. Here is a suggestion for America which might help in securing the kind of prison officials we sometimes dream of. Moreover, Japan has organized her educational and recreational work for prisoners on a national basis. So far no results have been published concerning this interesting adventure. The interest of Japanese prison officials in penological thought struck me when I visited a number of the institutions. Inquiries of all kinds were made as to how things were done in this country. One wonders if these training courses do not account for that significant interest. Why should not the authorities in charge of our prisons follow the Japanese example in providing adequate training for the officials and protection to them and their families against illness and death?

JAPAN'S SEGREGATION OF THE SICK

Another important provision of the Japanese prison system is the care of the sick prisoners. Not only has she fine hospitals, clinics, examining rooms, and isolation quarters for

those who are sick, each class separate from other classes, such
as those with infectious and those with contagious diseases, but
she provides special buildings inside the prison walls for epileptic prisoners and others with mental derangements of certain
kinds.   Here she has adapted Western methods to her own customs and ideas.   Her emphasis upon curative and preventive
medicine is surpassed nowhere.   Perhaps it ought not, but it
does astonish the Westerner to see how carefully she has looked
after these important matters with a thoroughness wished for
but not often realized in the United States.   Her prison physicians are specially trained in the schools for prison officials
already noticed.

An American must be very careful, would he not misin-
terpret what he sees in the prisons of Japan.   He must not
judge them on the basis of the social psychology of America.
The traditions of the Japanese are vastly different.   Their attitudes toward superiors, toward the aged, toward those of
different social status, and toward the erring are differently
motivated than ours.   An American finds it difficult to appreciate the sway of these Japanese mores, the emotional urge in
these age-old usages, and the repressive power of ideals of control which come down from an immemorial past.   Western
civilization is making inroads on these old folkways.   It is
breaking down, to some extent, the old sanctions to conduct
and is disturbing the easy flow of ancient sentiment and feeling.   Nevertheless, these ancient attitudes and customs are as
tough as an elm knot.   An American will misjudge Japanese
prisons, as he will misjudge all Japanese life, if he does not live
there long enough to feel his way into the spirit of Japan.

It is morning.   The steamer is nearing the coast of Japan.
Looking out of my window, I see an island rising out of the sea.
Sunlight washes the waves with glory.   Hurriedly we dress
and rush on deck.   From among the mists rising on the water
and covering the distant city with a diaphanous blanket appear
fishing boats making out to sea for their day's work.   It is the
harbor of Yokohama.   Slowly we come to anchor for inspection.   Suddenly as we look shoreward, there above the

mists rising like an unreal thing is the snow-capped top of Fuji. It has no base. Because of the mists and clouds around the bottom it seems to hang in mid-air as strange as a mirage of the desert. The sun from behind us strikes its summit into shining silver. Unreal but beautiful it seems to us. Strange, mysterious it would seem to one who does not understand the effect of mist and sunlight. No wonder that the Japanese worship it as a symbol of the divine. Fuji is the eternal symbol of Japan to Western ignorance. Japanese art, Japanese life and custom, Japanese houses, food, and ways of social intercourse seem to the stranger's eyes as without base, as unreal as Fuji seems to him as he sees it for the first time from the steamer's deck in the morning light. So in spite of the model on which Japan's prison system is formed the Japanese prisons seem to be different from those of any other country. In spite of extensive borrowing they are possessed by a genius all their own. The skeleton of the system is American-British-French. The spirit is Japanese. That structure I have described. I have only hinted at the spirit. I have felt it, but cannot do justice to it. Enough has been said perhaps to indicate that it must not be judged by our standards. Like ours, it must be judged by results. On that basis it does not suffer in comparison.

BIBLIOGRAPHY

Act Concerning Juveniles. (Translated by Caroline MacDonald in collaboration with Mr. Masataro Miyake, Councillor of the Department of Justice, Japanese Government.)

Endowment Act and Regulations of the Japanese Prison Association, "*Keimu Kyokwai*" (organized 1888). Tokyo, Japan, 1925.

Fifty-first Annual Report of Criminal Affairs, Department of Justice, Tokyo, Japan, 1925. (In Japanese.)

Prison Law of Japan.

Regulations for the Application of the Prison Law.

Twenty-seventh Annual Report of Penal Administration, Department of Justice. Tokyo, Japan, 1925. (In Japanese.)

Treatise on the Penal Law of Japan, by Dr. Shinkuma Motoji, Director of Criminal Affairs, Ministry of Justice, Tokyo, 40th edition, 1928, 2 vols. (In Japanese).

Vambery, R., "The Professional Training of Prison Officials," *The Survey*, January 21, 1911, pp. 660*ff*.

Work of the Japanese Prison Association and its Present Status, "*Keimu Kyokwai.*" Tokyo, Japan, 1925.

Miyake, Judge Masataro, *An Outline of the Japanese Judiciary and the Administration of Prisons in Japan*, Tokyo, 1930 (Reprinted from the Japan Advertiser).

CHAPTER II

FROM BILIBID TO IWAHIG

In the mountains of eastern Kentucky the natives have given picturesque names to various communities. These names are supposed to indicate the character of the places. Two such places are called by way of contrast "Kingdom Come" and "Hell fer Sartin." The one was supposed to be the antithesis of the other in life and conduct.

This narrative of a visit to two penal institutions of the Philippine Islands might well be named "From Hell fer Sartin to Kingdom Come." The difference between the two institutions, however, is not due to the difference in the former history and character of the inhabitants, but to the different methods of treatment applied in the two and the consequent results in the conduct of the inmates of the respective institutions. It must not be imagined that because of the different methods employed in the two institutions, in theory and practice, there is no relation between the two. You are assured that Iwahig is possible only because of the experience the convict has had in Bilibid. It looks as if the authorities think that a little taste of hell is necessary to produce a proper appreciation of kingdom come.

BILIBID PRISON

Bilibid is an old prison built by the Spaniards in 1865. A high wall encloses about seventeen acres of ground. Inside that wall the ground is divided into two equal parts by a wall running through the center. In the center of the wall is a circular building with a watchtower from which every part of the enclosure is visible. In this tower, constantly on duty, are two guards armed with rifles. At frequent intervals along the walls are stationed guards similarly armed, while in the tower over the entrance gate and at the corners of the wall are machine guns. At the entrance is the familiar double gate as seen in most American prisons. However, these gates are opened and shut by a man in a tower who operates the gates in response to electric signals from the outside gate. Moreover, he is in a barred enclosure reached by a circular stairway also surrounded by bars so that no one may reach him without a key to the lock at the bottom of the winding stair. Aloft the tower over the entrance is the central telephone switchboard from which a full view of the entire prison yard is provided. In the Spanish days the lower part of the central building referred to above was divided into dark cells, which, when the Americans occupied the city, were filled with political prisoners chained to the walls and floors. These are now used as storerooms, and only a few of the rings are to be seen. The former instruments of torture are to be seen in the museum.

Inside the walls on each side of the dividing wall, the various buildings are arranged like the spokes in a wheel from the central tower building as the hub. Then other buildings are arranged around the walls, workshops for the most part, for the prison is a great manufacturing establishment. Each of these spokes is a dormitory in which the prisoners sleep, or in which certain classes of prisoners are kept. Thus, one of the spokes houses 160 women prisoners. There they live and work. Moreover, their wing is shut off from the others by another wall. Another spoke contains the cells for the condemned prisoners awaiting execution, and the death house with its electric chair. There are no individual cells except the punishment cells, which were empty except for one or two in which were confined men who were suspected of being insane. All prisoners sleep in dormitories, in which there are triple-decked beds. These also serve as the dining rooms for each dormitory to which the food is carried and there eaten on a long center table. There is a large common kitchen.

The dividing wall through the prison serves to separate the

new arrivals from the other prisoners, the younger prisoners from the older, and the short termer from the long termer. Moreover, an attempt is made to classify the prisoners by segregation in different dormitories. In Bilibid Prison are also housed the jail prisoners of Manila. These, however, are worked outside the walls in gangs on the streets and public works of the city.

Bilibid is a great industrial prison. Various shops occupy some of the large buildings around the grounds. Here are various kinds of industries. There is an automobile repair shop, in which are repaired and repainted not only publicly owned cars, but also private cars, the work covering all the operations from adjusting a carburetor to putting on a new coat of paint. Another shop is devoted to the manufacture of bullock carts. All the work is done by hand in this shop as in most of the others, for it is the belief of the management that the work done in the prison should be as much as possible like that carried on outside. In connection with this shop is a carpenter shop in which lumber is sawed and planed partly by hand and partly by power machinery. The two large industries, however, are the wood and the rattan furniture departments. Bilibid furniture has a world-wide reputation. Here fine furniture is manufactured under the supervision of trained foremen. The work is done on orders from people on the outside. When we were there (January, 1928), the prison was eight months behind on the wooden furniture and a year behind on orders for rattan furniture. These two industries provide most of the profitable work of the prison. Most of the men are employed in them. However, other industries are carried on, among them being blacksmithing, carriage-making and repairing, tailoring, shoe-making and repairing, machine wood-working, tinsmithing, and hammock-weaving. The women make embroidery, do the domestic work of their department, make lace, weave and crochet. For their products, especially embroidery and lace, there is a heavy demand. One thing can be said, everyone able to do so works.

The industrial system in Bilibid Prison applies to only about

A Portion of the Shop Building

The Building in the Background with Two Flags is the Administrative Building

BILIBID PRISON

Foundry and Metal Sheet-smithing

Interior of the Automobile Shop

BILIBID PRISON

2500 prisoners out of a yearly average of 6500 in the entire
Philippine Islands. Thus for January 1, 1925, 6593 in custody were distributed as follows:

Bilibid Prison	2,474
Iwahig Penal Colony	1,538
San Ramon Prison and Penal Farm	628
Bontoc Prison	97
Fort Mills, Corregidor	458
Constabulary Stations	77
San Lazaro Insane Asylum	28
Luneta Police Station	52
City Boys' Reformatory	3
City Girls' Reformatory	1
Confined in Provincial Jails	1,237
Total	6,593 [1]

The organization of the industries in Bilibid Prison, designed
primarily to provide instructive employment for the inmates
and teach the earnest convicts a trade with which to earn a
living after they are released, provides for eight main departments in addition to certain miscellaneous activities which also
provide a measure of trade training. The following description of the organization by Mr. Alzate, Assistant Director of
Prisons in the Philippines, concisely states the organization:

We have at Bilibid Prison an Industrial Division which is operated
primarily to provide instructive employment for deserving inmates
and to teach every earnest convict a trade with which to earn an honest
livelihood after his release. With this end in view, all the industries
established in the various departments have been organized into courses
of training developed so as to fit the needs and peculiarities of all industrial classes of inmates. The courses of training in the various
shops and industrial plants are so laid down that an inmate, when he is
received in prison, can be assigned in the calling for which he is best
fitted by nature, ability, or past experience. Each industry is placed
under the direction of a thoroughly competent Superintendent or
Foreman, who is in charge of shop operation, production, and training
of the inmates.[2]

[1] Alzate, *Convict Labor in the Philippine Islands*, 1926, p. 31. Bontoc Prison
has since been abolished.
[2] *Ibid.*, p. 31.

The industries of Bilibid Prison are divided into eight departments, numbered from A to H.

In Department A are various mechanical trades. Here are the general machine shop, the electrical, the automobile, and motorcycle repair shops, the carriage shop, the blacksmith shop, the sheet metal shop, and shops for millwrighting, upholstering, and a few other trades. These trades have value as training for prisoners who will be discharged and also as profitable enterprises for the prison. Here you see three hundred men working and repairing all sorts of articles appropriate to such shops in the Philippines. Watch the men in the carriage shop making all kinds of vehicles from carabao carts, heavy wagons, trucks, trailers, street sprinklers, to the fine carriage for the grandee or the pony cart for his children. All kinds of vehicles are repaired and repainted.

In that next building is Department B, where three hundred fifty men make all kinds of furniture from the various fine Philippine hardwoods such as nana, acle, lumbayao, lauan, tonguile, tindalo, and camagon. A thoroughly competent furniture maker is at the head. His assistants are skilled woodcarvers and polishers. Go over to the storeroom where the finished products are kept until they can be sent to those who have ordered them. These artistic tables, chairs, stools, cabinets, etc., have been produced by prisoners from the cutting of the trees on the penal colony lands at Iwahig to the last polishing touch in Bilibid. While the main purpose is to provide occupational training for the prisoners, so much in demand is the product that they are usually behind orders. This department is one of the most profitable in the prison. The men on discharge are in demand by furniture manufacturers on the outside. This department is second only in importance to Department D.

Department C employs one hundred fifty prisoners on the construction and repair of buildings for the prison and on the manufacture and repair of equipment for the prison. Here the prisoner is trained as carpenter and concrete builder, remunerative occupations on discharge.

Department D employs the largest number of inmates, about six hundred prisoners. If you visit the storerooms you will see all kinds of wicker, rattan, and bamboo furniture—chairs of a great many designs, handsome tea-tables, stools, bookracks, flower baskets. Here are bedsteads made of the hardwoods mentioned above but with head and footboards woven of rattan and with rattan bottom in place of our bed springs. Such beds are considered "the thing" in that part of the world, although on the basis of my experience in sleeping on one, I prefer an American bed spring. Split bamboo shades and curtains are produced here. It is this furniture which first made Bilibid furniture world-famous. The medals the prison has received on this furniture at various expositions are as numerous and dazzling as those of a French or Italian World War veteran's. "Nuff said!" So popular is this type of furniture in the Orient that a prisoner who has become skilled in this department can easily get a job on the outside.

Department F is less fascinating to the Westerner. It is the tailoring department. It makes all the clothes for the inmates of the insular and provincial prisons and jails, as well as service uniforms for sailors, police, etc. Some civilian clothes are also produced for government officials. However, it cannot be said that the work of this department fits a man to become a master tailor. Eighty prisoners are engaged in the work of this department. The limitations of the tailor's trade in the Philippines may be suggested by the supposition that of approximately six million males in the archipelago, perhaps five million require only a breech-cloth.

One hundred inmates are employed in Department G. They run a steam laundry. It cares for the laundry of the prison and takes in civilian washing on a commercial basis. Fancy the derision visited upon an inmate who comes back to his mountain home and who in reply to the question of his neighbors as to what kind of work he did while in prison replies that he did the washing! What a blush of shame will mantle his swarthy face as the first astonished breath-holding is followed by a loud cry in unison, "What?" "Women's work!"

It will require a lot of explaining, perhaps considered as the Philippine equivalent of our defense reaction known as a lie, to disabuse his hearers of the picture summoned up in the minds of his neighbors by his word, "washing," the picture of him standing knee deep in a river among the women, sloshing the clothes up and down in the water and beating them upon a convenient stone. We are assured, however, by the prison authorities that the growth of sanitary laundries and cleaning establishments makes this trade a not undesirable one for ex-convicts. A Westerner wonders why this is not a part of Department H.

The last organized department is H, for the one hundred sixty women in Bilibid. Most of them are sentenced for theft, adultery, and prostitution. They are taught domestic economy, weaving, embroidery, lace-making, and crocheting. This is perhaps the least promising department from the standpoint of industrial training. However, their lace and embroidery command good prices. Women prisoners here, as in the United States, are poorly handled.

In addition to the organized departments just described, a number of other trades are taught, incidentally to small numbers, in the maintenance of the prison, such as shoe-making, cooking, baking, nursing, twine and rope making for prison use, gardening, poultry-raising, hair-cutting, clerical work, typing, stenography, and orchestral music. I fear, however, that the word "training" applied to such work of prison maintenance here, as in America, is an accommodation of language.

Yet it must be said of Bilibid, what cannot be said of many prisons in the United States, every prisoner is kept busy, from the unruly fellow, who in stripes and chains pulls monotonously back and forth the giant fan over the workers to keep them cool, or those others whom I saw industriously mauling a tough knot of Philippine hard wood—my back and arms ached for them from memories of my own boyhood exertions over dried elm knots—to the artistic woodcarver and rattan weaver or the 450,000 peso bank embezzler who kept the prison accounts.[8]

---

[8] *Ibid.*, pp. 31–36.

The inmates are graded into four grades. Entering the prison, a man is placed in the second grade. Those in this grade are clothed in blue denim and are allowed certain privileges. Those in the third grade have been demoted from the second grade for misconduct or lack of industry. These are clothed in stripes. They are denied most of the privileges enjoyed by those in the second grade. The first grade is made up of those who have been promoted from the second grade for good conduct over a certain period of time. These enjoy greater privileges and receive a larger wage. The fourth class is made up of trusties. These have still more extended privileges and receive larger pay. All these features are familiar to us in the United States.

Wisely the administration of the prisons of the Philippines has taken measures to keep alive the economic motive. The policy of the administration is to promote a prisoner from grade to grade as rapidly as possible and from one position to another. Ordinarily a prisoner may reach the grade of skilled laborer within a period of six months and then be entitled to receive a certain amount of compensation; until he reaches this grade he earns no wages. A convict who has served a tenth of his term without any bad conduct is made a trusty. A trusty has special privileges denied to others, such as sleeping in special dormitories, eating at a table covered with a tablecloth, served by waiters. He works in some responsible position and receives compensation for his work. There have been instances of convicts who left Bilibid with money enough to carry them through for a considerable period until they could get a job.[4]

The law passed by the Philippine legislature, regulating the compensation of prisoners, is as follows:

Insular prisoners who are or become skilled and semi-skilled workmen may receive compensation for their work from the profits accruing to the credit of the industrial division of the Bureau of Prisons by the sale of articles manufactured by the prisoners or from payments made for work performed by them: Provided, that such compensation does not exceed the difference between the gross cost of the prisoner's maintenance and the amount that his services are reasonably worth with the additional proviso, that all prisoners who are in the

[4] Victorio, *Prison Reform in the Philippines*, Manila, 1927, p. 20.

same conduct and workmanship classifications, regardless of nature of work, shall receive like compensation.[5]

Half of these earnings are withheld from the prisoners and deposited to their credit and paid to them upon discharge; the other half, on the request of the prisoner, is used for the support of the dependent members of his family or for such personal uses as may be approved by the director of prisons.

A very interesting feature of Bilibid Prison is the school. Every prisoner under thirty years of age gets two periods of schooling a day up to the fourth grade. These classes are taught by prisoners, but the whole school is under a civilian superintendent. Only the elementary subjects and such practical subjects as mechanical drawing, stenography, electricity, telegraphy, and accounting are taught. Since most of the prisoners are quite uneducated, the classes are large. These classes are held in one large building without partitions. When we visited the school the noise seemed very disturbing. I was told that in this prison school many a boy who has not had a chance at an elementary education learns to read and write and the elements of arithmetic. When one considers that all these prisoners are natives, many of them Igorrotes, who a few years ago were head-hunters, one wonders whether the education given them might not be more practical.

Discipline in Bilibid is of the semi-military variety. The chief question asked me by the newspaper reporters after my first visit was, "What about the discipline?" On inquiry I learned that the introduction of strict military discipline a few years ago was looked upon as a distinct innovation, and a progressive measure. This military discipline shows itself in the prisoners standing at military attention when the officers are met, and in the drills which occur each afternoon at five o'clock. The officers believe it has a salutary effect on the deportment of the men. The discipline is not obtrusive when the men are at work. Breach of discipline is punished by reduction in grade, deprivation of privileges, doing hard and

[5] *Ibid.*, p. 34.

PORTION OF THE AUTOMOBILE SHOP, BILIBID PRISON, 1928

The Wheel-making Shop

Women Inmates doing Embroidery Work

BILIBID PRISON

disagreeable work. I was struck by the sight of prisoners in stripes working the large fans hanging from the ceiling over the workrooms. I asked why these men were doing this work, and was told that it was a form of punishment. In another part of the prison we came upon a group of men in stripes mauling a tough knot of wood. It did not seem to me to be worth trying to split it, so I inquired why those five men were working so hard with maul and wedge. "They are being disciplined for something," I was told. A guard stood over them to see that they did not relax their efforts. The solitary confinement cells are kept for only the most recalcitrant. When I was there, there were no inmates. I looked at this large room and found that it was light and airy. Those who attempt to escape or are considered dangerous wear leg irons joined by a chain. These, however, are held up by straps tied to a belt around the waist so that they will not gall the ankles. Among the more than two thousand inmates I should estimate roughly that five per cent were undergoing discipline of some sort.

"Why do you retain stripes and leg irons here, when these things have been condemned by the best penological thought in our country?" I asked the director. "Ah," he replied, "we have to deal with people here in a different stage of social development than those you deal with in the United States. I use these punishments because they have a good effect upon those who see them." I had heard that argument before. Repress and intimidate by exemplifying punishment before their eyes!

At the daily "retreat" at five o'clock the prison band plays. At this "retreat" all the prisoners assemble from the shops to the space beside their respective dormitories. The outstanding group is the "Bilibid Scouts." This is composed of men selected because of good conduct, who live in a separate dormitory, enjoy special privileges, and are trained in maneuvers and gymnastic exercises. The "Scouts" and the band are the "crack" show units of the prison. Almost every day at five o'clock visitors fill a kind of rude gallery built on the roof of the central tower and watch these performers. It must be said that the maneuvers are very impressive. The director believes that through these exercises an *esprit de corps* is built up among the prisoners which has a wholesome influence. After the "retreat" the prisoners file away to their dormitories, take their baths, and eat their supper.

All executions in the Islands take place at Bilibid. While twenty-eight men were in the death house when we were there, it was uncertain whether any of them would be executed, as it is necessary in the Islands for each case to be reviewed by the Supreme Court of the Islands, and every one of the nine judges must sign the execution warrant. Even after that the defendant may take an appeal to the Supreme Court of the United States. However, in spite of all these difficulties, a number of men are electrocuted each year, depending largely upon the policy of the Governor-General. The only peculiarity about the mode of execution is the number of witnesses who must be present. On the floor about the chair are painted the names of the different officers who must attend. Not only must the director and his assistant be present, but also a representative of the Supreme Court and of the Governor-General.

There are very few escapes over the walls. No wonder! On the walls are fourteen guards besides numerous trusties and employees within the prison. Such a jail delivery as occurred at Joliet a short time ago, when a number of inmates murdered the deputy warden, took his keys, and forced the turnkey to open the gates, would probably have been impossible here by reason of the mechanism by which the gates are opened as explained above.

An attempt at a kind of self-government is carried on in Bilibid. As we went about the yard I noticed over a part of the old central tower, formerly the dungeon cells in Spanish times, a sign "The Court" painted on the wall. There was a room fixed up as a courtroom. All offenses are tried by a jury of inmates by judges selected from the prisoners. The sentence is reviewable by the director. Also from among the prisoners is organized a police force which assists the guards to keep

order. "How does that work?" I asked Director Victorio.
"Fine," he replied. "When a jury of his own peers and a
court composed of judges selected from among themselves pro-
nounces the verdict of 'guilty' or 'not guilty,' and when a man
is sentenced by his own fellows, he finds that he has no support
in his tendency to justify himself. He knows that they will
not convict him if he is not guilty. He feels that he is not
imposed on by a superior." He added that it makes discipline
very much easier for the officers. Here is a method of self-
government which seems to have won the support of a hard-
boiled warden.

I mentioned before that there are about 160 women prisoners kept in one of the wings of this prison. While they are
kept at useful work, and while the discipline is quite severe,
their presence within the walls in which men are confined is
an evil which the officers hope will soon be remedied by having
built for them an institution outside. It is impossible to prevent communication between men and women.

The most astonishing innovation in the prison is a hospital
under the direction of Dr. Estrada. While in most of our
American prisons the hospital is inadequate, at Bilibid abundant room is provided. I have seen nothing like it in the States.
Every prisoner is placed in quarantine, on entrance, for five
days. There is an isolation ward for those found to have infectious diseases. In the various wards special classes of diseases are treated. There are medical, surgical, contagious, and
quarantine wards, with special wards for convalescents. In
the laboratory connected with the hospital all kinds of examinations are made except Wassermann and blood chemistry.
These are made by the Philippine Bureau of Science. There
is a well-trained staff of doctors. There is an adequate staff
of nurses. Part of each are civilians and part inmates. For
example, two of the assistant doctors are inmates who were
well-trained medical men before they were incarcerated.
They have a nurses' training school manned by trained nurses
who instruct certain of the inmates to act as assistants. There
is also a good operating room with most of the modern appa-

ratus, and a dispensary adequate to the needs of the institution. Between the prison proper and the hospital is a wall the gates of which are shut after five o'clock at night and are not opened except on the orders of the director when a man must be transferred from the prison to the hospital on account of sickness. The only bad feature I saw in connection with the hospital was that in a certain building in the hospital compound there were confined twenty-eight civilian insane. This is done only because of the inadequate provisions for the care of the insane in Manila. Naturally if the civilian insane are not properly cared for one could hardly expect that the care of the criminal insane is what our best practice in the States provides. But the authorities are alive to the problem and are taking steps to improve the situation as soon as possible.

What has been the result of this rather interesting penal experiment? Mr. Alzate, the Assistant Director of the Bureau of Prisons, says: "Our prison records show that no convict accused of any of the crimes against property who has acquired skill and dexterity in some given trade during the period of his incarceration has been returned to any of our penitentiaries for offenses caused by inability to provide honestly for himself and his family or by a desire to live a life of ease which is not the result of his honest endeavors." [6] Perhaps the story of a case will show better than any mere statement what happens in some cases. The case of Emiliano Ramos is only one of a number of which I heard while in the Philippines.

I have killed three men and wounded several others. I killed them to defend the life of others and my own, not to rob them or because I was craving for human blood.

This was the statement of Ramos, who, on August 3, 1925, was granted a conditional pardon by the Governor-General. This man had served many years in prison and had two sentences of *cadenas perpetuas* (life imprisonment) hanging over him when pardoned. What strange kind of prisoner is this who in the face of such a record receives a conditional pardon?

[6] Alzate, *Convict Labor in the Philippine Islands*, p. 57.

I saw him first when Señor Victorio, Director of the Bureau of Prisons, was taking me through Bilibid for the first time. Close at the director's heels was this tall, slim, swarthy native. In the prison he was the director's shadow. Next, I saw him on the dock when I boarded the coastguard cutter, the *Busta-mente*, to go to the penal colony at Iwahig. There he was in his neat uniform assisting busily in getting aboard the prisoners being taken to the colony. The director and I were leaning on the ship's rail watching the last busy preparations for sailing. "Do you see that prisoner down there—the tall, slim fellow?" asked the director. "Yes, who is he?" I replied. "Wait until we get started and I'll tell you his story," he answered.

When the ship was at last slowly proceeding down the lazy Pasig River to the sea, the director motioned me to a seat on the deck and started to tell me the story of Ramos. We had not gone far, however, in the story before we were out of Manila Bay upon the rough sea. Victorio, the director, is a poor sailor and had to take to his cabin. He said that he would give me a booklet in which was the story. Here it is:

When I entered Bilibid I was only eighteen years old. Exactly thirty-five years ago last Monday I was born in the barrio of Balete, Calumpit, Bulacan. My people were engaged in farming and I, like my brothers, helped our father till the soil. One day, a date that I shall never forget, the 3d of April, 1909, I saw a man fishing in a pond situated within the boundaries of our land. I went to him and bade him to leave but he refused to go, claiming that he was on his own ground. In view of this, I went to my father and reported to him the incident, whereupon he came out with me accompanied by one of my brothers, and the three together went to the pond where the man was fishing. An argument ensued, two or three other men appeared on the scene, and seeing my father in danger of falling the victim of the aggression of a man much younger than he was, I pulled out the bolo we always carried as a necessary tool for our work and struck a blow on the man who imperilled my father's life. The next thing I knew was that a man was lying on the ground, blood gushing from his body. For this I got my first *cadena perpetua* and commenced to serve the sentence on March, 28, 1910.

My life in prison had been that of an underdog until the methods of enforcing prison discipline underwent a change for the better.

No matter how good I tried to be, no matter how closely I adhered to the rules and regulations of the penitentiary as best I knew how, no matter my efforts to refrain from committing the slightest infraction of discipline, I found myself rather too often with legs and arms chained and thrust into a cell known in Bilibid as the "bartoline." Despite all these discouraging experiences, I still persisted and tried to be good, realizing that I was up against it.   My persistency was not fruitless, for at last I gained the status of a first-class prisoner. My life then within the walls of the prison had been uneventful, my time and attention being devoted to acquiring the knowledge necessary to master a trade.   I was assigned to the Bamboo Department.

Another date written with human blood on the pages of my life is that of May 3, 1919, when a fellow prisoner died by my hand, and another fell badly wounded.   This was the result of what I regarded as an inhuman treatment accorded the patients in the prison hospital, among whom my father was one.   I noticed that the patients' rations were reduced to insufficiency—taking into consideration their condition—by fellow-prisoners who were in charge of the different wards, that they might trade the food taken away from the patients for articles of their own comfort.   On that day, I went to see the prisoner in charge of the patients' food and asked him why he persisted in starving sick fellow-prisoners, but as instead of a civil answer I saw a man in the attitude of striking me, I parried his blow with a blow which resulted in his death, and wounded another who tried to come to his aid.   For this, another *cadena perpetua* was added to the first imposed upon me, and I was transferred to Corregidor in chains, and demoted to third class.   While there, I had occasion to quell a fight among fellow-convicts who brandished bolos, knives, and staves, despite the chains which greatly handicapped the movement of my legs.   For the assistance I rendered on that occasion the chains were taken off my legs, I was restored to first class and made a chief squad leader.

In 1923, I was sent to Iwahig, where I was made foreman of a gang of colonists.   Having been informed by some of the men under my charge that Jacinto Pace, sergeant of the colony police and at the same time the acting superintendent's chauffeur, made it his hobby to report colonists—who refused to obey his bidding—for imaginary offenses which usually resulted in the punishment of the innocent convicts, due to the unbounded confidence the acting superintendent had in him, I decided, on the night of May 23, 1923, to see him to discontinue his unwarranted persecution, but my errand was so unsuccessful that to save my own life I had to kill him.   The Court pronounced me guiltless in this case, for it was established that I killed in self-defense.

Returned to Bilibid that same year, as a consequence of the unhappy incident I have just related, and as a reward of my efforts not only to be good but to do all I could to co-operate with the prison officials in enforcing discipline among fellow-prisoners, I was made a member of the Trusty Police. My record thereafter only the director can disclose to you.[7]

After two years of faithful service as a trusty, Señor Victorio recommended to the Governor-General, on April 14, 1925, that Ramos be classified as a free colonist with privileges much more restricted than those of the free colonists at Iwahig. The basis of his recommendation was that for the past three years Ramos had shown exemplary conduct. In fact, he had risked his own life to quell disturbances in the prison. On one occasion a crazed prisoner, Gonzalo Estrada, armed with a bolo, was chasing several convicts with intent to do them great bodily harm. Ramos intervened with great danger to himself, disarmed the man, and subdued him. More recently a convict, Pedro Adom by name, attempted to stab a fellow-prisoner, Severino Salvador. Ramos, who chanced to be near, jumped upon the would-be assassin, overpowered him, disarmed and delivered him to the authorities. The last of Ramos's exploits which led the director to recommend his pardon was his intervention in a fight between three Chinese prisoners and his bringing them all to the prison authorities. On the basis of his record, Victorio concluded that Ramos was "not a criminal by instinct or habit," and that "his complete reformation is not beyond the possibility of accomplishment."

Governor-General Wood remitted the penalties imposed on Ramos under the law, "on condition that he shall remain in Bilibid Prison for a period of five years to work as a foreman in one of the industrial shops of that prison and receive compensation therefor of one peso (50 cents) a day, without leaving the same prison unless given permission by the director thereof, and on the further condition that he shall not again be guilty of any crime or violation of the penal laws of the Philippine Islands." [8]

---

[7] Victorio, *Prison Reform in the Philippines,* pp. 144–150.
[8] Victorio, *op. cit.,* p. 150.

Other cases of reformation were cited by the director. Here as everywhere, men are committed to prison who are not hardened criminals. All they need is understanding by those in charge.

Considering all the circumstances, Bilibid was not so bad as I had been led to expect. True, it is overcrowded. The dormitories are inadequate to house properly the large numbers. The discipline is repressive, but not more so than nine-tenths of our American prisons—in fact, less so than in most I have visited. It is located within the crowded section of the city of Manila. It ought to be made into a receiving institution for study and classification, and for the medical treatment of those ailing or defective on entrance. Another kind of institution should be built out in the country where industry and farming, according to the Philippine methods, could be carried on as at Iwahig. Whatever classification is necessary would then be possible without the present crowding. All the incentives practiced in America are in operation there. The industries, for the most part, are adapted to the economic development of the Philippines. Bilibid is now used as a proving ground for the inmates on the basis of which selections are made for transfer to the Iwahig Penal Colony. There is no parole system in the Philippines. They still use the pardon to let men out before their sentences expire. That is bad, but it is not the fault of the prison, but of the legislature. The school is inadequate, but what prison school is not? The dormitory system, long condemned in the United States, is used. There the prisoners sleep three deep. That overcrowding none of the officers defend. It is a question, however, in their minds whether an adequate dormitory system for the Filipinos is not better than the isolated cell. "But," I asked the director, "what about sexual vice in these dormitories?" In his opinion there is not so great a likelihood of such practices as when two or four men are in a cell together. He adds that the Islands are not able to build cell houses with a cell for each man. There is no doubt that the present crowded dormitories are bad. On the whole it can be said that Bilibid is no worse than some American prisons, and a great deal better than many. That, however, is not enough for men who have done as much for penological practice in the Philippines as Director Victorio and Assistant Director Alzate. They appreciate the defects in many ways of the present system, especially in Bilibid and the provincial prisons. They must go on to further developments.

THE PROVINCIAL PRISONS

The fifty-two provincial prisons in the Philippines correspond to the county jails in the United States. I visited two of these, one at Puerto Princesa on the island of Palawan, and one at Lucena in the province of Tayabas. Director Victorio assured me that I had seen the worst and the best. The one at Puerto Princesa consisted of a long oblong room divided into three parts by iron bars. At one end was a part for women. There was nothing to prevent easy communication between the men at one end and the women at the other. Personal contact was impossible, but one can easily imagine what demoralization might occur in such circumstances. When we were there five men were confined awaiting trial. They had already been there for several months, and the court would not sit again for another three months. Doubtless there are jails as bad in the United States, but that is no way to measure jails. The one at Lucena was one of the finest jails I have ever seen. It has an infirmary for sick inmates; those awaiting trial are housed separately from those sentenced. There is a department for women entirely separate from the men's part, so that communication between them is impossible. One woman accused of adultery was there awaiting trial. In the men's part there were thirty-four inmates, eight of whom were awaiting trial. The prisoners here are not allowed to sit about in idleness, but work on the grounds of the municipal buildings. Except for the uniform you would not know that they were not ordinary laborers. The jail is clean, the food as good as most of these men ever had. In the writer's judgment, here as in the United States many of these men might be out on parole earning an honest living, had they a properly organized parole system. Neither they nor we have such a system for minor offenders. For the most part, according to the director, who is also inspector of provincial prisons, great improvement is needed in most of the provincial prisons of the Islands. However, the task of reforming some threescore of provincial prisons is trivial compared with the re-making of over three thousand county jails in the United States. Here all are under the supervision of the Insular Director of Prisons; in the United States they are under the forty-eight different states. Already a half dozen provinces have shown the way under the inspiration of the Director of the Bureau of Prisons, seconded by wide-awake provincial governors.

THE PENAL COLONY OF IWAHIG

"I suppose the colonists here are the less serious offenders," I remarked to Director Victorio as we walked up past the long line of inmates of the Iwahig Penal Colony on the Sunday morning we landed there to visit the colony. "Well," he said, "you see that man over there? That is Angel Saria. He was one of the most desperate bandits in northern Luzon a few years ago. He was finally captured, tried, and sentenced to Bilibid. After a period of training there, he did so well that he was allowed to transfer to Iwahig. He is now a trusty in a responsible position in the colony." He added, "You see that man at the head of the column." He was a sergeant of police in Manila, who was sent to prison for falsification of the police records. Today he is the chief municipal officer of the colony." He added, "Did you notice that small bronzed figure who came on the boat to get us at Puerto Princesa? That is a Moro Dato—a chief among the Moros. He was sentenced for life for insurrection. I transferred him to Iwahig because, when he came to San Ramon Prison, I put him in charge of the training of the Moro prisoners on good conduct. They respected him because of his position among his people. He did so well there that I thought he would be of service here. When he heard that we were coming for this visit, he left on foot through the wilderness and travelled from three o'clock Saturday until this morning in order to be here." So he went on, telling me of case after case in which there had been a most remarkable transformation of attitude toward society.

After we had been served refreshments at the superintendent's house, almost two thousand of these colonists with their band at the head marched past the reviewing stand in the plaza of the central station of the colony, a plaza named in honor of the Philippine patriot, José Rizal. At the end of the procession came about twenty water buffaloes with a convict astride each one, then the Indian humped cattle each ridden by a prisoner. It was a very remarkable sight. Even more remarkable in many ways was the assembly of the colonists at five o'clock that evening. They were led by the band to a position in front of the band stand from which the director made a speech to them. At the close of his address he asked if anyone had any complaints as to his treatment in the colony. There was silence for a few minutes; then an old man raised his hand. When asked to state his complaint, he said that the governor had promised to pardon him, but the pardon had not come. Then another old man said that he had been there twelve years and he thought he ought to be pardoned. These two were followed by perhaps a dozen more old men asking for pardon. The director finally remarked that he had asked for complaints, not requests for pardon, that he had no power to pardon, but would look into the cases and recommend certain of them to the Governor-General for pardon. There were no complaints. As evening settled down over the colony the colonists made their way to their respective stations.

In the dusk of the evening the memory of about a score of old colonists asking for pardon, men who were too old to be capable of repeating their crimes, stuck in my mind. "Why is there no parole system by which these old men can be set at liberty under supervision?" I thought. Languishing in every prison in the United States which has no parole system are similar sad cases which can be handled only by executive clemency.

When we left the colony to take the ship back to Manila, I had time to visit the little town at Puerto Princesa. I got into conversation with one of the provincial officers there. I asked him what he thought of the results on the men who had been at Iwahig. "Well," he said, "many of them when discharged settle down here with their families and take up a piece of land. They become our best settlers. They are industrious, as most of those here are not, and they make very substantial citizens." Remember that the provincial politicians at Puerto Princesa are not friendly to the prison administration. The island of Palawan on which the colony is located is mostly undeveloped land. The colonists have been taught to work under the supervision of trained agriculturists. They have learned the value of money and of good conduct in the colony.

What is this colony which has accomplished such results from which men come not as jailbirds with a stigma attached which prevents their success? It comprises some one hundred thousand acres of what was once untamed wilderness. It varies in character from swamp to mountains. It is cut up by rivers which rush down from the mountains, furnishing plenty of water for irrigation of the rice and coconut trees which the colonists have planted. Governor-General Luke Wright and later Governor-General Forbes are responsible for the inception of the colony. Mr. Quillen, who was one of the first directors of the Bureau of Prisons, took an active interest in it, but the colony has had its ups and downs. In the early days there were insurrections among the convicts, there were scandals in the administration, there were numerous escapes. After numerous trials and failures, the Director of the Bureau of Prisons, Mr. Quillen, sent Ramon Victorio, who was assistant superintendent of the San Ramon Prison and Penal Colony in Mindanao, to Iwahig as assistant superintendent. He was placed in charge of agriculture, and in charge of the discipline. He discovered that in the trouble there were about five ringleaders. These he called before him. He told them that he

Settlers and their Goods Are Transported to the Colony on Barges

Colonists on Parade, Riding Indian Humped Cattle

Lined Up for Lunch

IWAHIG PENAL COLONY, PHILIPPINE ISLANDS

Police Division (They are all Colonists)

Monthly Muster and Inspection

Praying for the Late Governor-General Leonard Wood

IWAHIG PENAL COLONY, PHILIPPINE ISLANDS

would not be bullied by threats of force on their part. He put pistols in their hands and charged them with the responsibility of putting down any disturbance among their fellows. He also told them for one week they would have the opportunity to kill him, for he would sleep unguarded and would carry only a walking stick for his protection. If they did not kill him during that week, he would expect them to obey him implicitly thereafter. At the end of the week the leaders met him again, handed over their weapons, and agreed to co-operate with the assistant superintendent. His physical courage and his business-like methods inspired confidence and there was no further trouble. Shortly thereafter he was made superintendent, the first native to hold the position. That action is characteristic of his dealings with the criminals under his charge. He knows criminal psychology.

This colony is intended for first offenders who have proved their good conduct and industry in Bilibid. Recidivists of more than two convictions are not sent to Iwahig.[9] Usually only first offenders sentenced to from twelve years to life are eligible. Of these, only those are eligible who have served a fifth of their sentences, at least two years, and have by good conduct attained the rank of first class and are ready to go into the highest or "trusty" class.[10] The following description of the organization of the colony will present in outline form the way in which matters are arranged:

Under the Spanish régime, exile was a method of punishment. The island of Palawan was used as this place of banishment. After the Americans took over the Philippines in 1898 nothing was done to change this place of exile into a penal colony until 1904. Then under Governor-General Luke Wright and W. Cameron Forbes, at that time Secretary of Commerce

---

[9] Victorio, *op. cit.*, pp. 114, 115.

[10] *Ibid.*, p. 40. In our administrative order approved January 1, 1926, eligibility for promotion to "penal colonist" or "trusty" was made to depend on having served at least one-tenth of the sentence imposed by the court and having attained a general conduct rating of 95 per cent for at least one year immediately preceding the completion of that period of one-tenth of the sentence. "Administrative Order, No. 1-S-1926," cited, Victorio, *op. cit.*, pp. 114, 115.

and Police, later Governor-General, a penal colony was established. Developments in many lines have occurred since that small beginning.

At present (1928) the colony occupies an area of over 100,-000 acres and has about 2000 inmates including the families of some 90 of the prisoners. The inmates are divided into two groups, "colonists" and "settlers." The latter are colonists who are allowed to bring their families to the colony, and live with them in separate dwellings in a *barrio* or district in charge of an officer called a *terriente del barrio* or village sheriff, elected by the "settlers" from their own number. These districts are near to the central station, so that the children may attend the schools established there for the education of the employees' children.

The "colonists" are scattered in some forty districts over the estate in groups of from 30 to 60, each carrying on some phase of colony activity. This group is divided into the following functional sections: (1) Animal husbandry; (2) band; (3) construction and repair; (4) engineering and machinery; (5) executive; (6) farming; (7) forestry; (8) health and sanitation; (9) horticulture; (10) information; (11) land transportation; (12) out-stations; (13) police; (14) bridges and roads; (15) water transportation; (16) miscellaneous.

The construction and repair section has charge of all building, repair and maintenance of all structures in the colony. They make the brick and tile, do the tinsmithing, and burn the lime needed.

The road and bridge section builds the bridges and have constructed all the roads in the colony.

The engineering and machinery section operates the power and electric plant, manufactures the ice, maintains the cold storage, operates the sawmills and planers, the sugar mills and the threshing machines.

The animal industry section has charge of the more than 2000 head of cattle, about 500 water buffalo, and thousands of other domestic animals and fowls. It carries on the dairying and butchers the meat for the colony. The care of the animals and fowls there, as here, has a wholesome influence on the colonists. Here are beings for which they are responsible. These animals they can subject and care for and thus feed their famishing instincts of dominance and sympathy. Here are beings which look up to them. Animals know no artificial social distinctions between a free man and a criminal.

The water transportation section has charge of the operation, maintenance, and repair of the boats, the hauling of firewood, and many other miscellaneous matters.

The land transportation section maintains the motors and other vehicles on land and hauls gravel for road construction and materials for buildings.

Those in the out-stations section are divided into two subsections—the agricultural and the fishing. The former has charge of the planting and the cultivation of coconut trees, tapioca, bananas, rice, corn, and fruit trees, the making of copra, and other agricultural work. The latter catches the fish used in the colony, often going out to sea in launches for a week at a time. They make and repair the fish nets, dig and care for the fish ponds, dry the fish, etc.

The police section, from the standpoint of penology, is one of the most interesting. Those in this section maintain peace and order, execute the punishments, disciplinary measures, and orders. The members are all colonists appointed by the superintendent of the colony and are under the immediate charge of a chief known as Lieutenant of Police.

The duties of those in the other sections are sufficiently indicated by their names.

The colonists work under a system which keeps the economic motive alive. Half of the net value of their products they get to their credit, the other half going to the government.

All the improvements in the colony, such as clearing the land, irrigation, planting the trees, etc., roads, buildings—all are products of the labor of the colonists.

Cultural institutions at Iwahig are not neglected. At the central station near which most of the "settlers" (practically all those with families) live are schools for the children. These schools both the children of the "settlers" and of the officers attend without any distinction between them. Moreover, the children of the convicts play with the children of the officers. One of the large buildings in the group at the central station is the community hall. This is a large recreation hall at which concerts, dances, plays, and exhibits are given. The colonists and the employees and their respective families attend these functions. One night we were there a dance was given. It was impossible for me to tell which were the families of the colonists and which were the families of the officers. They mingled indiscriminately so far as I could observe. Moreover, there are two churches at the central station attended by the officers and their families and by the settlers and their families. Certainly it was a new thing to me in the conduct of an institution for convicts. To them it did not seem to be anything out of the ordinary. Half of the officers had been convicts in former years!

The small number of employees necessary to run the colony is astonishing. They are: superintendent, first and second assistant superintendents, physician, nurse, chief clerk, cashier, property officer, farming instructor, two chaplains, eight foremen, bandmaster, and three teachers. Many of the employees are ex-colonists. Only the superintendent has a weapon! All the colonists carry bolos!

Does this colony pay? In 1925 the gross income of the colony was 113,808.43 pesos and the expenses 203,910.48 pesos. Thus the net cost was 90,102.05 pesos ($45,051), or an average of about $22.50 per inmate.

As at Bilibid the discipline is in the hands of a court under the police section which tries all offenders. There are also Justices of the Peace appointed from among the colonists to try petty offenders. All sentences are subject to the approval of the superintendent.

At the central station is a co-operative store conducted by the colonists at which they sell their surplus products and from which they buy their needed supplies.

Every station is connected by telephone with the central station. Each station reports to central thrice a day.[11]

THE SAN RAMON PRISON AND PENAL FARM

One other institution in the Philippine Islands completes the penal system of the archipelago. It is the institution known as the San Ramon Prison and Penal Farm near Zamboanga in the island of Mindanao.

This institution which combines the features of a penitentiary and a penal colony was established originally as a place of exile for persons convicted of political offenses and were engaged by the government in agricultural work. General Ramon Blancoy Erenas of the Spanish Army established the institution in 1870, in accordance with a royal decree of the Spanish king promulgated in 1869. The name of San Ramon was given to the institution in honor of its founder. Upon the withdrawal of the Spanish Government after the Spanish-American War, all prisoners were released and the buildings were destroyed. Everything movable was taken away or broken up except 5000 coconut trees which had been planted by the Spaniards. In 1907 the American Government re-established the farm. In 1912, when General Pershing of the United States Army was made chief executive of the Department of Mindanao and Sulu he reorganized the institution in its present form, combining a prison and a penal colony for all persons sentenced by the courts of justice of that department. In 1914 this prison and penal farm was placed under the control and supervision of the Bureau of Prisons of the Philippine Islands beginning January 1, 1915.

The San Ramon Prison and Penal Farm occupies an area of 2865 acres. On December 31, 1925, it had a total population of 758. 707 of these were prisoners at San Ramon, 10 were with the constabulary at Zamboanga, and 41 were prisoners living with their families on the farm. Of the total 758 all but 145 were Moros. One hundred forty-five Filipinos were

[11] Victorio, *Prison Reform in the Philippines*, pp. 39–41.

chiefly prisoners transferred from Bilibid to act as clerks, trade instructors, and musicians.

The prisoners are organized much as at Bilibid, and the penal farm is run on the same principle as the penal colony of Iwahig. Hence, it is a combined prison and penal colony chiefly for Moros.

The industrial activities, of course, are very much more limited than those at Bilibid, since most of the Moros are engaged in agricultural work and the institution is run for the purpose of training them for farm work. However, such industries as carpentry, cabinet-making, blacksmithing, etc., mostly related to the farm, are carried on. In 1925 the total cost to the Philippine treasury for running this institution was 66,434 pesos, over two-thirds as much as for 2000 prisoners at Iwahig. The same principles of reformation govern this institution as govern Bilibid and Iwahig.

The prison at Bontoc has been discontinued and the Igorrotes who formerly were incarcerated there are now kept at Bilibid.

CRITICAL ESTIMATE OF THE PHILIPPINE PRISON SYSTEM

Taking the whole system into account I think the following general statements can be made as to its value:

1. Compared with the prison system found in the Islands at the time of the American occupation, the present system represents a very great improvement. Industry has displaced idleness. The reformatory purpose has displaced repression. Some attempt has been made at the classification of prisoners, measures have been taken to maintain the economic motive within the prison on much the same terms as without. The training of the prisoners for a trade or industry has taken its place as a part of the reformatory discipline.

2. Gymnastic exercises, recreations of various kinds, music, and various forms of entertainment have been introduced to alleviate the monotonous temper of the prison.

3. A wage system has been introduced for those who have been in the institution for a certain length of time and who show promise of industrial interest and good conduct. This keeps alive the economic motive, aids discipline, and gives the prisoner an economic status in industry as well as helps him keep the economic lines intact with his family.

4. The continuance of leg irons as a method of discipline is a feature which is condemned by Western penology. As soon as possible that method of disciplining ought to be supplanted by a more humane and less disgraceful method.

5. A probation system adapted to the particular situation in each local community should be started as soon as possible. The absence of such a system probably accounts for the presence of such large numbers in the Philippine penal and correctional institutions.

6. The hospital arrangements in these institutions, aside from their care of the tubercular and the insane, is worthy of emulation.

7. Bilibid should be removed from the center of the city and made a receiving station for all prisoners from the upper part of the archipelago, the women should be removed to a separate institution, and for the short-time prisoners a special institution should be provided in the nature of a farm with some industries such as is found in the state farm for misdemeanants in Indiana or the farm for the District of Columbia misdemeanants at Lorton, Virginia.

8. A system of parole and an indeterminate sentence is badly needed, as the only method at the present time for the release of a man from the institution, aside from the shortening of his sentence by reason of good time, is executive clemency.

9. Special industries such as the manufacture of binding twine should be installed for the recidivists and habitual criminals who cannot be taught a skilled trade.

10. The continuance of men of experience with prisoners in office over long periods is very commendable and should be continued. The provincial prisons should be definitely brought under the control of the Bureau of Prisons and made a component part of the prison system of the Philippines as is done with the jails in England.

11. The chief menace threatening the prison system of the Philippines is politics. Would that were true only of those Islands! I am told the director constantly has to resist the pressure of politicians to have him recommend the pardon of some of their friends. Even less than in most of the United States are the prison and the prison official looked upon as a social institution and a social functionary respectively. Graft and influence are felt everywhere. That is the trouble with most of the provincial prisons, and that creates practically all the difficulties for the officials in the Bureau of Prisons. The declared purposes of the law and of the Bureau of Prisons are in accord with the best penological principles. But what demons of political demagoguery and graft they have constantly to fight!

12. Moreover, the breath of scandal has occasionally blown fiercely over this promising system. Both American and Philippine officials, whether justly of unjustly is not for me to say, have suffered from it. Men by nature are much the same everywhere, but how they act is

determined largely by the culture under which they find themselves. Peculation is not held in quite such bad odor among the Filipinos as among us. The rift between classes is greater. The ideals of democratic equality between man and man are newer there. Sex morals, thanks to hundreds of years of dominance of the white race there and to the mixture of different culture patterns, are not as puritanical as ours. Consequently graft, abuse of prisoners, and immorality have freer scope in the mores of the people. Now, impose on these people an American régime, and these conditions come to the surface with astonishing frequency.

13. At present every prisoner is at work. But the time is coming when the administration will have to face objections to Bilibid competing with free labor and with outside business and industry, in its public-account industries, and in its work for private individuals on orders. The Orient has yet to face these distressing problems, but not yet.

What has been done in an archipelago of scattered islands in the Philippines with 12,000,000 people can be done in any of our more populous states of the United States. Everywhere the development of penal colonies should go forward. The Philippines are unusually fortunate in that the Americans in the Islands and the leading Filipinos have taken great interest in the care of their prisoners. When that is done in the United States a better prison system will be in vogue here.

BIBLIOGRAPHY

Alzate, M. A., *Convict Labor in the Philippine Islands*, Manila, 1926.
Catalogue of the Products of the Industrial Division of Bilibid Prison, Manila, 1927.
Description of the Existing Penal System Including Brief Comparisons with Earlier Penalties, by Ramon Victorio, Manila, 1926. (mimeographed.)
Philippine Prisons Review. Monthly publication of the Bureau of Prisons beginning in 1925.
Rules and Regulations Governing Iwahig Penal Colony, Manila, 1914.
Victorio, R., *Needed Changes in the Legal Provisions Concerning Crimes against Property,* a lecture delivered before the faculty and student body of the College of Law of the University of the Philippines on July 9, 1925.

Victorio, R., *Our Prisons—as Educational and Vocational Institutions,* Manila, 1927.

Victorio, R., *The Adult Offender and the Community.* An address delivered before the First Annual Conference of Social Work, November 4, 1927, Manila.

Victorio, R., *Prison Reform in the Philippines,* Manila, 1927.

Victorio, R., *A Brief History of the Iwahig Penal Colony.* (Ms.)

CHAPTER III

THE PRISON SYSTEM OF CEYLON

PICTURE an island in the tropics less than half the size of Wisconsin or Iowa, with a population almost twice as large as the populations of either of these states. Heat and moisture have made this a veritable paradise. For half the year the sun shines almost directly down upon Ceylon. The southwest monsoon at one period of the year, and the northeast monsoon at another period, striking the high mountain ranges in the interior, bring down upon the land the moisture which, in combination with the heat, produce a luxuriance of vegetation seen only in the rainy tropics. Wherever man has not fought it, the jungle luxuriates. That is Ceylon.

Formerly conquered by the Dutch from the Portuguese and then by the English, Ceylon was made a crown colony in 1802 when it was separated from the Madras Presidency. Since that time it has been a crown colony of Britain. Its area of 25,332 square miles is one of the most fertile in the world. In 1921 it had a population of 4,504,549. The estimated population on December 31, 1927, was 5,288,792.

The population of more than four and a half million in 1921 was distributed as follows:

Race Distribution		Military, Shipping, and Miscellaneous
Europeans	8,099	838
Burghers and Eurasians	29,403	129
Low Country Sinhalese	1,926,892	623
Kandyan Sinhalese	1,089,078	66
Ceylon Tamils	517,189	684
Indian Tamils	602,510	635
Ceylon Moors	251,925	153

Race Distribution		Military, Shipping, and Miscellaneous
Indian Moors	32,923	875
Malays	13,395	66
Veddas	4,510	
Others	21,930	2,626
	4,497,854	6,695

It is apparent that more than half of the population are Sinhalese. The next largest contingent of the population are Tamils; the next are the Moors.

Moreover, this population in 1921 was distributed by trade classification as follows:

Agriculture	62.3 per cent (2,803,056, of whom 1,347,415 were earners and 1,455,641 were dependents).
Industrial	11.9 per cent (533,400, of whom 288,697 were earners and 244,703 were dependents).
Trade	7.7 per cent (345,824, of whom 162,376 were earners and 183,448 were dependents).

In spite of the fact that the population of Ceylon is four times as dense as that of Wisconsin or Iowa, only 12.9 per cent is urban. There are only four principal towns—Colombo, with a population of 244,163, Galle, with 39,073, Jaffna, with 42,436, and Kandy, with 32,562. The rest of the four and a half million were distributed in villages scattered chiefly over the non-mountainous region.

The population is divided among religions as follows:

Buddhists	2,769,805
Hindus	982,073
Muslims	302,532
Christians	443,400

Unlike India, Ceylon in her religion is predominantly Buddhist. Out of 320,000,000 Indians in India four-fifths are of the Hindu religion, and one-fifth are Muslims, whereas in Ceylon, Muslims constitute only one out of fifteen of the population.[1]

THE CRIMINAL POPULATION

Since 1924 there has been a considerable decrease in the admissions of convicted prisoners to the prisons of Ceylon. In 1924, 9357 were admitted, in 1925, 9061, and in 1929, 8631. Moreover, the total admissions of convicted prisoners from the higher courts show a decrease. In 1924 there were 1314; in 1925, 1212; in 1926, 1202; in 1929, 1172. In the higher courts are handled those who are charged with the more serious crimes. On the other hand, the number of convictions for murder and manslaughter have slightly increased since 1924. No clear trend is to be shown in the number sentenced to death. From 1924 to 1929 the number has fluctuated from 59 to 75. Only a little over half of these have been executed. Capital punishment has not lost its vigor in Ceylon. Of those committed to institutions from all courts in 1929, 6509 were males, 290 females, or 1 female to 23 males. This is in contrast to the commitment rate in the United States in 1926 of 1 female to 16.3 men. The distribution of the first offenders by age is of interest. They consist of three groups—from the ages of sixteen to twenty-one inclusive, from twenty-two to twenty-five inclusive, and above twenty-five years of age. The numbers committed in these three classifications in 1929 were respectively 797, 1820, and 4500. Almost three-fifths of them, therefore, were above twenty-five years of age. In Ceylon, consequently, the higher age groups include a much larger proportion than in most of the prisons of the United States. This fact is the more surprising when one remembers that in the United States often the adult reformatories take in a considerable number of offenders between sixteen and thirty.

Moreover, as in the United States, large numbers of those who go to the prisons of Ceylon are incarcerated because of default of the payment of fines. Of the first offenders between sixteen and twenty-one over half go to prison for that reason;

[1] *Statesman's Year-Book, 1928,* Art. "Ceylon."

of those between twenty-two and twenty-five years of age, about five-ninths; of those above twenty-five years of age, more than half. In this connection one must remember that the prisons of Ceylon include not only what we know in the United States as state prisons, but also the county jails.[2] In Ceylon from 1924 to 1929 there has been no marked increase in those convicted for crimes of violence. Such crimes include murder, culpable homicide, attempted murder, grievous hurt, and hurt with dangerous weapons. In these three years the largest number of those sentenced for crimes of violence received sentences of not over six months. For example, in 1929, out of 1185, 702 were sentenced for not over that period. Only 90 were given sentences of over ten years.[3]

There are very few escapes from the prisons of Ceylon. In 1924 there were only 7 escapes; in 1925, 3; in 1926, 5; in 1927, 8; in 1928, 4; in 1929, 5. During the same year the recaptures were respectively 6, 6, 4, 8, 4, and 6. It is apparent that some of the recaptures were escapes from previous years. The island is small, departures from the island are strictly controlled, hence it is quite possible to recapture those who escape. The problem is by no means so difficult as in such a country as the United States.

Reconvicted Prisoners. In 1926, 18.52 per cent and in 1929, 17.43 per cent of the admissions were reconvicted prisoners. Because of the excellent identification system in Ceylon in the Bureau of Criminal Investigation this figure is very much more exact than we could expect in a country like the United States. On the whole it seems very small when compared with the experience in the United States, where the recidivists in some prisons run to more than 50 per cent of the inmates of the prisons. However, one must bear in mind that the figures from Ceylon represent not only what we call the state prisons, but the local jails as well. Even so, however, the figure is small for Ceylon. Consider this percentage in

---

[2] *Administrative Report of the Inspector-General of Prisons for 1926*, Colombo, 1927, pp. 1–3; *Ibid.*, for 1929, pp. 1–6.

[3] *Ibid.*, 1929, p. 5.

comparison with 45 per cent of the inmates of the Wisconsin State Prison who were recidivists, 57.4 per cent in Massachusetts, 51 per cent in West Virginia, 42 per cent in Georgia, 26 per cent of the inmates of the State Reformatory in Wisconsin, and 17.5 per cent in the county jails of Wisconsin.[4]

While the total admissions into the prisons of Ceylon in 1929 amounted to 8631, the daily average of all convicted prisoners during the year was 3109. Into the minor prisons of Ceylon go also unconvicted prisoners, such as debtors, witnesses, those awaiting further examination, those committed for trial, those awaiting sentence, those arrested on warrant, and a small number of lunatics. During 1929 the average daily count of unconvicted prisoners was 492. However, during 1929 the total of 7263 unconvicted prisoners were admitted to these prisons.[5] Comparing the daily average of convicted prisoners in Ceylon prisons in 1929 with the number in prisons and reformatories in the United States in 1926 per 100,000, estimated population (for Ceylon, 1927) Ceylon shows up favorably with a rate of 60 compared with that of 85 for the United States.[6]

THE PRISON SYSTEM OF CEYLON

Profiting from England's experience with prisons and jails, Ceylon has the unified system of local and convict prisons. The Inspector-General of Prisons has charge of all these institutions. This system of unified control makes for efficiency throughout the island and permits the administration to follow a carefully worked out and integrated procedure in the treatment of all charged with crime.

There are six convict prisons. They are the Welikada Prison in Colombo, the Bogambara Prison at Kandy, the Mahara Prison some twelve miles out of Colombo, the Jaffna Prison on the northern point of the island, the Negombo Prison

[4] A Report of the Wisconsin Mental Deficiency Survey, Madison, 1920, pp. 2, 8, 17.
[5] Administration Report of the Inspector-General of Prisons for 1926, Colombo, 1927, p. 6; Ibid. for 1929, p. 7.
[6] Prisoners in State and Federal Prisons and Reformatories, 1926, Bureau of the Census, Washington, 1929, p. 4.

in the southwestern part, and the Anuradhapura, which is in the north central part of the island. The chief local prisons are at Galle, Bodulla, and Batticoloa, although sometimes Negombo and Anuradhapura are classed as minor prisons in the Reports.

Classification. One great advantage of a unified prison system is the possibility of classification of different kinds of prisoners in different institutions. The classification of the prisoner is not so much according to crime as according to length of sentence, and as to whether the prisoner is a first offender or a repeater. The Ceylon prison authorities believe that this classification aids in the rehabilitation of the prisoner. The major part of the responsibility of rehabilitation rests on the shoulders of the permanent prison official, who has under him prisoners with varying length of sentence. This gives him some opportunity of studying each individual with the assistance of the various social-service workers, usually privately supported, who work in the prisons.

The Welikada Prison is the receiving station of the prison system of Ceylon. It is also used for those sentenced by the Colombo courts for a month or less, and as the institution from which discharges and transfers from all prisons are made. Regularly confined in it are four classes: (1) All male convicted first offenders sentenced for over two years; (2) all "star class," *i.e.*, European and educated Ceylonese first offenders; (3) all juvenile (under twenty-three years) first offenders no matter what the length of sentence; and (4) all female prisoners other than short-term prisoners sentenced in other cities.

The Bogambara Prison at Kandy cares for the following classes: (1) First offenders sentenced by the local courts for a month or less, and all prisoners sentenced for less than two years; (2) Special Class "A," *i.e.*, specially selected reconvicted offenders with sentences of over two years; and (3) those sentenced to preventive detention, *i.e.*, habitual criminals to whose regular sentence is added an additional sentence of from three to five years.

The Mahara Prison receives chiefly reconvicted prisoners of the worst type with histories of more or less habitual criminal habits, but who have not yet been sentenced to preventive detention, and a few who have proved to be obstreperous in other prisons. These are subjected to a régime of rigorous imprisonment at very hard labor. Class "A" of this type of prisoners is at Bogambara Prison at Kandy, referred to above. Classes "B" and "C" are here at Mahara. Class "B" comprises recidivists with sentences of over two years rigorous imprisonment. Out of this class are recruited members of class "A" at Kandy. Class "C" consists of recidivists with sentences of from six months to two years. Each of these classes is kept in a separate ward so as to prevent intermingling.

The Jaffna Prison has four classes of prisoners as follows: (1) Prisoners of the Special Gang composed of prisoners of very bad repute, such as leaders of gangs, escaped prisoners, and those whose conduct in prison has been such that they must be kept from those of a better character. These are kept separate from the other prisoners and are forced to the most rigorous kind of labor. This group is divided into A and B sections. Those in the latter section are accorded better conditions and more privileges than those in section A. (2) Prisoners under monthly report who have been sent here because of their misbehavior in other prisons. (3) Short-term prisoners who have been sentenced for not more than six months. They cannot be trained in so short a time for any industrial job and are a nuisance in the other prisons. They are thus kept together and are put to such menial tasks as can be found for them. (4) Prisoners sentenced from local courts for a month or less chiefly for violation of the motor ordinances. Thus the Jaffna Prison is used for rather hopeless offenders and for those for whom, because of short sentences, nothing constructive can be done. Many of these short-term prisoners are used on reclamation works for the government.

The Anuradhapura Prison receives those with sentences of over six months and up to one year who are first offenders.

The Negombo Prison is a convalescent institution for all the prisons of the department.

At the local prisons are received both first offenders and re-convicted who are sentenced to one month and under. The prison administration admits that it is almost impossible officially to do anything constructive with those sentenced to so short a period, although it makes efforts to have volunteer social service workers in these institutions. Hence the official experiments are being tried out only in the convict prisons, and it is to them that special attention must be given.[7]

The prisoners in the prisons of Ceylon as a whole are divided into a number of classes. In 1929 the different classes with the daily average number in each one were as follows:

Penal stage	436.93
Class 4	1215.41
Class 3	507.09
Class 2	311.03
Class 1	434.30
Road Ordinance Defaulters	0.00
Simple Imprisonment	94.73
Preventive Detention	109.76

PREVENTIVE DETENTION

Ceylon is experimenting with England's preventive detention scheme. Anyone who has had four previous convictions for a felony may be sentenced to a preventive detention prison for from three to five years in addition to the regular sentence. In 1929 the average daily number in the class was 109 and there were 29 such cases admitted from Mahara Prison where they had finished their sentences of rigorous imprisonment. The experience in Ceylon has not yet been decisive as to the value of the scheme.

Those in preventive detention are considered the worst criminals. They have been convicted at least four times. Because of their incorrigibility they are given a regular sentence

[7] *Ibid.* for 1926, p. 23; *Ibid.* for 1927, pp. 10–26; *Ibid.* for 1928, pp. 10–34; *Ibid.* for 1929, pp. 12–22.

according to the crime which they have committed and then have added to that sentence from three to five years of what is called preventive detention. Simple imprisonment is for those who are sentenced to prison but do not have to work. These are the least serious offenders. Those sentenced to rigorous imprisonment are divided into four classes. They enter Class 4 which has the largest number. By good behavior and earnest work they may be advanced from class to class. Increased privileges go with each advance in class.[8]

On this preventive detention system in Ceylon the Inspector-General remarks:

One of the objects underlying a sentence of preventive detention is that the prisoner might be induced to learn a trade which would benefit him on discharge. All preventive detention prisoners are thus employed in industrial parties and every effort is made to teach them a trade. It is to be feared, however, that the majority of these prisoners have proved themselves incapable or unwilling to better themselves in any way. As a whole they do not take much interest in their work and close supervision is necessary or the result would be an outturn of bad work.

Since the introduction of the preventive detention system in 1914, 387 prisoners have been admitted, and of the 100 at present undergoing preventive detention only 10 are skilled and 37 proficient workers. Though by good conduct and industry they can earn badges which carry with them pay and privileges, and though they are also allowed to attend educational classes and to participate in games on two evenings in the week, and are further given every facility to attend religious meetings and lectures, little interest is shown, and this type of prisoner does not appear to regard these facilities as anything but a means of relaxation from the ordinary routine.

During the year, 32 prisoners have been discharged from preventive detention and 8 reconvicted.

There has been a marked improvement in the discipline of the prisoners generally, though the preventive detention prisoners are still a constant source of trouble to the staff. Quarrels not infrequently break out among them, necessitating prompt action to avert further trouble.[9]

[8] Ibid., 1929, p. 18. Previous reports should be consulted for changes and for details of the situation.
[9] Administration Report of the Inspector-General of Prisons for 1929, Ceylon Government Press, Colombo, 1930, p. 18.

WOMEN PRISONERS

As in all countries, the number of women prisoners is rather small in Ceylon. In 1926 there was an average of only 74.82 women prisoners in all Ceylon.

Only two of the prisons of Ceylon have departments for women, that at Welikada in Colombo for long termers, and the old prison at Kandy for short termers. In 1929 only one female was sentenced to death. In the same year, however, 290 women were committed to prisons from all courts.

There is no classification of the women in a prison. Private organizations like the Girl Guides' association, local social service leagues, and the Salvation Army teach the women needle and fancy work, basket-making, cloth-weaving, and educational classes in the vernacular. The administration is alive to the unsatisfactory arrangements for handling female prisoners, but has not yet been able to secure special treatment of women prisoners in a separate institution.

MEDICAL WORK IN THE PRISONS

All the prisons have hospitals in connection with them. Originally there was an old convict hospital at Borella which was abandoned in 1926 when the new hospital at Welikada, with 120 beds, was occupied. This prison hospital is the best one in the island and includes a special female hospital. Also in this hospital there is an infectious disease department with 60 beds.[10] Both from the reports and from my own observation at Welikada, the prison hospital there is well adapted to the needs of the people. The outstanding diseases in these prisons seem to be a form of hookworm and malaria. At all the institutions, the medical reports denote a progressive outlook. There, as here, prisoners are provided what is probably better medical care than they receive in free society.

LABOR IN THE PRISONS

In general there are three forms of labor in the prisons, public works, manufacturing, either for state use or for private

[10] *Ibid.* for 1926, p. 13.

demand, and a combination of public works and state use. In some of the prisons, also, the public-account system is in vogue to a small extent.

In Ceylon, prison labor does not suffer from some of the difficulties experienced in prisons in the United States. For example, there are no such things as I saw in New York, where only about one-third of the men are at work, or in Pennsylvania, where only half are working.

However, one must not infer that the present rather fine system of prison labor in Ceylon has just happened. It has come about as the result of careful planning. The emergence of Ceylon's prison industries from an unorganized and chaotic condition began in 1924 when a thorough reorganization took place. As a result the industries have expanded in variety and in total output. The prison management buys most of its raw materials from the Government Stores and from the Forest Department. Of the finished articles, 95 per cent are sold to the government departments and the remaining 5 per cent to private buyers. New industries are introduced experimentally, and if successful are retained. A measure of this expansion in total output is indicated by the value of the articles produced over a series of years. In 1927 the value was 117,-585 rupees, while in 1929 the value had increased to 299,365 rupees. While industrial work is carried on at the Welikada, Kandy, Jaffna, Batticoloa, Negombo, and Mahara prisons, at only the first two are there such necessary requisites as modern machinery, etc., which make possible large-scale production. By all odds the prison at Welikada is the most important from the standpoint of organization and output. At Welikada the following industries are carried on: Carpentry, blacksmithing, tinsmithing, brass work, gold and silver smithing, tailoring, shoe-making, and leather-working, laundering, weaving, fiber work of many kinds, rattan work, soap-making, the making of mail and treasury bags, and brush-making. The most important of these, both from the point of financial return and also from the value of these industries in training the prisoners for a useful job on discharge, are the first two. The following table indicates the relative value of each line of industry and also the growth for the last three years for which reports are available:

Workshop	Value of Outturn for 1926–1927		Value of Outturn for 1927–1928		Value of Outturn for 1928–1929		Daily Average Strength of Parties during 1928–1929
	Rs.	c.	Rs.	c.	Rs.	c.	
Carpentry	57,801	8	82,637	81	149,633	55	332
Laundry	34,076	83	38,085	33	43,861	38	93
Tailoring	31,225	43	19,182	44	40,581	75	102
Fiber works	8,947	59	10,030	73	12,751	94	75
Rattan works	7,931	56	8,775	87	10,652	65	32
Shoe-making	8,924	36	10,844	31	11,537	39	30
Smithy	7,547	81	7,706	86	9,079	46	37
Weaving	20,852	81	25,303	12	18,678	12	41
Soap-making	—	—	1,394	74	1,777	9	2
Brush-making	—	—	—	—	812	41	3
	177,307	41	203,961	21	299,365	74	747 [11]

Within the last few years a great expansion has occurred in a number of lines within the prisons. For example, all furniture required by the government must be obtained from the prison system when the latter is able to furnish the goods. While some furniture is made for private parties, most of it is for the government. The value of the amount of furniture produced rose from 82,637 rupees in 1927–1928 to 149,633 rupees in 1928–1929. With the government handing over to the Prison Department the repairing and making of mail bags instead of having them made on contract, a saving of 44 cents (Ceylon) a bag has been effected. Uniforms for the officers of the government, mattresses for the hospitals, and clothing for the prisoners are manufactured. Private orders for upholstering furniture and for private suits are executed by the prisoners.

The women make hospital clothing, such as shirts, jackets for women, pillow-cases, aprons, banias, mosquito netting,

[11] *Ibid.* for 1929, pp. 22–25.

bed sheets, dresses, etc. In two years the value of the output in these lines more than doubled. As the Welikada Prison an up-to-date laundry is operated. All laundry for the hospitals in Colombo, for the Asylum for the Insane, for the Railway, for the Police and the Prison Departments is done there. This industry increased from 38,089 rupees to 43,861 rupees in one year recently. Weaving has developed rapidly of late years. This industry is carried on at the Welikada and Bogambara prisons. The materials for prison clothing, bed sheets, towels, handkerchiefs, etc., are woven here. Also some materials for private clothing mentioned above are produced in these shops. Fiber industry is carried on at four of the prisons, the articles produced including rope, string, doormats, coir matting, brooms, etc. I saw some of the prisoners under discipline beating out the fiber from coconut husks. Shoe-making is conducted at two of the prisons. Boots for officers, shoes for certain classes of prisoners, baton straps for the police and prison officers, dog collars for local boards and municipalities, and private orders for shoes and suit cases are produced. In four of the prisons rattan work is done. Not only is wooden furniture rattaned, but whole articles made from rattan are produced. This industry not only is profitable but also provides good training for a job after discharge. If you wash your hands on the trains of Ceylon you will probably use prison-made soap, and all the soap used in the laundry at Welikada Prison is made by the prisoners. Brush-making has recently been introduced both for the government and for private use.

On the whole the prison industries of Ceylon are progressing rapidly. They are suited to the habits of the people and to the labor situation in the island. The question of prison-made goods has not become as acute as it is in the United States or in England. As a consequence, when I went into an office to confer with a government official, I sat in a chair made by prisoners, the mat on which I wiped my shoes at the door, the brushes which cleaned the floors were produced in the prison. When I took the railway train to visit Kandy, the sheets on

the bed were made in some prison, their cleanliness was secured
by the prison laundry at Welikada.   The macadam roads over
which I rode to visit the prison at Mahara were made out of
"road metal" quarried and broken up by prisoners.   The neat
shorts and other clothing worn by the officers who showed me
about and the uniforms of the railway officials were the products of Ceylonese prisoners.

Printing formerly was done for the Government Printing
Office and in 1926 38,362 rupees were earned.   In 1928 this
activity was discontinued.   At the convict prison at Jaffna
and at the local prison at Batticoloa reclamation work for the
public was carried on with earnings in 1929 of 30,712 rupees.
Prisoners are also used to clear jungle and to reforest for the
government.   In 1929 3,225 rupees were earned by the prisoners at this work.   Formerly the prisoners at Anuradhapura
operated a rice mill and engaged in the cultivation of rice
paddies.   This, however, has been discontinued.   Before it
was discontinued in 1926 they earned 369 rupees.   Breaking
stone occupies a good many prisoners, especially those in the
lower classes in the prisons who have not learned a trade before
they become prisoners.   For this work 75 cents a day is paid
by the government for adult male prisoners, 37½ cents for
juveniles, and 50 cents for females.   In 1929 the prisons
earned in this way 148,852 rupees. the prisons also supply ma-
sons for the Public Works Department and for repairing the
prison buildings.   In this way in 1929 they earned 18,207
rupees.   A few prisoners at Jaffna were used for sweeping
public buildings.   In 1929, the prisoners earned for the Prison
Department on Public Works a total of 383,421 rupees.[12]

Income from Manufactures.   Manufacturing carried on
in the prisons is partly state use and partly public account;
that is, a part of the materials manufactured is for government
departments and a part is on orders for the state acting as the
entrepreneur or for private individuals.   For example, in 1929
56,167 rupees were earned in making brooms, fiber strings,

[12] *Ibid.* for 1929, p. 7.   100 cents make a rupee.   The Ceylonese rupee in 1928
was worth 40 cents in United States money.

rugs, coir mats, tats, coal bags, etc., at 75 cents per head per day. 6,251 rupees were earned in making uniforms, boots for officers, and other private orders. 14,059 rupees were earned by tailors employed in executing orders from government stores and other government departments; 10,461 rupees from prisoners employed as blacksmiths, tinsmiths, etc., for government departments. Female prisoners earned 8,811 rupees in various industrial work such as tailoring, rope-making, lace-making, etc., at 50 cents per head per day. 87,849 rupees were earned by carpenters among the prisoners, making furniture for government departments. Practically all of this manufacturing is done by hand. Very little machinery is employed. In 1929 the total of 242,841 rupees were earned by the prisoners for the Prison Department in these various lines of manufacture. The total income produced by the prisoners for the Prison Department in 1926 was 626,262 rupees. The total expenditures that year were 938,959 rupees, leaving the net cost to the State of 312,696 rupees or a net cost per head to support the prisoner outside of his labor of 83.81 rupees.[13] The net cost in 1926 was 133.77 rupees. Thus, the prison industries in the last few years have greatly decreased the cost of caring for prisoners.

There, as here, however, the prison administration has difficulties to face. Here it is the agitation against prison-made goods, contract labor, and the difficulty of getting governing bodies to use prison-made articles; there to get freedom to buy raw materials in the market, and, as here, to get government departments to use the products of the prisons. At present in Ceylon the wood used in the prison industries may be bought in the open market, but other materials must be bought from the Government Stores.

The rapid development of prison industries in the island has led the administration to the belief that a special staff should be set up to manage the industries and thus release the regular staff for the other important aspects of their work for which they are much better fitted. Why is not the suggestion

13 *Ibid.*, pp. 7, 8.

sound? For years I have advocated that in addition to the warden there should be a manager of the prison industries in the prisons of the United States. At present the wardens in most prisons have to devote themselves so much to the business management of the prison's industrial activities that they have very little time to give to the other administrative duties.

Wages for Prisoners. In Ceylon there is provision made for a small wage to all first offenders and for the members of the special class of reconvicted prisoners. The wage is on a sliding scale based upon the badges won for good conduct and industry.[14] Hitherto, reconvicted prisoners have not been looked upon as hopeful convicts. The Inspector-General recently introduced this special class into which reconvicted prisoners are entered after careful study and observation. The purpose is to open up a new road for the reconvicted man which enables him to realize that an honest and hard-working life outside prison walls is infinitely preferable to a life drawn out in the quarries at Mahara Prison for the habituals. The Inspector-General reports that since the introduction of this special class a daily average of about 130 has been maintained with gratifying results both inside the prison and on their discharge.[15]

EDUCATION IN PRISON

In Ceylon for all prisoners under the age of twenty-four years education is compulsory. The classes are conducted by teachers appointed by the Education Department who conduct classes daily from 2:30 P.M. to 4:30 P.M. except on Saturdays and Sundays. The curriculum is the same as that of the government schools up to the sixth standard in Sinhalese and to the fourth standard in Tamil. In 1928 the daily average for the year was 90 as compared with 70 in 1926. The con-

---

[14] *Administration Report of the Acting Inspector-General of Prisons for 1928*, p. 31.

[15] *Ibid.*, p. 23. The wage for prisoners is not mentioned in any of the Reports since 1926. However, I assume that the payment of a wage continues for these classes. As stated before, this special class was transferred in July, 1926, from Welikada to Bogambara Prison at Kandy. The reason for this was that it was decided to make Welikada purely a prison for first offenders.

victs are promoted from class to class, subject to their passing the annual examination held by the inspector from the Education Department. It is interesting to notice that in 1929 out of 86 boys who took the examination 97 per cent passed.

In addition to these regular classes under the Education Department, voluntary evening classes are held from 5:30 to 7:00 P.M. These are confined to the teaching of English under the direction of representatives of the Royal College Social Service League, and Wesley College Social Service League three times a week. On the intervening days these people also train certain of the star class—that is, educated Europeans and Sinhalese—to carry on work prescribed by the syllabus. All educational work inside the Welikada Prison is under the direct supervision of a star-class prisoner of good educational qualifications. The Inspector-General reports that this system works well and has the additional advantage of enabling classes to continue uninterrupted under the guidance and unassisted direction of these star-class prisoners, when the attendance of the social workers from these two colleges is in temporary abeyance during the holidays. These voluntary evening classes are popular.

Furthermore, at Welikada conversation in English is stimulated by informal talks between star-class men and their pupils for a short time every day after class hour. The results of this system are to be seen in the fact that in 1926 out of 81 boys who took the examination 95 per cent were successful. This is all the more striking in view of the fact that while no less than two years before most of the boys had no knowledge of English, some of them had progressed as far as the fourth standard at the time of the examination.

Furthermore, in 1926, at Welikada, two Sinhalese and English classes were established for the benefit of the older and generally quite illiterate types of prisoner. The number of these classes have now been increased to seven, four for English and Sinhalese, and three for Tamil. These classes are entirely voluntary. They are conducted by some educated or star-class prisoners. The average attendance at these classes has been good. Many of the inmates have progressed as far as the third standard.

For the benefit of the more educated—that is, the star-class prisoners—a series of debates and lectures on general subjects of interest have been initiated. They are conducted by some members of the Royal College Social Service League. These debates, besides being instructive and interesting, have done much to relieve the dreary monotony of the evening hours after work.

In addition to these educational activities in 1926 steps were taken toward the formation of a commercial class among members of the star class for instruction in shorthand, typewriting, bookkeeping, and accounting. The purpose was to turn out some of the more educated and intelligent of this class of prisoners as experienced and efficient clerks, so that when they are discharged they may have better prospects of obtaining employment. These classes are conducted by an expert in all forms of commercial training from the Rodrigo Business College of Colombo. By arrangements with the Pitman Shorthand Institute and the Institute of Commerce in the United Kingdom these prisoners are allowed to take the necessary examinations, the papers being set and read in England.[16]

Most of these educational activities are carried on at the Welikada Prison which is used for first offenders. However, in addition to the classes for women in Welikada, voluntary classes are carried on by the private social service workers in needle and fancy work and useful arts both at Welikada and at the old jail in Kandy.

SOME NEW EXPERIMENTS IN CEYLON

We have already noticed the system of self-government in use in the prison systems in the Philippines. In the prisons of Ceylon, especially that for first offenders, the Welikada Prison at Colombo, certain further experiments have been made in the direction of placing responsibility upon individual prisoners. For some time there had been organized a group

[16] *Ibid.* for 1926, p. 9.

of prisoners known as "prison orderlies." This group was based upon the classification system in the prison system of Ceylon. In order to understand the arrangement a word must be said about this classification system in Welikada. On admission a prisoner enters the "penal stage." In this stage he remains for a month. Then he is advanced to Class IV. Here he serves eleven months. Then he is promoted to Class III, where he serves for one year. Then he advances to Class II. After a year in this class he is put into Class I. For misconduct he may not be advanced to the next class. Each succeeding class carries advantages in the shape of type of labor he must do, remission of sentence, gratuity, good-conduct badges, etc. Here you have the English system of classification.

From Class I, after six months good conduct, are recruited the prison orderlies. These orderlies assist the officers in the conduct of the prison. In 1923 the experiment was tried of taking forty of these prison orderlies and making them "disciplinary prison orderlies" on six months' probation. Their duties were to assist officers in the supervision of working parties. After the experiment got started the scheme of recruiting this group from the prison orderlies was based upon a system of badges. A prison orderly after six months of good conduct was given a good-conduct badge. After he had earned three such badges he might be promoted to be a disciplinary prison orderly. Hence behind a disciplinary prison orderly lies six and a half years of continuous good conduct. Later provision was made whereby the badge system was extended down the line to the lower classes so that a prisoner might earn earlier a maximum of four badges; that is, on entry to Class II. The purpose was thus to create a class of badge prisoners from which disciplinary prison orderlies would eventually be recruited.[17]

This system met with such success that in 1925 it was decided to increase their number to a total of 100. These orderlies assist the disciplinary staff by being placed in charge of small working parties inside the prison. They are selected

[17] *Ibid.* for 1928, p. 11.

with extreme care and are subjected to very close scrutiny by the prison officials during their probationary period. Through a roster system each individual "disciplinary prison orderly" never spends more than six months at one time away from headquarters at Welikada Prison. Their smartness, loyalty, reliability, and high sense of duty are stimulated by granting them extra privileges, such as association during meals and sleeping hours, more frequent opportunity to shave, permission to play games, etc., during recreation hours. A part of them are termed disciplinary prison orderly instructors, whose numbers also have been increased. The latter serve in teaching and training raw hands in the various industrial parties. Experience has shown that they have done much to improve the standard of work all around.

As the result of the good work of these disciplinary prison orderlies and with the purpose of increasing their responsibilities further, a new class called "prison monitors" was created on March 15, 1926. Three selected disciplinary prison orderlies and three selected star-class prisoners were appointed to this class. These monitors have powers inside the prison equal to regular prison officers except for the handling of keys, and are distinguished by a red armlet with the letters P. M. in black on the right arm. Experience has shown that by example and precept they have contributed in no small measure to the tone and discipline of these classes in particular and of the prison in general.[18]

A further experiment was inaugurated in 1927. The reports of Osborne's mutual welfare league in the prisons of New York had reached Ceylon. It seemed to the management that its experience with the disciplinary prison orderlies at Welikada indicated that a further step should be taken which would place further responsibility upon them. After a long period of preliminary work had been done in explaining the scheme to the men, and in working out adaptations of the plan to the peculiar situation in Ceylon, it was decided to organize what is called the Disciplinary Prison Orderlies' League.

[18] *Ibid.*, for 1926, p. 9.

It is based upon the Osborne plan but with certain modifications, as may be seen by the following quotation of its constitution:

1. This League will be known as the League of Disciplinary Prison Orderlies of Welikada, with Inspector-General of Prisons as President.
2. The objects of the League are:
   (1) To promote in every way the true interests and welfare of the men of this class confined in prison.
   (2) To cultivate a sense of understanding in and responsibility to the League laws as a community, and thereby to arrive at a wider understanding of the necessity for similar adherence to the laws of society.
   (3) To obtain a willing co-operation with the Prison Authorities in producing order, a high moral tone, and good discipline.
3. Membership will be open to all persons of this class who are prepared to make the promise referred to below.
4. The general management of the League will be in the hands of a committee of management consisting of:
   Ex-officio. The Superintendent, Chairman; the Head Jailer, Vice-Chairman; the Deputy Jailer, Secretary.
   Elected. Six Disciplinary Prison Orderly delegates.
The right to veto the election of any member to the Committee of Management is invested in the Chairman.
5. Every member prior to admission into the League will be required to make the following solemn promise:
   "I ————— hereby declare that I will adhere in spirit and in letter to the rules and regulations of the League of Disciplinary Prison Orderlies, and to further give my word of honor to assist the Superintendent and staff by doing all that may be required of me."
Such promise will be made in the presence of the Committee of Management.
6. General meetings of the League will be held once in every quarter and meetings of the Committee of Management once every month or as often as required.
7. Members of the Committee of Management, individually and collectively, will be held responsible for the good order, high moral tone, and general discipline of the members of the League. All cases of misdemeanors or breach of rules will be reported direct by the elected delegates of the Committee of Management to the Vice-Chairman, whose duty it will be,

after making thorough inquiry into the matter, to bring the offender up for disposal before the Chairman's court— such court to be composed of all members of the Committee of Management.

8. Elections of members of the Committee of Management will be held once every six months at a general meeting of the League. Existing members of the Committee will be distinguished by a red star to be worn on the right breast.

9. No member of the League will be eligible for election as a member of the Committee of Management unless he has served six months in the League.

10. Any member of the League found guilty of an offense shall have the right of appeal to the President against the ruling of the court.[19]

The Committee of Management is also the court of the League. The chairman is judge and the six elected members are the jury. This court tries all cases of misdemeanor and breach of the rules. The Committee of Management is held regularly once a month for a free discussion of all sorts of matters relating to the conduct of the prison and the welfare of the prisoners from arrangements for recreation, evening classes, etc., to matters of clothing, diet, and the details of the routine duties of the disciplinary prison orderlies. The six elected members are not only responsible for the good behavior of their men, but act as the leaders of the prison community and as the mouthpieces of the League. Elections of these six members are held every six months. They are eligible to re-election, thus showing whether they have discharged their duties to the satisfaction of the other disciplinary prison orderlies.

The plan is an attempt to get away from the repressive atmosphere of most prisons and to lay emphasis on the positive and constructive elements in human nature. The prison administration does not conceive this plan to be in any sense "self-government," but a combination of selected prisoners and the prison administration in co-operation for mutual benefit. The purpose is to establish a means of co-operation, plain deal-

[19] *Administration Report of the Inspector-General of Prisons for 1927*, pp. 12, 13.

ing, and honesty of purpose in making the life of the prison as agreeable as possible consistent with the safe detention of the men, productive work, and correction of the conduct which brought them there. Speaking of the spirit of this League, the Administration says:

It is in a sense a small world containing within itself many of the problems of the world outside. There is, however, one basic difference; namely, that a community in prison is an isolated and secluded one which they cannot leave at will and in which actions by individuals almost always react on the whole group. They are knit together by virtue of their position in a way that free men are not, and the interests of the League are so bound up with the behavior of the individual, that he is under constant pressure to conform and to play the game, not only while in the small world of prison life, but in a wider sense in the world he will reënter some day equipped, it is hoped, with at least some knowledge of the rules of the game.[20]

What have been the results of this experiment? In 1929, three years after its inception, the Administration says:

The passage of time has proved that the members of this League respond fully to the trust that is placed in them. The Committee take their responsibility seriously, and it is becoming more evident that the men who belong to it have their general tone and standard of thought and action raised in consequence. The public opinion of the League is brought to bear upon each individual, and public opinion of this kind has a very salutary influence in moulding the conduct of its members.

The following are the figures with regard to Disciplinary Prison Orderlies:

	1926	1927	1928	1929
Daily average	100	100	100	100
Disrated	2	1	5	5
Reinstated	5		3	4
Discharged from prison	16	28	20	31
Reconvicted	—	—	—	—

As will be seen from the number of disrated there have been five individual cases of failures. Such failures have to be expected, but the League as a whole has proved a successful experiment, fitting the prisoners (sic.) for free life by developing his honour, his self-

20 Ibid., p. 13.

reliance, and a sense of citizenship. The main object of such a League being the training of first offenders to fit them to re-enter the world as good citizens, it would be interesting if the after careers of those who belong to the League could be watched and compared with those of other prisoners. However, the absence of reconvictions from among the members of the League who have left the prison is not without significance, and indicates that the lessons learnt in prison through the medium of this League have not gone to waste.[21]

In August of the same year in which the League of Disciplinary Prison Orderlies was organized there was organized the Badge Prisoners Mutual Welfare League. This was an endeavor to extend to those who were not yet ready to become disciplinary prison orderlies, but who for a number of years had a record of good conduct, the same principles found in that organization. As already mentioned, prisoners can begin to accumulate badges for good conduct on entrance into Class II. Anyone who has accumulated four badges may become a member of the Badge Prisoners Mutual Welfare League. It has its own constitution, its Committee of Management and Court similar to the League of Disciplinary Prison Orderlies. The results here also have been so good that those with three badges have been admitted, and it is a question whether those with two badges should not be admitted.[22]

Curiously in contrast to the results in these two Leagues the League for Star-Class Prisoners, which was organized at about the same time as that for the disciplinary prison orderlies, proved to be a complete failure. Recall that the star class is made up of educated European and Ceylonese first offenders. Says the 1927 report:

It was not unnatural in a way to expect that this type of prisoner, by reason of his higher education and social status, would have the more readily appreciated and assimilated the spirit and principles underlying the system of a Mutual Welfare League. Curiously enough the reverse has actually proved to be the case, and the establishment of the Star-Class League has been as signal a failure as the two others have been successful. Right from the beginning and

21 *Administration Report of the Inspector-General of Prisons for 1929*, p. 14.
22 *Ibid.*, p. 14.

during the period of preparation it was felt that the atmosphere amongst these educated prisoners tended to be inimical to the spirit of a League of this nature. No coercion of any description was made, and after many checks, the preliminary preparation only culminated in the League being actually inaugurated at the outwardly expressed desire of all these prisoners. Trouble, however, was soon to come and it did not take long to discover that the elected delegates of the Committee of Management could not or would not control their members. Dissension was rife, and in spite of many chances being given to enable these star-class prisoners to pull themselves together, this League was forcibly dissolved in May last.[23]

The failure of this experiment casts a very interesting light on the social psychology of prisoners from different social strata of society. It showed that there was lacking and that it was impossible to develop any *esprit de corps* in this group. The jealousies, envies, and suspicions among the members of this educated group could not be sunk, but came to expression in the League. The selfishness and conceit of these prisoners were so great that they could not work together for their common welfare. Their felt superiority to each other and to all the less educated prisoners reminds one of what is often seen among educated prisoners in this country. Hence in the same year in which this League was born it was put out of its miserable existence. The attempt was then made to accomplish something by dividing this group into sub-classes so as to prevent the building up of a united resistance to discipline through group solidarity. The worst ones are now transferred to Mahara or to Jaffna.

I have already noticed briefly the "special class" of reconvicted prisoners which was established some time ago. This is an effort to pick out the most hopeful of the reconvicted prisoners and by certain incitements encourage them to prepare for a hopeful and useful life upon discharge. This experiment was begun in the Welikada Prison in Colombo. However, in July, 1926, this special class was transferred to the Bogambara Prison in Kandy. Here they continue the training on lines originally initiated at Welikada with the hope that they may

[23] *Ibid.*, for 1927, p. 14.

be rehabilitated so as not to return again. The scheme is best described by the administration. The report says:

Having passed through the initial training and preparation in section B at Mahara, these reconvicted prisoners are on promotion to A section at Kandy treated in all respects as if they were first offenders, every facility being given and every inducement held out to arrest the criminal tendencies latent in many of them. As has been pointed out before, the whole system requires the closest co-operation between the Superintendents of Mahara and Kandy Prisons, who share between them the responsibility for the desired object being attained. The former is chiefly concerned with the careful selection, out of the mass of reconvicted prisoners at his disposal, of only those likely to be suitable material and likely to respond to the reformative influences inherent in the system, and with paving the way for such influences to take root, while the latter is charged with the far harder though not more important task and ideal of so training and shaping the finer instincts of these men that on discharge the balance of probability will lie in favor of their refraining from committing further crime. As can well be imagined, this task is in many ways far more difficult than in the case of first offenders, among whom the commission of a crime is more often due to a combination of more or less accidental or impulsive causes than to the urge of a criminal instinct, and it is only natural that the percentage of failures must of necessity be higher. The means adopted to attain the desired object for this section of the special class are similar in many ways to those in Welikada for the first offender, and no effort is spared to afford them every opportunity of making the best of their second chance.[24]

The Inspector-General is well pleased with the results of this experiment and hopes to extend it further as experience shows its value and indicates the methods necessary to handle this class successfully. After three years with the experiment, he says:

The daily average strength of this class which represents the second grade in this classification—the first stage being at Mahara Prison—was 142.21. During the year under review 60 prisoners were received from the Special Class "B" at Mahara, and since the inauguration of this class 394 prisoners have undergone this training. Of the present number (149), 20 prisoners have been classified as skilled and 61 as proficient in the various trades. As a group

[24] Ibid., for 1928, p. 31.

they have generally responded to the efforts made to improve them, and show great interest in their work, which is of a high standard. This is borne out by the fact that 18 prisoners are in possession of one, 13 in possession of two, 20 in possession of three, and 17 in possession of four Good Conduct Badges respectively while 10 prisoners have been appointed instructors. They are allowed to be in association and to attend educational classes and to participate in games on two evenings in the week. During the year 67 prisoners were discharged from this class and 18 reconvicted.[25]

In the chapter on the Philippine Prison System we noticed that one of the most interesting experiments in that institution was the Philippine Scouts. The Inspector-General of Prisons in Ceylon has tried a similar plan in the Welikada Prison. The orderlies and disciplinary prison orderlies reach only those who have been in the institution for some time. Some plan had to be devised to train those who had been in prison a shorter period. The organization of Scouts suggested itself as a solution. In 1922 the Prison Scout Troop was organized in Welikada for the purpose of experimenting with selected prisoners. The program of training had been to a large extent haphazard and unsystematic. Gradually more men were introduced into this troop. It began with 16 boys in 1923 and in 1925 had reached the number of 90. The troop during that experimental period had had no connection with the Scout movement at large and were Scouts only in name. However, by the beginning of 1926 the condition of the troop had developed to such an extent that some of the members of the Boy Scout Association, who had been interested in this troop in the prison, in conjunction with the prison staff felt that the Boy Scout troop in the Welikada Prison had ceased to be an experiment. It was, therefore, officially organized and is run as a recognized unit of the world-wide Scout movement. The imperial Scout headquarters gave formal approval to the registration of this new prison troop with the stipulation that in the future entry into the troop should be very carefully supervised and that troop of-

[25] *Ibid.,* for 1929, p. 18.

ficers should undergo a special course of training. So far as known this is the only officially recognized prison troop of the Boy Scout movement in the world. It is known as the Welikada Rover Troop. Since its organization, developments have occurred intended to perfect the adaptation of Scout principles to the particular situation in a prison. The experiment is under trial of extending the Scout movement to the special class of reconvicted prisoners at Kandy. Thus, a second troop of Scouts has been organized in the prisons of Ceylon, this time among this special class of the reconvicted. To start this troop at Kandy three of the members of the Welikada troop were sent to the Bogambara Prison at Kandy to instill the spirit there which had been developed at Welikada.[26]

The immediate purpose back of the Scout work in the prisons is to provide ideals of conduct within the prison and a sufficient social motivation to live up to these ideals to make these men strive for adaptation to the conditions of life outside. It breaks down the wall of prejudice which surrounds persons with the stigma of prison upon them, it stimulates and encourages them to better things while in prison, and it affords them on discharge a bond or tie through this international organization which enables them to ask for and obtain admission to any outside Rover troop, and entrance into the universal brotherhood of Scouts, which, it is hoped, will greatly facilitate the reconstruction and rehabilitation of these men. A committee composed of the inspector-general of prisons, the superintendent of the Welikada Prison, the assistant jailer, the chief commissioner of the Boy Scout Association of Colombo, the assistant commissioner of Rovers, and the deputy camp chief of the Scout headquarters in Colombo, exercise a careful supervision over the admission into the troop of specially selected and suitable juvenile-adult first offenders who have passed their probationary period in six months and have qualified in the necessary Rover tests.

There is a subsidiary body of juvenile prisoners hitherto

[26] *Ibid.*, for 1927, pp. 14–17; *Ibid.*, for 1928, pp. 14–16; *Ibid.*, for 1929, pp. 16, 17.

known as the Attached Scouts. Of this organization, originally every juvenile-adult who entered Welikada Prison was considered a member. Experience, however, early indicated that the short termers, some of them with sentences of only a few weeks, got no benefit out of the plan. Hence, all newly admitted juvenile prisoners were taken out of the Scout organization and put into two classes, A and B. Those in the first class are those with sentences of less than a year. These not usually admitted to the Attached Scouts. Those of class B after three months may be admitted. Both these sections are assigned to hard labor, but they are kept separated in the prison. Out of the Attached Scouts are recruited members of the Rover Troop.

Troop meetings are held regularly three times a week for recreation and instruction in scout craft both practical and theoretical. Instruction is carried on by the scout master according to a program and arranged to conform with the existing prison conditions. All questions affecting discipline and internal administration are dealt with by the court of honor. By the creation of rover dens, patrol corners, troop and patrol flags, frequent inter-patrol competitions coupled with complete absence of supervision by the prison staff, loyalty to the patrol, to the troop, to the leaders and troop officers, above all, loyalty to the scout ideal, are fostered and raised to a high degree. There is a sense of belonging to a corporate entity and a definitely organized institution, which has brought about a transformation in the lives of these boys. In order to overcome the limitations of a prison with high walls, for purposes of practical instruction, permission has been granted provisionally for six days in camp each month outside the wall. Patrols four at a time have been taken away from the prison every month in charge of the scout master, entirely free of any sort of supervision, to a camp some distance from the prison, where from 7 A.M. to 5 P.M. a crowded and enjoyable day is spent. Thus far there has been no difficulty. In addition, camp-fires have been held at frequent intervals, generally when the troop has been visited by outside troops.

Through this Scout organization, plans are under way for more definite after-care of the members of the Rover Troop. With the co-operation of the Scout headquarters, all Rovers on discharge are given a certificate from the scout master and must report themselves to the Assistant District Commissioner of Rovers who arranges to obtain employment for them. This official also communicates with the scout official living nearest the destination of the Rover, with a view to helping the latter to join a local troop and providing him with a friend to whom he can go for assistance or advice, if necessary.[27]

Even before the changes took place which made the prison troop into a regular Scout Troop, a study of the discharges from the Troop and of reconvictions shows that it has been quite successful. The following table of discharges and reconvictions up to 1927 speaks for itself.[28]

	DISCHARGED	RECONVICTED
1923	48	4
1924	28	9
1925	55	2
1926	39	1
1927	28	1
	198 *	17 †

* Of this total of 198 discharged, 31 were previously convicted.
† Of this total of 17 reconvicted, 11 were previously convicted.

During 1928 and 1929 no discharged Rovers were reconvicted.

This experiment in prison discipline and education will bear watching. Those in charge hope that with further experience more careful work may be done. The experience thus far with these juvenile-adult first offenders is very promising in view of the fact that they are not in a special institution of their own as in England and in most other countries.

After-Care in the Ceylon Prisons. In addition to this special after-care for the members of the Rover Troop, some attention is given to the after-care of the other prisoners. Ceylon's prison administration has recognized what is so often

[27] *Ibid.,* for 1926, p. 11.   [28] *Ibid.,* for 1927, p. 17.

forgotten by prison administrators and legislators, that if the full effect of the work in the institution is to be obtained in the lives of the prisoners, attention must be given to him when he leaves the prison. Help, then, to the man who wants to go straight is of as much importance as the various devices in the prison contrived to get him into the state of mind of wanting to make a place for himself in society. Otherwise often the work done by the institution is wasted. Terrible is the moment for the first offender when he enters the gates of a prison. But vastly more terrible often is the moment when he is released with no one to help him get reëstablished. In Ceylon the after-care work in 1929 was confined chiefly to the two prisons of Welikada and Bogambara. It is the conscious purpose of the prison administration to insure that prisoners are better trained and fitted for employment on discharge than when admitted. Various industrial parties are organized and run mainly with this objective in view. All prisoners, especially in these two prisons, on discharge who so desire may obtain a very full and carefully worded certificate detailing their ability, character, etc., together with an introductory letter to some firm requesting employment. A list of firms willing to employ such men is kept on file. As far as possible a history of the ex-prisoners is kept after discharge.

In the attempt to centralize the after-care work hitherto done by private organizations like the Salvation Army, the Girl Guides, and the Colombo Discharged Prisoners' Aid Society in 1927 the Ceylon Discharged Prisoners' Aid Association was organized. A Central Committee at Colombo was set up to direct the work, and sub-committees were to be organized at a number of the important centers both where prisons were located and other places to which discharged prisoners were likely to go on discharge. A number of such sub-committees were set up, but at the last report (1929) only those at Colombo and at Kandy were functioning in a promising way. However, in 1929 this association helped a total of 135 discharged prisoners. It found employment for 106, assisted financially 20, paid the passage of 1, and helped 5 others in various ways. The development of the work hangs on the creation of an active and intelligent interest in the ex-convict among the people. Ceylon's plan is a replica on a small scale of the English system, but without the well-established reputation of the English Society, and without subsidy so far from the government treasury.

I suppose we shall have to struggle along with these private associations doing the work which the public should do through agencies set up by statute and financed from the treasury as any other public enterprise, until such time as the public awakens to the fact that after-care of the prisoners is as much a governmental function as his arrest, his trial, or his incarceration. The job is not done when the government turns him out of the prison door. It recognizes that fact in the case of the paroled man by providing after-care for him. Is it not just as logical for the government to recognize its responsibility to society and to the discharged man by setting up a department of after-care for the discharged prisoner?

Entertainment and Recreation in the Prisons. The most extensive provision for recreation for the prisoners is to be found in the Welikada Prison. Even here recreational privileges are not allowed indiscriminately, but are limited to the Rover Scouts, the Attached Scouts, the members of the two Leagues described above, to instructors of trade parties, and the "A" section of the Star Class. At the Bogambara Prison, Kandy, prisoners holding certificates of industry and conduct are allowed out for exercise and games and to attend English classes two evenings each week. Evening recreation for those prisoners is provided by grounds for volley-ball and cricket. There is also a stage complete with scenery, wings, overhead, and footlights, which serves also as an auditorium for concerts, lectures, etc. The various private organizations also provide entertainment for the prisoners. These entertainments have been found to help much in the discipline of the prison by relieving the monotony of imprisonment after work hours. At Bogambara, recreation in the open air is permitted to certain prisoners after working hours. Private organizations also hold

religious services and supply the prisons with books and maga-
zines. It should be borne in mind that in addition to such
forms of recreation as the Scouting activities already described,
attendance at classes and the social service activities to be mentioned provide release from monotony during spare time.

On the whole it can be said that the experiments made in
providing recreation hours for prisoners in Ceylon might
seem to an American not very far advanced. However, recreation in any form is looked upon as a privilege and is accorded
only to certain classes. In this respect, Ceylon has extended
our practices relating to recreation much farther and applied
them in another way. We deny recreation to those under
punishment. Some of the prisons seem to have absolutely no
provision at all. In Ceylon, where recreation privileges are
accorded, recreation is integrated into a system intended to
motivate the prisoner's good conduct and industry. The attitude of the Administration towards the whole subject of
leisure-time activities is shown by the following statement:

> It is very evident that where concessions have been made in the
> way of lectures, concerts, games, etc., the moral effect has been ex-
> cellent. The prisoners do not regard this otherwise than a desire
> on the part of the officers that the monotony of their daily life shall
> from time to time be broken by an appeal made to their intelligence
> and their higher feelings; the whole idea is to interest them in the
> right type of things apart from the fact that they are touched by the
> interest taken in their welfare by strangers.[29]

Social Service in the Prison. In contrast to the situation in
most American prisons, Ceylon, like England, has been able to
interest a large number of outside organizations to work within
the prison walls. I find a list of nineteen organizations and individuals who are working within the prisons, giving their
time voluntarily to the helping of the inmates. The Inspector-
General in his report says:

> In reading through the list of these associations and individual help-
> ers who have done and are doing all in their power to help the prisoner
> both inside the prison and on discharge, the many difficulties which
> each and all have to contend with can be realized. . . . It is plain

[29] *Ibid.*, for 1928, p. 17.

fact that no amount of reformative correction and training within a prison which aims after rehabilitation of the prisoner as a true member of society, can be completed without co-operation of the public through the medium of a thoroughly sound and earnest society of voluntary and willing helpers.[80]

One gains the impression, however, that the service is spasmodic and inadequate. In spite of the fact, however, that such service is not what it might be much good is accomplished. With the passage of each year it becomes more evident that the prisoners who come in contact with these outside workers derive nothing but benefit. The prisoner comes to have a feeling that the great society outside has an interest in him. This feeling helps to cultivate in the prisoner the consciousness that he has not entirely lost status in society. There are still some who have not forgotten him.

Anyone acquainted with the work of John Howard and Elizabeth Frye will remember that volunteer social service workers in the prisons of Ceylon are not a new thing. However, in the last hundred years of prison work, the co-operation of outside agencies with the prison itself has been greatly neglected. Here in Ceylon, as in England, we see a revival of this ancient interest. Private work with the prisoners in the institution is a promising experiment. In the United States more of this needs to be done. Too often there is no body of public opinion outside the prison which knows intimately by firsthand contact the problems within the prison, and the difficulties the prisoner faces on discharge. Hence, the difficulties in the United States of getting progressive legislation concerning the treatment of discharged prisoners. As for social work within the prisons by volunteers, we are doing almost nothing.

THE TRAINING OF PRISON OFFICIALS

Ceylon's Prison Administration has no such formal system of training of prison officials as Japan. Nor has it followed England's example in this respect. However, since the prison's

[80] *Ibid.*, for 1926, p. 20.

official personnel is comparatively small, it is possible to train the officials informally. This the administration tries to do. With a unified system it is possible to train a few new officials each year, without any formal instruction. The administration selects the official personnel with as great care as possible. The Inspector-General dominates the system. He can realize his ideals as to policies, selection of personnel, and training within the limits made possible by his budget. So far as possible the personnel of the other prisons is supplied from Welikada, at least the chief officials. That fact has significance for the training process. In a small prison system like Ceylon's that may be adequate.

SOME NEEDS NOT MET IN CEYLON

As in the United States, prisons and jails are still used for the detention of the unconvicted awaiting trial, and also for the convicted. Ceylon, like most countries with the fine system, still has imprisonment for debt to the state, hence these debtors are in the jails. The local prisons, there as here, are chiefly for the detention of these people awaiting trial, awaiting further examination, debtors, and short-term local prisoners. There, as here, separation of the convicted from the unconvicted is necessary, but not yet reached. As a matter of fact, from the reports and from talking with the Inspector-General, there is evidence that the separation of the unconvicted from the convicted is recognized as important, but facilities have not yet been provided.

The prison administration appreciates the fact that it has no training school for young offenders. The question is before the government, and a site has been tentatively decided upon. There is no institution for delinquents below the age of sixteen years. There is no separate institution such as corresponds to our adult reformatory. What they call there the juvenile-adult offenders—that is, between the ages of sixteen and twenty-three—are in the prisons, although, as we have seen, first offenders are segregated chiefly in the Welikada Prison. Evidently the administration has in mind the Borstal

Institutions in England in urging the establishment of an institution for juvenile-adults.

The prison administration in Ceylon also recognizes that a
thoroughly organized society of prison workers in a true sense
is badly needed. More or less haphazard work of the private
organizations, while thoroughly appreciated, does not meet
the needs of the situation. Agitation is going on within the
informed circles in Ceylon for the establishment of such an
organization.

The administration also recognizes that a more complete
system of after-care is desirable. A step towards providing
this is the newly organized Ceylon Discharged Prisoners' Aid
Association.   Nowhere in the world, so far as I know, has any
state or nation provided by law for the public after-care of
discharged prisoners. In Japan, in the Philippine Islands, in
France, in Great Britain, private societies and individuals are
entering this field.   Probably these private agencies will have
to pioneer the way.

The prison administration in Ceylon craves a greater degree
of sympathy on the part of the government and the public
with the discharged prisoners. It recognizes that without
this co-operation recidivism will continue; the police and the
public will hound the discharged man or at least have him
under suspicion.

In Ceylon, as almost everywhere else, adequate educational
facilities are not provided for in the prison. The promising
attempts made in some of the prisons of Ceylon are only
partial. That the prison may be an educational institution in
the larger sense of the word has not yet appeared upon the
horizon of many of our prison administrators. Avowedly in
Ceylon the educational facilities are provided for the most
part for first offenders only, on the theory that the others
are not hopeful, and therefore society should not spend effort
upon them, although the administration is moving to extend
educational privileges to other classes, especially in industrial
training.   Let us grant that education of these convicts is a
more difficult problem than the education of unconvicted

people. Nevertheless, the necessity exists that education, if it is a panacea in some sense for crime, ought to be applied to these convicts for the sake of society. If they were remaining perpetually in prison, the need for education would be less. Since, however, practically all of them are to be discharged sooner or later, it would seem that an endeavor should be made to give all trainable men a chance at some kind of education to prepare them for life on the outside. The time ought to come when every prison would be looked upon as an educational institution with a definite, specific purpose of preparing men to live in society usefully and happily. From my observation, I am inclined to the opinion that in Ceylon's prisons the promising inmate has as carefuly devised plans for his education for life after release as he receives anywhere.

Probation in Ceylon is in an unsatisfactory condition. In spite of frequent mention of the matter in the reports of the Inspector-General, progress has been slow. A Probation Committee was appointed to study the question. Its report recommending probation for first offenders whose sentences are short has been published. If probation is ultimately established, the difficulties hitherto experienced with the short-term first offender at Welikada will be lessened.

No system of parole from the institutions is found in Ceylon. One wonders at the absence of such a system, since it has long been known in England under the name of ticket-of-leave and is rather widely operative in the United States. No discussion of the matter occurs in the reports. There may be some special reason that the Prison Administration does not consider it desirable. Whatever the reason, the need of such a system is not felt.

HOW DOES THE SYSTEM WORK?

So far as the prison system of Ceylon is concerned it is an attempt to adapt the English system to the situation in this island. As in England, the fundamental characteristic of the prison system is classification. Classification in Ceylon is on the basis chiefly of length of sentence and number of convictions, although age and conduct also enter into the scheme. However, because of the law concerning sentence to simple imprisonment and to rigorous imprisonment, this classification scheme is not thoroughly carried out. There is no unifying principle of classification rigidly carried through. If this scheme is to attain its purposes it should be based upon a fundamental principle and carried through thoroughly. Nowhere has this been done.

In discussing the results, one must bear in mind that Ceylon is a small island thickly populated and with few large cities. Also it should not be forgotten that while the population is composed of different linguistic and religious groups, ethnically the various elements of the population are not so diverse. More important, culturally the population is probably as homogeneous as that of England. Furthermore, because Ceylon is an island and passage from Ceylon to India can be carefully controlled, the escape of a prisoner is very difficult.

With all these conditions in mind, and with a clear appreciation of the fact that the prison system of Ceylon in some respects has not been touched by modern penology, one is prepared to appreciate that a reconvicted rate of 18.52 in 1926 of all the admissions to the prison indicate a low recidivist rate.[31] Judged by this standard, therefore, the Ceylon prison system works very well as compared with the system of England or the systems of the United States. I came away from studying the prison system of Ceylon with the feeling that in most matters the experimental spirit lives there. While naturally England's models have been normative in the development of Ceylon's system, they have not been slavishly followed. Witness the variation in the period of preventive detention from England's from five-to-ten-year period to Ceylon's three-to-five-year period. Witness, again, the adaptation of England's classification system to the peculiar social system of Ceylon. Witness yet again the independent development of the various leagues

[31] Cf. with England's 66 per cent of the men and 86 per cent of the women received on conviction, 1925–26. See *Report of the Commissioners of Prisons and the Directors of Convict Prisoners for the Year 1925–26*, London, 1927, p. 8.

of selected prisoners, and especially the independent introduction of the Scout movement among certain inmates of Ceylon's prisons. Moreover, recall the development of her prison industries and the emphasis upon training for a job upon discharge and upon reformation as a primary object of the system. Doubtless much of this success is due to the progressive vision of such men as Mr. Walker, the Inspector-General, and other interested authorities in Ceylon who are responsible for some of the more recent experiments which are there being carried out. The world may well watch these experiments with hope.

BIBLIOGRAPHY

Administration Report of the Inspector-General of Prisons for 1926, Colombo, 1927.

Ceylon Discharged Prisoners' Aid Association: Rules and By-Laws. (No date.)

Administration Report of the Inspector-General of Prisons for 1927, Colombo, 1928.

Administration Report of the Acting Inspector-General of Prisons for 1928, Colombo, 1929.

Administration Report of the Inspector-General of Prisons for 1929, Colombo, 1930.

CHAPTER IV

THE CRIMINAL TRIBES OF INDIA

IT MAY seem strange to go to a country as backward as India to learn something about the treatment of the criminal. It would be audacious were one to claim that India has anything to teach us about the treatment of the ordinary criminal. Her jails and prisons do not merit any special comment from the student. They are just others copied from models which just now are under considerable criticism. But India's problem with the criminal tribes forced her administrators to face in new ways the problem of organized crime. Here India set out along new lines, unique and daring, which deserve close scrutiny by the student of new experiments with the criminal.

So far as the literature of penology is concerned, little is known in the West about these adventures in penology. Although for years I have been a rather careful student of penology, I was surprised, on visiting India, to find such a radically different scheme from the orthodox methods of the West. Whether it has lessons for us or not, it is a new thing under the sun and deserves careful description, so that our penologists may consider it for the light it may throw upon our efforts to readjust our own methods of dealing with criminals. It is possible that in this case light may come from this new experiment.

Vizualize 320,000,000 people living on an area about two-thirds the size of Continental United States. Consider a stage of industry about the same as it was in England before the Industrial Revolution. Remember also that aside from a few large cities like Calcutta and Bombay, the most of this huge population is scattered in villages over the face of the land.

Agriculture is of the most primitive sort and the bulk of the products consumed by the population is made in the household. Picture a standard of living in which a family of five or six can be maintained for three or four dollars a month.[1] It is easy to see that the bulk of the population lives on the verge of starvation most of the time. Let a famine come along and millions die unless they are assisted by the government or relief organizations. Under such conditions, which have extended over decades, there is small wonder if whole families and tribes of people finally have resorted to criminal methods to get a living. Hence from time immemorial there have existed in India large numbers of people who became marauders, living by illicit methods, chiefly robbery and thieving. These people constitute the so-called "criminal tribes."

NUMBERS IN THE CRIMINAL TRIBES

There were thousands of these gangs or tribes scattered all over the country. It has been estimated that there are one and a half million members of them in all India. The crimes they committed amounted to thousands of dollars of damages besides the violent deaths they caused and the personal injuries inflicted. While the comparative numbers are small in any given area, they were troublesome by reason of their being organized in tribes and hence were centers for the perpetuation of their criminal customs, ideals, and mores through all future generations.

WANDERING AND SETTLED CRIMINAL TRIBES

The criminal tribes are of two sorts, those who wander about like gypsies and those who are settled in villages. In the old days, the gypsy sort was the more difficult to handle. However, since the coming of the railways, even men of family among the settled tribes are frequently found as leaders or members of the gangs which commit burglaries or robberies

---

[1] Review of Zimand, *Living India*, in *Information Service*, Department of Research and Education, Federal Council of the Churches of Christ in America, November 24, 1928, p. 1.

with violence. A criminal tribe in Rajputana, for example, can come up into the Punjab, commit a dozen burglaries, and be back again in Rajputana within the week, leaving no trace of their identity. Frequent cases of this sort are cited in the reports. They are very difficult for the police to handle.

PHYSICAL, MENTAL, AND SOCIAL CONDITIONS
OF THE TRIBESMEN

When the government began to register these criminal tribes and bring them into settlements, the physical condition of many of them was very bad. The following description illustrates the situation:

When the first batches were brought into the settlements most of the men were clad in rags, the women had hardly enough clothing to cover their shame, and the children up to twelve years or so were stark naked. . . . But they were by no means poor. Cash and jewelry were, in many cases, carefully deposited in their quilts, which consisted of rags of all sizes stitched together, or secreted in false bottoms of hukkas or by other ingenious devices. This money was gradually taken out of the hiding places and invested in the Savings Bank or War Loan.[2]

The mentality of the members of criminal tribes varies. Some of them have fine mental ability and others are of low mentality. In either case, however, if left to themselves it was felt that they would all soon become habitual criminals. In the pre-settlement days they made no secret of their criminal profession. By reason of the long practice in criminality and the traditions handed down over long periods of time, these people do not look at crime as do others. For example, the Buhra Brahmans of the Kangra district think that in their case stealing is not a crime. They interpret their acts as merely the exaction of a form of charity which was given willingly in the good old days, but is withheld in these more degenerate times. Again, the Chhamar think that the little that they steal from the house of a *bania* (money-lender) who robs others by falsifying his accounts, or from a goldsmith who

[2] *A Note on the Administration of Criminal Tribes in the Punjab, 1917 to 1919,* by Hari Singh, Lahore, 1920, p. 3.

cheats by mixing his alloys, is no crime. They form a criminal profession, but a profession like many professions and occupations in India tribally linked, circumscribed, and accepted. Moreover, one must not forget that the lower classes in Indian society are controlled by all sorts of superstitions which sometimes lead to crime. For example, a Katkari, of Nadhal, lost three of his children by death, and the fourth was ailing. He suspected that someone had cast an evil spell over them. This is a common belief among the people. After resorting to a local deity where a kind of ordeal was carried out to ascertain the guilty one, one Pangya was declared guilty by the oracle. This Katkari by the name of Tambdia, and his brother-in-law, demanded five rupees from Pangya. They then proceeded to a neighboring village and got drunk. At this place they met a woman, Bhagi, who boasted that her daughters were capable of casting evil spells over people. Tambdia and other Katkaris with him attacked her and beat her at once. The next morning her corpse was found floating in a well.[3] With such a background, economically and socially, it is easy to see that the situation is such as to promote instead of to repress criminality.[4]

CHARACTERISTIC CRIMES OF THE CRIMINAL TRIBES

In order to get a picture of the kinds of crime committed by these criminal tribes I reproduce the following instance from the police report of the Bombay Presidency for 1922:

All were numerically strong, well mounted and well armed. Mirkahn's gang was also in the habit of wearing khaki uniforms, impersonating government servants. The *modus operandi* of these gangs was to swoop down on a village at about three in the afternoon, to picket all the exits so as to prevent the villagers from going out to give information, to loot at their leisure until sunset, and then to leave for their base. They usually travelled some forty miles during the

[3] *Police Report of the Bombay Presidency, including Sind and Railways, for the year 1922*, Bombay, 1923, p. 26.
[4] The sociological backgrounds of crime are not being attacked very persistently in the present scheme of caring for the criminal tribes. The major emphasis is on economic prevention.

night and thus had a considerable start before the police could follow their tracks.[5]

Another instance runs as follows:

On the 4th of May, 1922, information was received that Magan Nana, a famous outlaw, was at a village called Kesra. The sub-inspector on arrival there with a party was informed that Magan was holding up a wedding party about a mile from the village. The sub-inspector proceeded to the spot immediately. The outlaw, a desperate criminal, though taken by surprise, being armed with a 410 B. L. gun and a pistol, put up a fight. He took shelter behind a tree and was taking his gun out of his case when sowar Kalaskhan attacked him with a sword. Although the outlaw managed to avoid the blow, the plucky action of the sowar prevented him from opening fire on the police. But for the sowar's brave act casualties would have inevitably occurred among the police, for the outlaw was a very good shot. He was finally shot dead, a bullet passing through his head.[6]

Among some of the more intelligent and clever tribesmen, counterfeiting was a special hobby. While such instances illustrate the more ambitious misdeeds of the criminal tribesmen, the majority of their crimes consists of petty pilfering, cattle stealing, small-scale swindling at fairs and bazaars, and imposing on the credulity of the natives for profit. Their chief aim and end is to deprive other people of their property without violence, if possible, by murder, if necessary. This is the easier by reason of the fact that for a long time prior to the occupation of India by the British it was a land of political instability. No man ever knew when his life and property were safe, consequently the tendency was to put as much as possible of his material wealth into such concentrated forms as precious stones, gold and silver ornaments and trinkets, and in coin. Wealth of this kind is easily secreted and transported. Furthermore, this custom fitted in with the tendency to decorate the person with gaudy ornaments. This practice of carrying about the person precious property lends itself to the practice of robbery with violence.[7]

[5] *Police Report of the Bombay Presidency, including Sind and Railways, for the year 1922*, Government Central Press, Bombay, p. 23.
[6] *Ibid.*, p. 24.
[7] Coatman, *India in 1925–26*. Government Press, Calcutta, pp. 189–190.

FIRST ATTEMPTS TO DEAL WITH THE PROBLEM

Up until 1908 the usual method was to cast into prison those who were caught. It was discovered, however, that the families of these men are usually involved. If the men were thrown into prison, the families either had to continue their depredations or else were in great distress. The authorities found, furthermore, that as soon as the man was released from jail he was worse off than before, at once returned to his group, and showed no evidence of any reformation.

In the meantime the Salvation Army and some other religious organizations had been experimenting with some of the criminal tribes and with released prisoners to see what could be done to turn them into honest channels of life. Finally in 1908 the first Criminal Tribes Settlement Act was passed, permitting the various provincial governments of India to make plans whereby tribes suspected of living by crime could be registered and supervised by the police, and those members of criminal tribes which had been convicted could be placed in settlements. In these settlements they were taught to work, were given instruction in an honest life, their children were sent to school, all in the hope that complete reformation might be the result.

THE PROVISIONS OF THE ACT OF 1911

In 1911 the weak act of 1908 was replaced by a law passed by the Indian legislature which set up a scheme for the control of these tribes. This act was known as the Criminal Tribes Settlement Act. It has been amended a number of times on the basis of experience, the last changes being enacted in 1924. Any presidency or province of the Indian Empire is permitted to set up the machinery necessary to put it into effect. The main features of the law are as follows:

If the local government has reason to believe that any tribe, gang, or class of persons or any part of a tribe, gang, or class is addicted to the systematic commission of non-bailable offenses, it may by notification in the local official gazette declare that such person or group is a criminal tribe as the term is used in this act. There are two methods of dealing with these people

—registration and settlement. Registration attempts to keep track of them under police surveillance in the communities where they live, or, if they are wandering tribes, where they may be found when suspected of crime. Settlement means locating them in a special place provided so that they can be more closely controlled than by registration. In the settlements they are under the control of the "Criminal Tribes Settlement Officers."

The government of the province or presidency called in the act the "local government" may direct the district magistrate to register the members of any criminal tribe or part of a tribe within his district. The magistrate then publishes a notice calling upon those to be registered to appear at a time and place specified before a person appointed by him for the purpose of registering them. This person makes up the register and takes their finger prints. This magistrate is given power to exempt any member of the tribe or gang from registration and may cancel any such exemption.

The register, when made, is placed in the keeping of the superintendent of police, who acts as adviser to the district magistrate from time to time as to any alterations which should be made in the register. No person's name can be placed on or erased from the register except on written order of the district magistrate. Any person who feels himself to be aggrieved by being registered may complain to the district magistrate who takes action according to the facts found.

Registered members of any criminal tribe must report themselves at fixed intervals, and must notify the magistrate of their place of residence, of any change or intended change of residence, and of any absence from the locality. Thus, the Act provides for control over the criminal tribes by registration and police supervision in the local communities.

In addition to these provisions the movements of criminal tribes and their registered members may be restricted. The local government may restrict the movements of a tribe or a member to a certain specified area or settle it in any place of residence. However, before making any such order the local government is required to consider (1) the nature and circumstances of the offenses in which members of the tribe are believed to be concerned; (2) whether the criminal tribe, part, or member follows a lawful occupation, and whether such occupation is a real one or is claimed merely as a pretense to facilitate the commission of crimes; (3) the suitability of the restriction areas or place of residence; and (4) the manner in which it is proposed that persons so restricted or settled shall earn their living, and the adequacy of such economic arrangements.   This is the settlement plan.

Moreover, the local government may establish industrial, agricultural, or reformatory schools for children and may have them separated from their parents or guardians.   So far as this law concerns schools and reformatories for children, all persons under the age of eighteen and above the age of six are included.

Furthermore, the local government or some officer acting as "Criminal Tribes Settlement Officer" decides when to discharge anyone from the settlements or to transfer to some other settlement or school in the province, or to any settlement or school in some other province if the consent of the local government is first obtained.   The local government also makes rules to carry out the purposes of the Act.

Penalties are provided for any member of a criminal tribe who fails to appear when notified, intentionally omits to furnish information required, gives information which he knows or has reason to believe is false, or who refuses to allow his finger prints to be taken.   Penalties are also provided for breach of the rules concerning those whose movements are restricted or who abuse pass privileges.   On first conviction, imprisonment for one year is the penalty; on second conviction, two years, and any subsequent conviction, three years, or a fine of 500 rupees or both.

This Settlement Act is also connected up with the Indian Penal Code so as to provide severe punishment for members of criminal tribes who shall break that code.   Among these punishments are sentences for not less than seven years for a second conviction, and on a third or subsequent conviction transportation for life.

Village officials, including the headman and the watchman in any village in which any members of a criminal tribe reside, any owner or occupant of land who hires these criminals, and the agent of such owner or occupant are to notify the nearest police officer of the failure of any person to appear when notified for registration, or of the departure of any registered member from the village or land. Any such village official or landlord may be punished for non-compliance with this law.

Each local government may, with the consent of the prince or chief of a native state, remove thither any criminal tribe or members thereof who may be residents of the native state.

Thus the purpose of the law is to control the criminal tribes either by keeping them under very careful supervision in the places where they are permitted to live, or if that is not successful, to remove them to settlements where they are very much more carefully restricted and guarded. The system, so far as the administration is concerned, is a double one. The superintendent of police in a province and his men have charge of enforcing the restriction of tribes who have not been placed in settlements, but who have been registered. They also have the responsibility, as we have seen, of arresting those who have broken the restrictions laid upon them. The settlements, however, are usually under the supervision of a criminal tribes settlement officer. Sometimes the settlements are under the authority of these two—the superintendent of police and the criminal tribes settlement officer. Under this plan the larger number of the tribesmen are merely registered and so are under the control of the general superintendent of police.

The original intention in connection with the control of criminal tribes was to make the village, or *thana*, the basis of the scheme and to use the settlements only as a place for the reformation of the most depraved and for the encouragement and reward of the more promising. In practice, however, it soon appeared that, while supervision by the police in the villages had some good results, the more serious cases had to be

handled in the settlements.   In the villages the school attendance by boys was considerably diminished, the number of absconders remained high, and there were accusations of criminality brought by the police of the various districts.[8]   It was
soon learned, once the members of criminal tribes were placed
in settlements, that provision had to be made for the education
of the children.

The purpose of the whole scheme, to use the words of its
originators, was "an effective but sympathetic control of the
tribes combined with the provision of sufficient opportunities
for earning an honest livelihood."   In other words, the object
is reformation through providing economic avenues of self-
support and social pressure through the schools and other activities of the settlements.

EXTENT OF REGISTRATION

The Criminal Tribes Settlement Act contemplates placing
in settlements or otherwise restricting their movements those
members and families of criminal tribes which are a menace
to the community.   We must keep in mind that this began
as an experiment.   Consider also that the settlements had to be
built up from the beginning, involving considerable expenditure, and that there were no precedents on which to begin.
The experiment varied in different parts of India, and changes
were made from time to time.   Let us take two provinces of
India to illustrate the extent of registration, the Punjab and
Bombay.

Keeping in mind that the experiment began in earnest only
at the close of the World War, it is significant that in the early
days large numbers were registered and as time has gone on
the numbers have decreased.   Thus on January 1, 1919, there
were 33,498 on the registers of the Punjab, while at the end of
the year the number had decreased to 31,473.[9]   However, experience showed about 1923 or 1924 that the reduction in the

---

[8] *Report on the Administration of Criminal Tribes in the Punjab, 1925,* pp. 1, 2.
[9] *Report on the Administration of Criminal Tribes in the Punjab, 1922,* Lahore,
1923, p. 1 of Third Letter.

number of those registered had led to bad results. As a result the authorities tightened up registration and placed more of the tribesmen in settlements.[10]

The same thing took place in the Bombay Presidency, although there a more steady increase has taken place. During 1923 in the Bombay Presidency, the registrations increased from 18,962 at the beginning of the year to 21,242 at the close. The increase was due to two facts—the registration of criminal tribes for the first time in the Ahmednagar district and in the Belgaum district, two districts in which the registration had never been complete before, and the registration of those who had been discharged from jails and had never before been registered.[11]

As the number of settlements has increased in the various provinces, naturally the number of inmates has slightly grown. Most of the increase in the Bombay Presidency is accounted for by members of criminal tribes who had been sent to the government under Section 16 from Bombay City or from the districts or from jails. As a result of experience the tendency has been to place in settlements all discharged from jails and those having multiple convictions.[12] However, owing to financial stringency, the number of registered persons in the settlements had decreased to 3,226.[13] The same fluctuations took place in the Punjab for the same reason. Because of the expense of keeping these criminals in settlements, the policy was established of placing only those with numerous convictions in the settlements and supervising the others carefully in the restricted villages.

TYPES OF SETTLEMENTS PROVIDED

There are four types of settlements besides the institutions for children and loose women: (a) Industrial settlements near

[10] Ibid., 1926, p. 1.
[11] Police Report of the Bombay Presidency, including Sind and Railways, for the year 1923, Bombay, 1924, especially Part II on Report on the Working of the Criminal Tribes Act in the Bombay Presidency for the year 1923, pp. 2, 3, 7, 8.
[12] Report on the Working of the Criminal Tribes Act in the Bombay Presidency for the year ending March 31, 1926, Part I, p. 1.
[13] Ibid., p. 8.

some large industrial plant such as a cotton mill, railroad shops, or a large tea plantation; (b) agricultural settlements. In these settlements lands are provided by the government which the settlers are allowed to cultivate at a certain rental; (c) forest settlements where the settlers work in the woods getting out timber and reforesting land either for the government or for private owners. So far as the Bombay Presidency and the Punjab are concerned, these are mostly government forests; (d) reformatory settlements. The last are intended for those who cannot be trusted and who attempt to escape. Since these settlements are the most unique and interesting part of the scheme, let us look at three of these types more carefully.

A peculiar feature of all the settlements is that the men restricted to the settlements are allowed to keep their families, to appropriate their entire earnings, and when necessary to go out on leave. In the early years of the settlements many of the men refused to bring their families. Experience showed that they were harder to control and more likely to try to escape if their families were not present. Hence more recently the families have been sent with them into the settlement. As a result of this compulsory settlement of families along with the males, and the provision of necessaries of life, where needed, discontent among the inmates had decreased. In the Punjab in 1919, the first year after the compulsory settlement of families was put into operation, only 120 escapes took place as compared with 193 the preceding year.[14] The inmates are allowed to keep whatever they earn because the scheme contemplates that the economic motive shall be kept alive. In some cases the inmates were not able to make a good living inside the settlement; therefore, they were permitted to go out on leave, if necessary, to make a living. The reformatory settlement, which deals with the worst type of men, has to provide work in the settlement for the inmates. This, of course, has not been very remunerative, hence has not fitted into the general scheme. As those within the reformatory settlement show themselves to be amenable to discipline, they are given liberty

[14] *Report on the Administration of Criminal Tribes in the Punjab,* 1920, p. 7.

and are found a better economic position. Close supervision and restriction are relaxed as the inmates show an earnest attempt to make an honest living, and to observe the rules.

INDUSTRIAL SETTLEMENTS

I have mentioned above the industrial settlements. These are of two kinds, manufacturing settlements and labor-supplying settlements. In the manufacturing settlements the settlement carries on its own industries. I visited one of these at Kalianpur near Cawnpore. The labor-supplying settlements are a modification of our own lease system of the South. Labor is supplied from these settlements to industries near by. In some districts these are housed by the government and in others they are housed by the employers. The experiments in housing by the employers do not seem so successful as housing by the government. At Moghalpur the settlement supplies labor to the railroad shops. The inmates work for wages. On certain of the tea estates to which labor was supplied the wages were insufficient and conditions were bad.

AGRICULTURAL SETTLEMENTS

The highest type of settlement was the latest to be developed, the agricultural settlement. As the reformatory settlements were for the worst offenders and the industrial settlements for those who were quite trustworthy, but who still needed some supervision, the agricultural settlements were begun for those who could be depended upon to work in the fields without much supervision and at a kind of work which is followed by most of the inhabitants of India. In these agricultural settlements members are allotted a piece of land amounting to about ten acres when that much is available. To be a success the family must have irrigated land. These allotments are given them for fifteen years on probation. During this time the grant is liable to reversion for proved misconduct.[15]

This provision has been found to be the strongest incentive

---

[15] *A Note on the Administration of Criminal Tribes in the Punjab, 1917–1919,* Lahore, 1920, pp. 6, 7.

to these criminal tribesmen to behave themselves and make an honest living. One of the reports says that land hunger is as strong with the inmates placed in settlements as with any non-criminal tribes. One of the incentives to good behavior in the industrial settlements is the possibility of being transferred to an agricultural settlement and getting a piece of land.[16] It is the belief of the leaders in this work that settling the tribes permanently on agricultural tracts is the only real and lasting solution of the problem. Early in the experiment, Sir Michael O'Dwyer, then Lieutenant-Governor of the Punjab, said: "In the long run, settlement on the land is the goal which all aspire to, and in any future scheme of colonization provisions should be made for them." [17] Moreover, the agricultural settlement takes these people away from the large towns where there are temptations of all sorts not present in the settlement.

Three of these agricultural settlements I visited, one at Bitragunta, one at Stuartpuram in the Madras Presidency, and one at Sholapur in the Bombay Presidency. A brief description of each will make the plan clearer.

At Bitragunta, eleven miles south of the Kavali settlement, is the agricultural settlement of the Nellore district, of the Madras Presidency. Part of the inmates are transfers from the Kavali reformatory settlement who had shown their trust-worthiness. These had been allotted land which they farmed or pastured. Even here, however, there was one enclosure of cactus in which some who were not totally trustworthy had to stay at night.

At Bitragunta there are about 250 houses besides the assembly hall, schoolhouse, and the attendants' houses. These houses form a village occupying about 102 acres. It is a high, well-drained piece of land sloping eastward toward the Allur Swamp. In this low land the people are assigned tracts for cultivation. There is also plenty of land on which to locate the settlers' houses as soon as they are released from the settlement and are ready to settle upon these tracts. Allur is a good site

[16] *Report on the Administration of Criminal Tribes in the Punjab, 1925*, p. 8.
[17] *Ibid.*, 1920, pp. 3, 4.

of nearly eight acres which furnishes space for forty-eight families who are still members of the settlement. At Allur is the mission compound with its church and school about two miles from the settlers' fields in the swamp lands.

I was at Bitragunta on a Sunday morning. The morning religious services had just been finished and Sunday-school classes were being held when we arrived. These are held in an assembly hall either open at the side or closed only with matting. The top is made of thatch and is of very simple construction. All the houses are Indian huts built of mud with thatched roofs. The animals belonging to the settlers were wandering about the streets and out over the unenclosed land.

I was interested in the way in which individual initiative was stimulated in these settlements. In addition to the ground for his house the settler is also given a piece of ground on which he builds his granary or other buildings needed. The granary is a hole dug in the shale rock underneath one of the huts. A part of this settler's grain was threshed and in this pit. There are also settlement granaries into which those who have not granaries of their own may place their grain as in one of our modern grain elevators. These pits are dry and the grain keeps well until it is required for use or sale.

At Stuartpuram, in the Madras Presidency, I visited another agricultural settlement under the Salvation Army. In this settlement is a combination of sandy loam and irrigated flat land. The irrigating canal is not large enough, however, to supply water sufficient at all times. During dry seasons the situation is somewhat difficult. The sandy loam land is fertile if water is put upon it. Many of these settlers have dug wells from which they get water to put upon the land. It was very interesting to see a number of these men on a Sunday afternoon drawing the water out of the wells with their cattle, carrying it over the little patches of ground, and watering the grain. In each of these agricultural settlements the ordinary economic motives prevail. In this particular settlement I saw a sort of family house, the largest in the settlement, occupied by a man and his brothers, who not only farm land but also deal in live stock. They have proved to be such dependable men that they are permitted to go out of the settlement on passes to buy stock and to sell it. They rent land in the settlement on which they graze the cattle while they have them there. The manager told me that this man and his brothers were worth about $10,000.

The other settlement I visited that had an agricultural feature was the one at Sholapur in the Bombay Presidency. While most of the families in this settlement work in the mills in the town a mile away, a great many of them farm. This is a combined industrial and agricultural settlement. A barbed-wire fence surrounds the area in which the living huts are placed and to which all return at night. The farm land is out around the settlement as is the case with most Indian villages. Aside from the wire fence, the community well, and other buildings, like schools, etc., the settlement is like any ordinary Indian village. Here the people seem to be contented and are doing well financially.

I was not privileged to visit a forest settlement and know nothing about these except from reports.

REFORMATORY SETTLEMENTS

The reformatory settlements are for the worst offenders. Kavali in the Madras Presidency is such a settlement. Amritsar is the reformatory settlement in the Punjab. There is usually only one in each presidency or province. After various experiments one had to be provided near Bombay for that presidency at Bijapur. The Indian Jails Committee in 1919 recommended that one at least be established in each presidency.[18]

I found one settlement in India which was under the police instead of under the Criminal Tribes Settlement officer. This was a settlement of bad-acting Hurs at Visapur. Just before I was there the great irrigation project on which they had been working had been finished and they had been removed to another place. This really was a work colony instead of a settlement.

[18] *Report of the Indian Jails Committee, 1919–20*, Simla, 1926, Vol. I, p. 330.

Criminal Tribesmen at Sunday Morning Roll-call at Kavali
Repairment Settlement, Madras Presidency

From Left to Right, the Author and Officers of the Salvation
Army in Charge of the Agricultural Settlement for Criminal
Tribes at Stuartpuram, Madras Presidency, India.

Living Quarters

CRIMINAL TRIBES SETTLEMENT, VISAPUR

This was a settlement of Hurs under the control of the Police. It had been abandoned at the time of the author's visit because the irrigation project on which they had been engaged was finished.

Usually, as the men in the reformatory settlement and their families show ability to control their activities, they are transferred to a settlement in which the restrictions are less rigid. For example, from Kavali they go to Bitragunta.

At these reformatory settlements, strict control is kept over the inmates. Patrols are stationed about the settlement which is usually enclosed with a high wire fence. It is very much like a prison except that there are no walls and the inmates are classified in different departments within the wire fence.

In the Madras Presidency and the Bombay Presidency these reformatory settlements are enclosed with high wire fences so that the inmates cannot escape. At Kavali in the Madras Presidency I found three areas in the reformatory settlement. The inner one was surrounded by a barbed-wire fence ten feet high outside of which there was a cactus bed eight feet wide. Within this enclosure were men without families, who were more likely to try to escape than those with families, and any other who had misbehaved or attempted to run away. Outside of this enclosure and surrounding it was another enclosure, surrounded by a barbed-wire fence within which were confined at night those who worked outside in the daytime. Outside of these two enclosures were a lot of huts in which lived those who had been found faithful and were cultivating ground or working at wages for people.

One of the things pointed out by the Indian Jails Committee in 1919 and 1920 is that wherever the settlements provide a living income for the inmates there is little difficulty. The number of absconders is small, and contentment prevails. That is one reason why the labor-supplying settlement and the agricultural settlement seem to give the best results.

LOCATION OF SETTLEMENTS

In choosing the locations of the settlements, consideration is given to opportunities near by for profitable work.[19] For example, the one at Sholapur is near large cotton mills at which

---

[19] *Report on the Working of the Criminal Tribes Act in the Police Report of the Bombay Presidency, including Sind and Railways, 1923,* Bombay, 1924, Part II, pp. 6, 7; *Report on Administration of Criminal Tribes in the Punjab, 1926,* p. 4.

the inmates of the settlement may find employment. The industrial settlement at Moghalpur is there because the Northwestern Railway employs large numbers of the settlers in the shops. The labor-supplying settlements are located near large tea plantations or near forests in which the settlers may be employed.

EXTENT OF THE SETTLEMENTS

In 1919 all of British India had settlements for criminal tribes except Burma, Assam, the Central Provinces, and the Northwest Frontier Province. It is uncertain from the reports whether all of the native states have them.[20]

In the Punjab in 1919 there were twenty-six settlements besides the reformatory settlement at Amritsar. Of these, twelve were industrial, one semi-agricultural, three old agricultural, and seven new agricultural, together with three old settlements which had no supervising staffs.[21]

ADMISSION TO SETTLEMENTS

The larger proportion of the inmates are sent to the settlements by the authorities.

In the early days of the experiment in the Bombay Presidency, it was usual to ask a gang or tribe to select the settlement where they would like to be placed. This was done on the theory that they would be much more contented and yield more readily to discipline if they had their wishes consulted in the matter.[22]

In addition to those who are sent to the settlements by the government, there is provision in the law for voluntary inmates. However, in order to be admitted, they and their dependents must make a statement to the effect that they wish to enter and be recorded by a magistrate or by the manager or by the settlement inspector in charge of a settlement

---

[20] *Report of the Indian Jails Committee, 1919–20*, Simla, 1920, Vol. I, p. 321.

[21] *A Note on the Administration of Criminal Tribes in the Punjab, 1917–19*, Lahore, 1920.

[22] *Report of the Indian Jails Committee, 1919–20*, Simla, 1920, Vol. I, p. 327.

and this statement must be forwarded to the inquiry officer. That officer considers the reasons offered and if he thinks they should be placed in the settlement, a copy of his opinion with his reasons are forwarded to the government for orders under Section 16 of the Criminal Tribes Act.[23]

In the Bombay Presidency, conditions of admission into settlements were tightened up in 1926 as a measure of economy. Persons with their dependents were admitted only after they had at least five convictions or two convictions if the total sentence amounted to seven years' imprisonment.[24] The result of this rule has been to increase the number of more serious offenders. This makes the tasks of the settlement staffs more difficult.[25]

LIFE IN THE SETTLEMENTS

The following description does not fit all the settlements throughout India, but will give some idea of the general features of their life. Features vary from settlement to settlement. We must not forget that some settlements are industrial, some are agricultural, and some are reformatory. Moreover, in certain cases, a given settlement will have two or more of these features.

Consider that when the people come into these settlements usually they are in a filthy condition. When they were ordered to bathe once a week in May and June, the early inmates of one settlement vigorously resented a departure from their tradition which tabooed this unnecessary function. Moreover, usually they are averse to work. They have made their living by dishonest methods. Booth Tucker reports one of them saying: "We never work; we only dance and sing." Another asked, "What does the government think? Do they take us for coolies?" Still others said, "Why should we work? Even if we get a rupee a day it would be nothing to us. We

---

[23] *Bombay Criminal Tribes Settlement Rules*, 1926, pp. 1, 2.
[24] *Report on the Working of the Criminal Tribes Act in the Bombay Presidency*, 1926, Part I, p. 10.
[25] *Ibid.*, 1927, Part I, p. 6.

can secure one thousand rupees in a single night by one our dacoities." [26]

Picture an area of land covered with native huts built by the settlers themselves, arranged along streets, and usually surrounded by a wire fence. The fence, however, is not characteristic of all the settlements. The agricultural settlements at Bitragunta and at Stuartpuram have no fence, while the combined industrial and agricultural settlement at Sholapur has a fence. The huts look untidy, they are built of mud, thatched with palmyra leaves, or straw. Most of the settlements are built on land well drained and wind-swept so that the location is sanitary. The huts themselves are open and therefore admit air and sunlight. They are used chiefly for sleeping, and as a place in which to store articles belonging to the family.

Remember that these people, if they are able to work, must make a living for themselves. Therefore, in most of the settlements, the women as well as the men work either in the fields, if it is an agricultural, or in the mills if it is an industrial settlement. That means that someone must take care of the small children. Some of the settlements have *crèches* where the mothers can leave their children while they are at work. Sometimes the settlement itself pays those who take charge of the children. In other settlements the people have to hire some old man or old woman to take care of the children while they are away. The older children are in school provided by the settlement. Therefore, during the day the settlement seems to be comparatively deserted, except for the children and the old or sick.

The sun was sinking toward the horizon when I visited the settlement at Sholapur; the people were beginning to come in from the fields; women and girls were going to the settlement well in order to get water for household purposes; children were playing about in charge of their attendants; the boys and girls had come from the schools, and were playing about. Aside from a quarrel which was going on between two women and their friends the settlement seemed very quiet. However, after the sun had set, the workers began to come from the mills a mile away in long streams of people. Preparation of the evening meal began, the guards at the gates were checking up on the people. Then evening roll call was attended to. Finally the gates were shut for the night and only a guard remained in charge. Those who had been released from the enclosure and were living in huts outside were attending to their evening duties in their huts and preparing to settle down for the night.

Yonder on the hill stands a school for boys who have proved to be incorrigible or whose parents have absconded or are considered unfit for association with their children. A half mile away on another rise of ground is the girls' school for similar purposes. As evening closes down the fires under the cooking boxes begin to gleam, and make a very pretty picture as we wend our way from the settlement to the railroad station. This régime is modified only on Sunday. While it varies in different settlements, Sunday is a day of rest with just enough activities to keep the inmates from plotting escape or planning robberies. Thus at Kavali Reformatory Settlement and at Bitragunta there is a roll call at seven o'clock in the morning, with a two-hour religious service, followed by Sunday school of an hour. Then in the afternoon again there is another hour for religious services. At Stuartpuram, under the Salvation Army, religious services are held in the morning with Sunday school; in the afternoon the Boy Scouts and the Girl Scouts meet, and still later a general meeting is held of a Salvation Army character. However, while this was going on I saw a number of the settlers drawing water and watering the land, attending to their cattle, and such like. In the agricultural settlements the chores have to be done.

In every way the managers of the settlements endeavor to instil a spirit of optimism in these people as to their ability to make an honest living. However, they confess that their chief hopes are in the children and the young people.[27] Economically, the program is designed to encourage the people to earn their own living and take pride in it, to instil in them ideals of manhood and womanhood through the Boy Scouts, the Girl Scouts, and the Salvation Army organizations for young people and children. If any one is sick in the settlement, medical aid is furnished free.[28]

ROLL CALL

In order to ascertain whether inmates are present or not, frequent roll calls are necessary. The rules vary, of course, from local government to local government. In some settlements the most untrustworthy are required to report for roll call twice or three times a day, while those for whom the restrictions have been somewhat loosened must report only once a day or even weekly. Thus the whole plan is built on the policy of making the restrictions as light as possible and gradually relaxing them as the individual shows himself to be trustworthy.

Roll calls are held in the reformatory and industrial settlements morning and evening, and in industrial settlements morning and evening with surprise roll calls occasionally at night. Roll call is also effective in the Bombay Presidency for those registered in the village. However, the aim is to release them from roll call as soon as it appears that they are behaving themselves. For example, in the Bombay Presidency at Satara, of 1271 persons registered, 161 were in settlements, the remaining 1110 persons were registered and on roll call. However, during the year 1923, 509 were released from roll call.[29] Exemption from roll call depends, both within and without the settlements, upon good behavior for a certain length of time. Leave is also permitted on pass for necessary

[27] *Report on the Working of the Criminal Tribes Act in the Bombay Presidency for the year ending March 31, 1924,* Part I, p. 6.
[28] *Report on the Administration of Criminal Tribes in the Punjab for the year ending December, 1926,* Lahore, 1927, p. 7.
[29] *Report on the Working of the Criminal Tribes Act in the Police Report of the Bombay Presidency, including Sind and Railways, 1923,* Bombay, 1924, Part II, pp. 6, 7.

business outside the settlement or outside the restricted area of the village.

LAW AND ORDER IN THE SETTLEMENTS

Various devices are used in order to bring about reformation. One of these is the lessening of the rigor of the roll call, and its removal at the earliest possible moment. Three successive stages of release are in general use. (a) A change from a daily to a weekly roll call; (b) a change from a weekly roll call to freedom from roll call, and freedom from the necessity of taking a pass when proceeding on a journey; and (c) cancellation of registration. This increasing relaxation sometimes results in abuses, but the theory is that these people will learn to control themselves only by doing so.

There are guards, or police, at most of the settlements. At some of the reformatory settlements, as at Kavali, the regular police of the district are employed for the reformatory settlement. These are drawn from among the discharged members of the settlement, and paid monthly salaries by the police department as special police.

At Bitragunta, with its 850 people, there are only 10 special constables, and no regular police at all, and in such a place as Allur, which has 164 people, there are no police, because these people are about ready to be released from registration.[30] However, these special police have to be watched. For example, at Kavali, the assistant superintendent rode around the fence one morning and found the special constable supposed to be guarding the west side fast asleep. He lost his job. After midnight one night, perhaps fifteen minutes after the time clock had made its rounds, the superintendent of police made a surprise visit and found six out of eight patrols sitting comfortably on the ground instead of alert and on duty.[31]

Absconding is one of the prices that has to be paid for giving these criminal tribes comparative freedom. Aside from those

---

[30] Bawden, *The Kavali Repairment Settlement; The Report of the Erukala Industrial Settlement, 1924,* pp. 16, 17.
[31] *Ibid.,* p. 18.

settlements which are surrounded by a fence it is comparatively easy for a man or a woman to run away. For example, a few days before our visit to the Kavali Settlement, during a storm one night, twelve of the inmates of the reformatory settlement climbed the ten-foot barbed wire fence and jumped an eight-foot cactus bed outside and all got away except one who missed his footing and fell in the cactus bed. Formerly the absconders when arrested were sent to jail, but recently these reformatory settlements have been set up in order to take care of just such cases. The first offense in the Madras Presidency means six months, the second offense two years, of which part or all of the second year may be remitted by the manager if the conduct of the individual seems to warrant it. The third offense means three years, while the fourth offense is counted as proof that the individual is incorrigible, which means close confinement for the minimum of four years. This may be extended further if the man has shown no further proof of improvement. Since the close confinement within the reformatory fence is irksome, in most cases men of normal mentality respond and in the course of a short time are let out to a less restrained life.

In general, the methods of discipline consist of close restraint, and deprivation of privileges, with the positive reward of relaxation of restraint and extension of privileges for good conduct. The psychology of having to answer to roll-call twice a day compared with exemption from roll-call seems to be a strong incentive to good conduct. Furthermore, the issuance of passes is dependent upon the good conduct of the inmates. Many times these passes are of distinct economic advantage and therefore are very much desired. They are to be carefully guarded, however, else they will be abused.

(For Bibliography, see following chapter)

CHAPTER V

THE CRIMINAL TRIBES OF INDIA (Continued)

WHEN the government earnestly set about putting the criminal tribes into settlements, the initial difficulties were very great. In the early stages the task was of enormous magnitude in bringing the wild tribesmen under control, in inducing them to give up their dirty and lazy habits, and to take continuous hard work in place of their spasmodic, though often adventurous, efforts at making their living by robbery. Moreover, the introduction of this class of rather indifferent, if not hostile, labor into the labor market and obtaining good wages for the members was no small task. They were unprepossessing in appearance as well as averse to hard work. When the first batches were brought in, most of them were clad in rags. Furthermore, most of the potential employers of labor were hostile to these criminal tribesmen. One of the first tasks, therefore, was the removal of these prejudices. For example, the Northwestern Railway was approached to ascertain if it could not give employment to a number of these men. It was reluctant to try the experiment with 100 families at first, even though the government offered to pay the cost of building the settlement. The first two attempts at such an arrangement were unsuccessful. The railway thought the criminal tribesmen were not capable of becoming skilled workmen, and were likely to steal some of the valuable articles lying in the workshops. It also thought that their employment would be resented by free labor. It even refused to give land for the building of settlements as an experimental measure. It was not until 1917 when the War created a shortage of labor that the railway was willing to listen. It then permitted a settlement to be built at government expense on railway land, and agreed to take 200 workmen for the signal engineer for a period of one year. So successful was the experiment that criminal tribes labor is now preferred to other labor on this railway. The railway has recently agreed to build a large settlement at railway expense to enable more inmates to be brought in. In order at first to get them to work in the mills at all, often comparatively low wages had to be accepted to begin with. The employers of labor looked upon these criminal tribesmen as wolves, and the tribesmen were stubborn in their determination to avoid work under the new environment at all costs. However, a man who would not take employment in the mills was sent to a reformatory settlement where he had to work, and gradually they learned that it was better to work for a private employer.

In the agricultural settlements are kept the best behaved and most completely reformed members of the criminal tribes. This is done to reward them for their good behavior and as an inducement to others to follow their example.

In the agricultural settlements the settlers are allotted ten acres of canal irrigated land each on probation for fifteen years, during which the land is liable to confiscation for proved misconduct. At the end of this period they are eligible to occupancy rights. In these settlements, at least in the Punjab, the village buildings are erected at government expense and the government foots the bill for the supervising staff.[1]

Another type is the semi-agricultural type of settlement. We have an instance of it in the Punjab. These criminals were settled as tenants at will on a plot of land made up of parts of three distinct villages. The proprietor was to provide seed, cattle food, fodder, and clothing until the tenants could earn enough to maintain themselves. The amount advanced was to be repaid by easy installments from their share of the produce. This plan, however, is not generally followed in the settlements.[2]

[1] Hari Singh, *A Note on the Administration of Criminal Tribes in the Punjab,* 1920, p. 7.

[2] *Report on the Administration of the Criminal Tribes in the Punjab for the year ending December, 1919,* Lahore, 1920, Appendix, p. viii.

The agricultural settlements are the most hopeful, but in order to be a success they must be on good lands where the tenants can make a living. Also they have been most successful since the local governments have required that the families go with them. This tends to keep them satisfied and to reduce absconding. Those who have no families with them are kept in a separate part of the settlement and are under stricter supervision.

Many of the old people who cannot make a living for themselves in agriculture or in the industrial plants take care of the cattle, goats, pigs, and children of settlers who are working. Some of them are employed also as servants in the houses of the staff, in the school, and in sweeping the streets and cleaning the camps.[3]

In the industrial settlements, sometimes some settlers work for a wage, and others, where that is possible, are employed at piece work.

It is of interest to note the wages which are paid these people when they are employed in industry. When the settlements were first begun, in order to get them employment in industries, often they had to work for less than the current wage. However, in 1919, about the time that earnest work began in the settlements, while the fixed daily wage in Indian society was from 6 to 12 annas (an anna is the sixteenth part of a rupee, and the rupee is worth about 36 cents), in the settlements on piece work the individuals were able to earn from 1 rupee to 1½ rupees.[4] In the Indian Jails Committee Report it was stated that the wage earnings of a man in the mills over the three years previous to 1919 had been 12 rupees a month, for a woman 6 rupees, and for a child 6 rupees. The employer also added a grain allowance of 3 rupees per month. Thus a family of two adults and two children could not earn more than about 30 rupees a month.[5] In the weaving mills the wage was somewhat higher, but always greater for men than

[3] *The Kavali Repairment Settlement*, Madras, 1925, pp. 24, 25.
[4] Hari Singh, *A Note on the Administration of the Criminal Tribes of the Punjab, 1919*, Lahore, 1920, p. 5.
[5] *Report Indian Jails Committee, 1919–20*, Vol. I, p. 317.

for women.[6] In some other occupations, the wages were higher. As wages advanced in Indian society, the wages in the settlements likewise rose.[7] By 1923 some of the more industrious families were earning as high as 60 rupees per month, a very much higher wage than was to be earned outside.[8] In the Moghalpura railway settlement in the Punjab the average monthly earnings per family in 1925 was 22–4–0 rupees.[9] On the whole it is clear that these people in the settlements earned more than they could have earned by honest, unskilled labor outside.[10]

That these wages are appreciably above that which is paid the free laborer is indicated by the fact that about 1900 the estimated average income for all India per annum was 30 rupees. However, later studies in the Madras and Bombay Presidencies have shown an annual average of 100 rupees for the 42.3 million persons in the former and in the latter 100 rupees for urban localities and 75 rupees for rural areas.[11]

That these wages throughout India are a mere subsistence or below a subsistence wage in some cases is indicated by the fact that in Bombay the poorest classes of the population were compelled in 1921 to spend 68 per cent of their income on food, 15 per cent on clothing, 11 per cent on compulsory expenditure of various kinds, leaving only 6 per cent for voluntary expenditures. A study of the working-class budgets in Bombay City about 1921 or later showed that out of a total family income averaging just over 52 rupees per month, 56.8 per cent went for food, 9.6 per cent for clothing, 7.7 per cent on house rent, 7.4 per cent on fuel and lights, and 18.5 per cent on miscellaneous activities.[12] Thus is apparent what has been learned wherever studies of income and expenditure have been made,

[6] *Report on the Administration of Criminal Tribes in the Punjab for the year ending December, 1918*, Lahore, 1919, Appendix A, p. iii.

[7] *Ibid.*, 1922, Lahore, 1923, p. 1 of Second Letter.

[8] *Report on the Administration of Criminal Tribes in the Punjab for the year ending December, 1923*, Lahore, 1924, p. 6.

[9] *Report on the Administration of Criminal Tribes in the Punjab*, Lahore, 1925, p. 7.

[10] *Ibid.*, 1926, p. 6.

[11] Williams, *India in 1924–25*, Calcutta, 1925, p. 235.

[12] *Op. cit.*, p. 237.

that with increased income a lesser proportion is spent on the bare necessities of life.

FINANCING THE SETTLERS

Many of these criminal tribesmen come into the settlement without adequate finances of their own to carry on. Early in the experiment it was learned that some arrangements would have to be made by which these people in the agricultural settlements could live until they had earned something.

In the early years of the experiment following the War a special indigent grant was made by the government of the Punjab to enable the settlement officer to provide for the necessaries of life where needed. Free food and free clothing had to be provided for helpless indigents, but so as not to encourage pauperism among the people. Some of them were already inclined to dependency, and, as already indicated, to many of them any form of work was galling. Therefore, to all able-bodied persons who were needy a recoverable loan was made from this fund which was cancelled, if, owing to circumstances beyond their control, and in spite of their best efforts, they were unable to repay it within a reasonable time.[13] After a year or two with this experiment, it was discontinued, because the tendency of many of them toward pauperism was thereby increased.

Then the experiment was tried of allowing shopkeepers to locate in the settlement on the express understanding that no credit was to be given to a tenant unless authorized and approved by the superintendent. This kept a check on the borrowing tendencies of the tenant.[14] Some local governments, because of the abuse of their privileges by the traders in the settlement, had to limit their operations.

In addition to these various devices, with the growth of the co-operative movement in India, some of the local governments have organized co-operative societies in the settlements for members of the criminal tribes. These were established in

[13] *Report on the Administration of Criminal Tribes in the Punjab, 1920*, pp. 1, 2.
[14] *Ibid.*, 1922, Lahore, 1923, p. 6.

the early part of the present decade, and their growth has been steady in certain of the local governments. Thus Mr. Starte, the criminal tribes settlement officer in the Bombay Presidency, says that these societies serve not only a very useful purpose in helping the settlers to obtain credit for their needs, but many of them are producing societies also. In Bijapur and Gadag, carpentry shops have been maintained by the societies, and they have also undertaken building construction.

The Bagalkot Society undertook the business of cutting wood from the forest and selling it as fuel. Some of the others have established small weaving factories.

At first the rules of these societies were very elastic and full control could not be given to the settlers. Later, however, the effort was made to bring these societies into line with the other credit societies. For example, the societies at Hubli and Baramati have become registered co-operative credit societies, and others are being registered.[15]

In the Bombay Presidency the criminal tribes settlement rules provide that the criminal tribes settlement officer is authorized to make advances free of interest on good security: (a) To members of the criminal tribes whether such be settlers or not; (b) to credit societies, producer societies, or factories run by or in the interest of the criminal tribes under the control of the criminal tribes settlement officer for the following purposes: (1) The purchase of bullocks, tools, and other articles; (2) building of houses or huts; (3) railway fare and maintenance; (4) financing of industry.[16] Any amount advanced under this rule may be recovered in installments by the criminal tribes settlement officer. Where there is wilful default in payment, the amount due may be recovered by attaching and selling the movable property of the defaulter or of his sureties.

In 1924–25 in the Madras Presidency there were five societies for members of certain criminal tribes. At the end of the year

---

[15] Starte, *Report on the Working of the Criminal Tribes Act in the Bombay Presidency, 1922*, Part I, p. 7.

[16] *The Bombay Criminal Tribes Settlement Rules, 1926*, p. 6.

these societies had 499 members and a paid-up share capital of 5,388 rupees. All of them in that Presidency had worked at a profit, the net profit earned amounting in the aggregate to 636 rupees.[17]

In a number of the presidencies, for example in the Bombay Presidency, these societies continued their steady expansion and were in a good financial position in 1924. In that year the share capital was 10,405 rupees, and the total of deposits was 48,069 rupees; the reserve fund, 9,475 rupees.

EDUCATION AMONG THE CRIMINAL TRIBES

When one remembers that in 1921 only 82 out of every 1000 persons 5 years of age and over and in 1926 only about 18.6 millions out of some 300 odd millions of the inhabitants of India are literates, he will see the significance of the provisions for the education of children in the criminal tribes settlements.[18]   In the Bombay Presidency, for example, in 1925, the average number of children attending primary schools in all the settlements during the year was 176 per 1000 of the population, while the average number of children attending the primary schools in the entire presidency was only 76 per 1000.[19] Primary education is compulsory for all boys and girls in the settlements between the ages of five or six and twelve or fifteen years.   In the Bombay Presidency all children over twelve and under sixteen years who work as half-timers in the mills must go to school the other half time.[20]   Attendance in night schools is in force for boys up to the age of eighteen years who are working in the mills, and for boys who have left the day school, in order that they may maintain whatever literacy they have achieved.

In order that more of the children of criminal tribesmen who are not in settlements may be induced to go to school, in some

[17] Coatman, *India in 1925–26*, Calcutta, 1926, pp. 159, 163; Census of India, 1921, Vol. I, p. 187.
[18] Starte, *Report on the Working of the Criminal Tribes Act in the Bombay Presidency for the year ending March 31, 1925*, Part I, p. 5.
[19] *Report on the Working of the Criminal Tribes Act in the Bombay Presidency for the year ending March 31, 1925*, Part I, p. 5.
[20] *Ibid.*, 1924, Part I, pp. 4, 5.

of the local governments scholarships have been provided in order to induce the parents to allow these children to attend. While these scholarships are very small, as small as 2 rupees per year, even that small sum has a decidedly stimulating effect.

When it became apparent to those managing the settlements and in control of the tribes in the villages that economic prosperity is one of the best means of reforming the criminal tribes, those interested in the education of the children of the criminal tribes saw that manual education or training for a job was one of the important matters to be considered. This was not introduced into most of the presidencies until along in 1923 and 1924. In practically all of the settlements, in the Punjab and Bombay at least, and also to a degree in other presidencies, manual training classes are now held for the boys and domestic science classes for the girls. In addition, those working in the mills are receiving apprenticeship training for future jobs. A skilled young fellow is always in demand in the mills and is paid a good wage. In 1927 in the Bombay Presidency 498 boys in school were receiving training in agriculture or woodwork, and in tin work or tailoring or weaving as part of the school curriculum of the settlements.[21] The aim of the settlements in the Punjab is that every boy who leaves school shall have had the opportunity to learn a trade.

Moreover, great attention is given to scouting work in the settlements in the belief that through play these children can be taught many useful lessons. In addition, every year in the Bombay Presidency and in some of the others an industrial exhibit is held of the objects made in the industrial school. This excites great interest and has a good effect upon the people as well as upon the children, because they see that these criminal tribesmen are able to produce beautiful and useful articles.

The philosophy back of this insistence upon education of the criminal tribesmen's children is that by educating the children new habit patterns are established, new ideals are set up, and in the end they will not want to follow the same lines as

[21] *Report on the Working of the Criminal Tribes Act in the Bombay Presidency, 1927,* Part I, p. 4.

their fathers. Furthermore, the idea in connection with manual training and the trade schools is to provide these children with a trade before they are turned out of the settlement. Evidently, there is going on in India in the settlements what went on at an earlier date in the juvenile reformatories of this country; namely, that the children guilty of delinquency are more highly privileged in getting a trade education than those in free society. All the reports indicate the utmost enthusiasm on the part of the officials as to the results obtained by this educational system. There is no question that it is more thorough and that more children are reached in the settlements than where the criminal tribes are restricted in villages. However, even in the villages progress is being made. The school presents the finest opportunity for the molding of these young criminal tribesmen into honest and efficient citizens.

SPECIAL INSTITUTIONS FOR CHILDREN AND WOMEN

In a number of the settlements scattered throughout India, day nurseries are provided for young children so that their mothers can go to work. While in this country the day nursery is a problem, in India, where the situation is somewhat different, those in charge seem to think that they are doing good work.[22]

Early in the settlement experiment, especially under the religious societies, and for the most part with the worst among the criminal tribesmen, the question arose as to whether their children could not be educated in an institution separate from their family. For example, in the Kavali settlement in the Madras Presidency the children are taken away from their parents, boarded and educated in the mission school. In some of the Salvation Army settlements, the children have been taken away and sent to the Salvation Army school some distance away. The Indian Jails Committee commend this practice in their report in 1919–1920.[23] However, there has been

---

[22] *The Kavali Repairment Settlement*, Madras, 1925, pp. 41, 42; *Report of the Administration of Criminal Tribes in the Punjab, 1919*, Appendix A, p. iii.
[23] *Report of the Indian Jails Committee, 1919–20*, Vol. I, pp. 327, 328.

a tendency to limit it to the children in families where the parental influence was bad, and to those whose parents died or absconded.   In the Bombay Presidency there are three such homes for children—at Bijapur, Hubli, and at Baramati. However, in these three institutions there is a total of only 76 children.   The children are sent to these schools only when there are no other means of controlling them, or when their parents have been proved to be irreclaimable criminals.[24]   In some settlements, as in Sholapur in the Bombay Presidency, the settlement itself has a special school for incorrigible children or the children of those who are not fit parents.

In the Bombay Presidency they have felt the necessity of providing a special home, a kind of a rescue home, for certain women of the criminal tribes.   Some of these have been guilty of living by prostitution.   Consequently, a woman's home was set up at Hubli and fulfills the function of a rescue home. In 1917 this home had only 17 occupants.   The officers in charge feel that real progress is made in reforming these women.[25]

HEALTH CONDITIONS IN THE SETTLEMENTS

In the early days of the settlements, some were poorly located and the health of the inmates suffered very materially. When one remembers that these criminal tribes have been used to a free, open-air life, he can understand how a restricted life in a settlement especially in a bad location, or employment in mills to which they were not accustomed, seriously affects those who are adapted to the outdoor life, the wandering tribes particularly.[26]   This lesson had to be learned at a great expense in the lives of these settlers.   For example, in the industrial settlement at Ghariwal in the Punjab in 1917, 11 per cent of the population of the settlement died; in 1918, 10 per cent;

---

[24] *Report on the Working of the Criminal Tribes Act in the Bombay Presidency for the year 1922*, Part I, p. 9.

[25] *Report on the Working of the Criminal Tribes Act in the Bombay Presidency for the year ending March 31, 1924*, Part I, p. 8; *Ibid., 1922*, p. 9.

[26] *Report on the Administration of Criminal Tribes in the Punjab for the year ending December, 1919*, Lahore, 1920, p. 1.   Introductory.

1919, 7 per cent; 1920, 12 per cent. At another settlement, Bhiwani, in 1917 the death rate was 22 per cent of the population, in 1918, 12 per cent; 1919, 18 per cent; 1920, 17 per cent.[27] In 1920 these two settlements were discontinued. When the settlement is well located it has been found that the health of the inmates has, on the whole, been good. This is shown by the fact that in the Bombay Presidency in 1922 the average death rate in the settlements was 19.3 per 1000 of the population, which is considerably lower than the average death rate throughout India. The average birth rate in the settlements was 32.42 in that year, showing an excess of 13.29 of births over deaths.[28] In 1926 the situation was still further improved. The average birth rate for 15 settlements in the Bombay Presidency was 42, which is higher than the average for the presidency; the death rate was 18.2, which is less than the average for the presidency.[29] Evidently those in charge of the settlements are learning how to take care of the health of their people.

RELEASE OF CRIMINAL TRIBESMEN

For the criminal tribesmen who are registered and are not placed in settlements, the difficulty of control is great. We have already noticed that in the early days of this decade such great numbers were exempted from registration largely owing to the inability of the police to check up on them carefully, and that it was felt that many had been exempted who should not have been. In recent years, less exemptions have been made. Increasingly it has been emphasized that those who have been exempted are still on probation, and if they again show signs of criminality they are re-registered. Up to the present this is an unsolved problem in the handling of the criminal tribes.

Once a man or family is in a settlement, however, the restraints are, step by step, relaxed as he shows good conduct, until

---

[27] *Ibid.,* 1920, p. 7.
[28] *Report on the Working of the Criminal Tribes Act in the Bombay Presidency for the year 1922,* Part I, p. 4.
[29] *Ibid.,* 1926, Part I, p. 4.

he is released from the settlement. He may be conditionally released and still be on what they call probation. When so released, he may go back to his own village or he may settle down on land near the settlement, or in the adjacent town. In the Punjab, the rule has been that after detention for five years in the case of either a settled or a wandering tribe, the question of release is considered in consultation with the local officers. If he is released it is on two years' probation, and he is only released if he can find a paying occupation and a house to live in. Final discharge is allowed only if the conditions of release are fulfilled and his conduct has a good report from the local police.[30] The reports show that some of those released on probation have to be recalled. Mr. Starte, the criminal tribes settlement officer of the Bombay Presidency, feels that this conditional release is a valuable and important factor in the work of reformation, because the criminal tribesman knows that should he be caught committing any offense, not only will he be punished for that offense, but the remitted part of his previous sentence will be reimposed.[31] The numbers exempted from registration and the numbers conditionally released from the settlement, both in the Punjab and in the Bombay Presidency, seem to be very small.

In the Bombay Presidency a person discharged from a settlement remains on probation for six years before his registration is cancelled. From all the settlements in the Bombay Presidency in 1925 only 75 were discharged under probation.[32]

In the Bombay Presidency these probationers are visited by officers from the settlements because of the conviction that experience the world over shows that after-care is just as important a branch of institutional work as the organization of work within the institution itself. This visitation, however, is not universally practiced on discharged criminal tribesmen from the settlements.[33]

[30] Report on the Administration of Criminal Tribes in the Punjab for the year ending December, 1926, p. 7.
[31] Report on the Working of the Criminal Tribes Act in the Bombay Presidency, 1922, Part I, p. 8.
[32] Ibid., 1925, Part I, p. 8.   [33] Ibid., 1927, Part I, p. 7.

Out of this experience has grown the conviction that if the persons discharged from settlements could be established on the land, they would do very much better than to go back to their own villages or to try to find employment in the large towns. In a number of the presidencies, attempts have been made to settle them upon land. In the Bombay Presidency a special settlement for such people has been established at Hotgi. However, most of the available land there has now been settled.[34] At Kavali, in the Madras Presidency, such a settlement has been provided at Allur, two miles from the Bitragunta agricultural settlement. Moreover, the families of the criminal tribesmen are now beginning to grow up and it is the belief of those in charge of the settlements, especially of Mr. Starte in the Bombay Presidency, that after-care must be given these discharged people. Some of them, as a matter of fact, do not wish to be discharged. Mr. Starte says that in 1926, 43 heads of families and their dependents, 106 persons, though offered their discharge on probation, preferred to remain in the settlement. They have secured regular work in the town, and they also appreciate the amenities of the settlement and the help of the settlement staff. This situation presents a problem which Mr. Starte considers serious. He is endeavoring to solve it by establishing free colonies adjacent to the settlements. At Sholapur he has such a settlement in addition to the others already mentioned, on which there are now 255 persons from the settlements. In that particular instance the colonies are financed by the mills who employ these people.[35] This extended after-care, while it involves added expense to the government, seems to be the only way to insure that these people do not relapse into crime.[36]

In the matter of discharge, these Indian settlements for criminal tribes are experimenting in a pioneering way which is of the utmost value to penology all over the world. It is apparent that gradual release from restraint, additional release for discharge, probation, and patient after-care bring

[34] *Ibid.*, 1927, Part I, p. 9.   [36] *Ibid.*, 1927, Part I, pp. 8, 9.
[35] *Ibid.*, 1926, Part I, p. 10.

results from these people who might be called habitual criminals.

CHANGES IN THE APPLICATION OF THE ACT

As experience with the Act proceeded, many changes had to be instituted. Frankly the whole Act contemplated a new experiment. As an experiment, changes had to be made. Most of these could be carried out by means of rules provided by the local government and authorized by the Act itself. Some of these changes will throw light on the difficulties encountered in any such experiment. Thus in the Punjab, as I noted above, the tendency to place convicted members of these criminal tribes in settlements overloaded the settlements, and interfered with the effective working of the Act. An amendment was therefore added in 1923 providing that no criminal tribe should be placed in a settlement unless the necessity had been established to the satisfaction of the local government after inquiry by such authority.[37]

Furthermore, while in the first enthusiasm the restriction of these criminal tribes to certain areas in their villages seemed to bring about the lessening of criminality, excessive exemptions from registration followed. The result was that in 1925 it was decided that an annual examination into the conduct of the exempted persons with a view to re-registration should be initiated. As a consequence, in the Punjab 896 men out of a total of 6700 exemptees were re-registered, and future exemptions were curtailed.[38]

Furthermore, the problem of providing paying work for those registered in the villages so as to relieve the economic distress has been a difficult one. The authorities in the Punjab recommended in 1926 that at least a thousand more families be taken care of in the settlements within the next two years. Moreover, vocational schools are also needed for the youths who are being corrupted by bad associations in the vil-

---

[37] *Report on the Administration of Criminal Tribes in the Punjab for the year ending December, 1922*, Lahore, 1923, p. 3.
[38] *Ibid.*, 1926, Lahore, 1927, pp. 1, 2.

lages. If the nomads are settled in the villages instead of being put into settlements, more productive work must be found for them, and more careful supervision given.[39]

In the Bombay Presidency, while some of the same problems occurred, others appeared. The Hurs were a peculiarly troublesome tribe, but after they were put into the special settlement at Visapur, under the control and supervision of the police, they gave little trouble. One of the large problems in that presidency was to provide a sufficient amount of irrigated land for the formation of agricultural settlements. As a result of experience in this presidency, a number of the gangs like the Bestars of the Madras Presidency were transferred to the Hubli settlement, absconded, and committed a number of depredations. They finally surrendered to the settlement officers after they were in danger of being caught and sent to prison. This and other experiences convinced the authorities that the settlements are making headway in showing these criminals that the best thing to do is to settle down and reform.

Constant changes are going on as experience indicates the necessity therefor in providing better settlements on agricultural land. For example, at Sholapur, the old settlement was in the city. Most of the inmates have now been transferred to the settlement a mile outside the city with very much better results.

Another lesson learned by experience with these people is that instead of notifying criminals by villages, the whole tribe, no matter where scattered, must be registered as a tribe and placed together in settlements where that seems to be necessary.[40]

Again, it came to be seen in the Bombay Presidency that the members of criminal tribes who had not been registered because they were in jail, should be registered and placed in a settlement immediately upon dismissal.[41]

[39] *Ibid.*, p. 4.
[40] *Police Report of the Bombay Presidency, including Sind and Railways, 1923,* Bombay, 1924, Part II, p. 1.
[41] *Ibid., 1924,* Bombay, 1925, Part II, p. 8.

Other changes which have been going on are in the nature of experiments to try better to adjust the system to the ends in view.   In the Bombay Presidency, for example, the settlement officer proposed that the government introduce a more uniform method of revision of the registration, in order to carry out the purpose of providing for the progressive lightening of the restrictions imposed in accordance with improvement in the behavior of those registered.   Only as such uniformity prevails can the act work automatically and without too much injustice to people in the different districts.[42]

With increasingly stricter control in the villages in the Bombay Presidency, many expert and dangerous criminals gravitated to the city of Bombay.   This made necessary the establishment of a settlement outside the city where the worst criminals could be segregated.   They were employed in a match factory, in woolen mills, and chemical works.

Another new experiment was tried in Bombay in 1925. Certain settlers who were believed to have progressed toward reformation were allowed to settle in the city of Bombay under as few restrictions as possible.   They were subjected to the supervision of probation officers appointed by two mission boards.   Two thousand six hundred and eighty-one were put under this probation.   The probation officers are responsible for providing labor, for maintaining some sort of check upon the movements of the settlers, and for securing the children's regular attendance at school.   If any of these probationers revert to crime they are sent back to a settlement.   In order to make this supervision easier and the control more effective, it was proposed to bring all of these people on probation to one place and for this purpose a new site was selected at Dharavi near Bombay.[43]

DIFFICULTIES EXPERIENCED

From time to time certain difficulties have been experienced in the application of the Criminal Tribes Settlement Act.

[42] *Ibid.*, p. 4.
[43] *Report on the Workings of the Criminal Tribes Act in the Bombay Presidency for the year ending March 31, 1925*, Part I, p. 2.

This act puts it within the power of the police to recommend that any individual member of a registered tribe be selected for removal to a settlement, where he may be detained for an unlimited period. This was thought to place the power of blackmail in the hands of the subordinate officials almost without limit, a danger to be guarded against as pointed out in the report of the Indian Jails Committee in 1919 and 1920.[44] This report suggests that the law should provide for a magisterial inquiry not only in case of registration, but in case of the decision of the police to remove a registered member to a settlement. They point out that in case it is a whole gang or tribe a full and regular inquiry be held before the removal to a settlement. Where official integrity is as poorly developed as in India such power is not without danger.

Managers and other officials of the criminal tribes have many difficulties to face. Some of these are due to conflicts between different individuals in the settlement which would arise even on the outside. For example, one settler comes and complains that, having been invited to a meal with a fellow caste man, the family of the latter during the heat of a subsequent quarrel insulted him by alleging that he had eaten in a gluttonous manner. Or, again, a group of criminal tribesmen want a pass because their particular enemies have bewitched their nets and therefore they cannot catch game and hence wish to go to a certain place and perform some ceremonies which will remove the spell from their nets. What is a busy manager to do in such cases? When I was visiting the settlement near Sholapur, as we passed between the huts we came upon a group in the midst of which two women were pulling each other's hair and fighting. The official accompanying me endeavored to find out the trouble. He learned that one of the women was accused by the other of beating the latter's child. All such differences of opinion have to be settled by the officials.

Another difficulty is in connection with employment both within the settlements and in the notified villages. Often

____
[44] *Report of the Indian Jails Committee, 1919–1920*, Vol. I, p. 324, 325.

these tribes have had no settled occupation in the village where they lived or they have wandered about from place to place. Restrict them to a certain area and it is difficult for them to find work and earn an honest living. In the Punjab it was suggested in 1921 that some authority should have the responsibility in the villages to find work for those registered and restricted. The police have supervision over them, but have their hands full without endeavoring to find them employment.[45] Difficulty of making an honest living was one of the original causes of criminal bands. How to find them employment in an overpopulated country is a serious problem.

Again, with the double authority over these criminal tribes, already described, there is the possibility of diagreement between the police and the criminal tribes settlement officer. As pointed out when describing the plan, one authority, the police, has charge of the supervision of those registered in the villages. The activities of this authority are mainly repressive or restrictive. It deals with the procedure before it seems necessary to place a tribe or gang or individual in a settlement. On the other hand, the authority who has charge of those in settlements and of those on probation is the criminal tribes settlement officer. There is only an imperfect liaison between these two authorities.[46]

Then, there is the difficulty that while the original intention was to make the village or *thana* the basis of the scheme and use the settlements only for the reformation of the most depraved or for the encouragement and reward of the more promising, the major attention, at least in the Punjab, has been devoted to the settlements. There seems to be an inherent difficulty in making the police responsible for the village end of the treatment.[47]

Another difficulty has risen by reason of the practice of notifying by whole villages rather than by tribes. In notify-

[45] *Ibid.*, 1923, Lahore, 1924, p. 12.
[46] *Police Report of the Bombay Presidency, including Sind and the Railways,* 1924, Bombay, 1925, p. 12.
[47] *Report on the Administration of the Criminal Tribes in the Punjab for the year ending December, 1924,* Lahore, 1925, p. 2.

ing by a village, some innocent people are restricted when they should not be.   However, the same difficulty, it would seem, is encountered if the tribe scattered through various villages is notified and registered when it is likely that there are some members of the tribe who are not criminal.[48] Other differences between the police and the criminal tribes settlement officer are detailed in the reports.   A further complication arises in connection with the wandering gangs.   They do not seem to belong anywhere.   Therefore, if they are registered in the district or province where their depredations have been committed, even though they may be from another state, the whole burden of their care either in the village or in settlements devolves upon the district in which they are registered.   In spite of the provisions in the law that such gangs may be returned to the state to which they belong, or from which they have come, many times the officials of that state will refuse to receive them.[49]   These wandering criminal tribes are the most difficult problem to solve.

CO-OPERATING SOCIETIES

The criminal tribes settlement plan grew out of certain experiments made chiefly by the Salvation Army.   Before the Criminal Tribes Act was in operation the Salvation Army had co-operated with the police in forming settlements for some of these criminal tribes with the hope that they might be able to lead them to a new course of life.   The Government of the United Provinces first invited the Salvation Army to deal with the criminal tribes.   Soon afterwards the Punjab, the presidencies of Madras, of Bengal, and of Bombay, as well as of Bihar, Orrissa, and of Burma, made contracts with the Salvation Army to place certain of these criminal tribes in settlements.   In 1916 the Salvation Army had 29 settlements and 5 children's industrial homes in which various tribes were

---

[48] *Police Report of the Bombay Presidency, including Sind and Railways, 1924,* Bombay, 1925, Letter No. 13, p. 11.
[49] *Ibid.,* Part II, p. 7.

settled. These settlements took care of 8000 members of these tribes.[50]

At the present time many other organizations, Christian, Hindu, and Mohammedan, are conducting settlements on contracts with the various governments. The following is a partial list of these agencies:

1. Salvation Army.
2. Hindu Maha Sabha (Matunga branch).
3. Servants of India Society.
4. Anjumans Islamia and Ahmadiyya.
5. Canadian Mission.
6. Dev Samaj.
7. Anjuman-i-Islamia.
8. Anjuman-i-Ahmadiyya Ishayat Islam.
9. Arya Samaj.
10. Chief Khalsa Diwan.
11. Qadian Society.
12. Hindu Sabha.
13. Sanatan Dharam Sabha.
14. American Board of Commissioners for Foreign Missions.
15. Mission Board of the Northern Baptist Convention.

The reports seem to indicate that most of these societies are doing rather poor work. Exceptions are made in the reports for certain of the native Indian societies, the Salvation Army, and some of the settlements under American mission boards. Among the Indian societies, Anjuman, Ahmadiyya, Ishayat-i-Islam, and Dev Samaj are decidedly the foremost ones in producing practical results.[51]

I visited three of these settlements under religious organizations—the one at Kavali in the Madras Presidency under the American Baptist Mission, the one at Stuartpuram under the Salvation Army, and the one at Sholapur, Bombay Presidency, under the American Board of Commissioners for Foreign Missions. I also visited one under government auspices at

---

[50] Booth Tucker, *Criminology or the Indian Crim, and What to Do With Him,* 4th ed., Simla, 1916, p. 43. *Report on the Administration of Criminal Tribes in the Punjab for the year ending December, 1919,* Lahore, 1920, p. 5.

[51] *Report on the Administration of Criminal Tribes in the Punjab for the year ending December 1919,* p. 6.

Kalianpur near Cawnpore. All of these seemed to be doing excellent work.

It is a question, however, whether the actual management of the settlements should be retained in the hands of government officials or should be entrusted to a private agency. The Madras Government has expressed the opinion that there should always be some religious or philanthropic agency attached to each settlement, if not actually in charge of it. Mr. Starte, the criminal tribes settlement officer of Bombay, thinks there should be a combination of government and private control. He believes that to exclude voluntary agencies would lead to disaster.

Difficulties, however, are met in connection with those run by private agencies. What shall be said when criminal tribes are placed under an American religious organization or the Salvation Army when their ancestral religion is either Hinduism or Islam? The Indian Jails Committee in 1920 suggested that so far as possible only persons of the religious faith of the organization having them in charge should be placed in a settlement. This, however, has proved thus far to be impossible. This committee agreed that a great part of what had been accomplished for the advancement of the criminal tribes was due to the self-sacrificing efforts of many missionary bodies and of the Salvation Army. The Hindu and Mohammedan faiths up to that time had given little attention to the matter and even in more recent times many of them have failed to take seriously their responsibility.[52]

Perhaps a few words describing how some of the religious organizations took up this work of dealing with the criminal tribes may be of interest. The Salvation Army seems to have been first on the ground. In 1908, three years before the enactment of the first criminal tribes settlement act, the Government of the United Provinces invited the Salvation Army to deal with the criminal tribes. At that time there was no law compelling these people to go to a settlement. They could be induced to do so only by persuasion and in some cases

[52] Report, *Indian Jails Committee, 1919–1920,* Vol. I, p. 326.

by the alternative of imprisonment. Then for a time after the enactment of the law in 1911 pressure was not exerted upon the criminal tribes to enter settlements, and the same policy of inducing them to enter the Salvation Army Settlements had to be pursued. However, after a few years the government saw the necessity of exerting force and hence many more entered these settlements. From the very beginning the Salvation Army endeavored to make them economically independent, to treat them fairly, and to teach them an honest trade. This organization set up industries at which they could make a living, helped the young people to produce various things which they could sell for a profit, and set up schools for the education of the children. This work was so successful under the enthusiasm and the good sense of the Salvation Army officers that a number of other provinces also asked the Salvation Army to undertake this kind of work.

One example of an American Missionary Society shows how the work grew up under this organization in a slightly different way. In 1912 the district superintendent of police in the Nellore District of the Madras Presidency rounded up a gang of Erukalas about ten miles west of Kavali, consisting of about twenty-five families or one hundred persons, and ordered them to the Kalichedu Settlement which had been organized by the government under the Act of 1911. It was the rainy season and this group was proceeding by road toward this settlement with their goats and donkeys and a few household effects, consisting of a few cots and some bamboos for their miserable huts. They camped across the road from the mission bungalow at Kavali. They pleaded with the Superintendent of Police for permission to stay with Mr. Bullard, the missionary, and promised to work hard and support themselves and their families if permitted to stay. In this way the Kavali Settlement with 100 members opened. The chief industry was the gathering of palmyra fiber for sale as thatch for huts. This single settlement has now become the reformatory settlement for the worst characters, and three other varieties of settlements have grown up in connection with it.

It can be said without fear of contradiction that some of the best work being done in the settlements is done in those under religious organizations, especially under the missions and the Salvation Army.

LESSONS TAUGHT BY THE EXPERIMENT

In the course of this novel and widespread experiment with criminals, certain lessons have been learned by those in charge. Most of these lessons were not anticipated. They have been the outcome of carefully studying these criminal tribesmen in actual situations.

The first great lesson appeared when comparisons were made between settlements which gave the inmates opportunities to make good money and other settlements which were located where the family income was meager. This had become apparent as early as the study by the Indian Jails Committee in 1919 and 1920. They say:

The main point to which we would invite attention is the predominant importance of the economic factor in dealing with the question of criminal tribes. The facts collected seem to establish beyond doubt the proposition that the first essential of success is the provision of a reasonable degree of economic comfort for the people. Mr. O. H. B. Starte, I.C.S., whose long experience in work among criminal tribes in Bombay makes him probably the leading authority in India on this subject, inclines to the belief that in many cases economic causes are at the bottom of the criminal habits of these people. In the case of the wandering tribes, so long as they were constantly passed on from district to district by the police, it was hardly possible for them to settle down to any steady form of industry. Under the organization created under the Criminal Tribes Act, 1911, they are now able to adopt a settled life, and in many cases are glad to do so. Even in the case of the more stationary tribes, the poor quality of the lands they held may have something to do with the adoption of predatory habits, a case in point being that of the Kallars of south India. The necessity of providing adequate and remunerative work, if these criminal communities are to be weaned from criminal courses and converted to habits of industry is, we think, clearly established by the experience acquired in the settlements already noticed.[53]

[53] *Report of the Indian Jails Committee, 1919–20*, Simla, 1920, Vol. I, pp. 321–22.

As time has gone on, this point has been increasingly clear. The administrator in the Punjab admits that the results achieved can be but temporary at best even for those settled in the villages under registration unless some agency is organized to solve the economic problem for the criminal tribesmen thus restricted.[54] The behavior of these tribesmen in the villages and in the settlements varies apparently directly with economic conditions. It has been found that, except in a few cases, if they are given opportunities and are controlled and directed properly, most of them have been found to be as industrious and as well behaved as any other class of men.[55] Numerous illustrations of this truth are provided in the reports. Repression was tried and failed. Even religion and education without good economic conditions cannot succeed. Wherever these settlers are found to be dissatisfied and where absconding occurs in large numbers, there is to be found bad economic conditions. When the harvest yield, or any other condition, results in the lowering of wages or lack of employment in the mills, or when settlements or villages are located on poor land, everything that can be done seems to get no results with these people. Place them, however, where they can earn a good living, and then treat them with consideration, and they respond heartily. Even the Huns, which repression has been unable to tame, are said to be able and willing cultivators and their great ambition is to own a piece of land.[56]

As a result of this lesson the recent settlements have been established where there is opportunity for good earnings and the agricultural settlements have given attention to location on as good land as possible, well watered, and productive.

Out of this experience has also grown a penological lesson which has been learned in some of the institutions of the Occident. The cornerstone of success must be reliance on other than physical force for restraint. Kindliness, firmness,

---

[54] *Report on the Administration of Criminal Tribes in the Punjab for the year ending December, 1923*, p. 12.

[55] *Ibid.*, 1922, p. 2 of Third Letter.

[56] *Police Report of the Bombay Presidency, including Sind and the Railways, 1924*, "Report on the Working of the Criminal Tribes Act in 1924 in Sind," p. 7.

attention to the physical needs of these people, economic opportunity, succor in case of unavoidable need, have wrought wonders.

The experiment has also shown that segregation of different classes is of very little importance. Of much greater importance is the keeping intact of the usual social ties. Hence the families are now brought into the settlements whenever possible. It has been found that if a man has his family with him he is not nearly so likely to abscond, and is a much better worker. Often, also, the presence of children keeps the feeling of responsibility upon the man. As much as any men they love their children, and in the experience of the settlements many problems are solved by keeping the family intact. By placing the responsibility squarely upon the shoulders of the criminal tribesmen for support of himself and family the economic motive is not destroyed as it is in most of our prisons.

The system of gradual release from restriction either in the villages or in the settlements reminds us of Crofton's Irish System. The conditional release and "probation," the exemption from registration in the villages, the follow-up work after absolute release, have proved to be very important factors in the work of reformation.[57]

At first the incorrigible criminals in the settlements, such as absconders, etc., were punished by being sent to jail, and even yet, as we have seen in the case of those who have not become amenable to the conditions of settlement life, after a number of convictions, are handed over to the police. Early, however, it appeared that the reformatory settlement for the worst members might be worth trying. In 1925 it had become apparent to a number of those concerned with the settlements that the punishments inflicted by the magistrates for infringement of the rules under Section 20 of the Act are inadequate.

The importance of after-care became clear as those who had

---

[57] *Report on the Working of the Criminal Tribes Act in the Bombay Presidency for the year 1922*, Part I, p. 8.

been in the settlements for some time were released.   To Mr. Starte, who probably knows more about this question than any other man in India, it appears that "It would have been a very short-sighted policy to turn such people adrift compulsorily without making some provision for their future." Such provision must be adequate arrangements for their support and follow-up during the period of their so-called "probation" following release.

In the course of these years it has appeared that the most successful of these settlements are the agricultural settlements. The Indian has always lived from the land.   More than 90 per cent of the population still live on the land, and all of them are land hungry.   It is therefore in the agricultural settlements where the best results are appearing, according to the officials.[58]

With the development of the close supervision of the registered criminal tribes in the villages, added to the threat of removal to a settlement, the exemptions from registration have been increased without evil results.   This is in contrast to the experience of exemptions during the early years when the system had not been so carefully worked out.   The following table shows the situation in the Punjab in 1923.   This indicates the very large number of exemptions which occurred from 1917 to 1923.[59]

	WANDERING	SETTLED	TOTAL
Figures at the close of 1917	22,678	10,820	33,498
Additions which have taken place since	5,859	1,850	7,709
Total	28,537	12,670	41,207
Figures at the close of 1922	9,417	3,092	12,509
Figures at the close of 1923	8,282	2,844	11,126

[58] *Report on the Working of the Criminal Tribes Act in the Bombay Presidency for the year 1923*, Part II, p. 21; *Report on Administration of Criminal Tribes in the Punjab for the year ending December, 1920*, p. 4; *Ibid.*, *1922*, pp. 1, 7; *Ibid.*, *1923*, p. 9; and p. 2 of First Letter of November 10, 1924.

[59] *Report on the Administration of Criminal Tribes in the Punjab for the year ending December, 1923*, Lahore, 1924, p. 3.

Main Street

Criminal Tribesman and Wife returning from their Fields

CRIMINAL TRIBES SETTLEMENT, SHOLAPUR,
BOMBAY PRESIDENCY, INDIA

Typical Hut in the
Settlement

Left to Right, Guards and Author
at the Settlement

Family of One of the Criminal Tribesmen

CRIMINAL TRIBES SETTLEMENT, SHOLAPUR,
BOMBAY PRESIDENCY, INDIA

PENOLOGICAL PRINCIPLES IN THE SETTLEMENTS

What penological principles govern these settlements? What are the aims which they attempt to carry out? Perhaps no better statement of the matter has been made than by the Indian Jails Committee:

> We think it is very important that they should not be allowed to degenerate into a novel type of jail where members of the criminal tribes can be locked up indefinitely without the usual formalities of a trial. There was perhaps at first a tendency to regard them rather from this point of view, as a useful police measure for the prevention of crime. That view has, however, gradually altered. Through the influence of officials, of many missionary bodies which have generously assisted, and last, but not least, of the Salvation Army, which although we differ from its views on some subjects, possesses the special merit of having come forward as a pioneer in the operations under the Act and has thrown itself heart and soul into the work, it is now recognized that the true aim is the reformation of the people in the settlements by a combination of economic, religious, moral, and educational agencies. The result ultimately to be hoped for is the absorption of the settlers into the general body of the community, when the settlement, having served its purpose, will disappear. This ultimate aim should, we think, be clearly borne in mind by all who are engaged in this work, and whenever a new settlement is planned or an existing one remodelled it should be so located, arranged, and directed as to promote this final result.[60]

It is apparent that the penological aim of these settlements is reformation, so that the inmates may be restored to good citizenship among the general population. The methods of accomplishing this are partly familiar to us from penological practices in other lands, but some of them are new. One distinguishing characteristic stands out—they are not to be a new type of jail with a repressive atmosphere. It is almost a hundred years since Crofton established his system of treating prisoners in Ireland. That was a system of gradual relaxation of discipline through a series of different establishments until the prisoner was finally released under the supervision of the police of his city or village. Here, on the other side of the world in old India, similar lessons have been learned out of experience with these criminal tribesmen. However, this ex-

---

[60] *Report of the Indian Jails Committee, 1919–20*, Vol. I, p. 331.

periment has gone very much farther than Crofton's and farther than anything elsewhere tried in prison discipline and control.   In the registered and restricted criminal tribesmen in
the villages you have a form of probation, although on a very
much larger scale than anything seen elsewhere.   In the conditional release, and what they call there "probation," you have
our parole system.   In the different kinds of settlements, from
the reformatory to the industrial and agricultural, in which
very little restriction is practiced, in the relaxation as to the necessity of passes, and in the placing of people who can be trusted
on pieces of land outside the settlement, you have the principles of relaxation of punishment practiced to some extent
in Western countries but here extended more widely than
anywhere in the world.   In the organization of these colonies
with agricultural land at their disposal, you have the prison
farm colony more widely used than anywhere else.   There are
no walls here; in some places there are, however, wire fences.
This experiment demonstrates as nothing else how even desperate criminals can be controlled with other methods than
walls and guns.

However, in this experiment you have some entirely new
practices not seen in Europe or in the United States.   Whole
families are brought into the settlement, not just the individual.   This experiment has shown that keeping the family
ties intact has solved many problems in connection with these
criminal tribes.   In making these people entirely self-supporting and keeping economic responsibility upon them, an
important step in reformation has been made.   Does it not
suggest that in our own country, when we take people out of
the economic order, relieve them of responsibility of making
a living, take from their shoulders the responsibilities of caring
for their families, that we have destroyed some of the most ancient and well-grounded motives to good conduct in human
nature?   So far as I know only here and in the Philippines
colony at Iwahig have we those two features worked out to
their logical limit.

Again, it is the avowed purpose of these settlements to assimilate the criminal tribes to the general body of the community. Even the industrial settlements, as organized, aim to provide a means of livelihood for the inmates, break them into habits of systematic work, and provide a means for their reformation by the combination of economic, religious, moral, and educational agencies.[61] Here under close supervision, proper restraint, and sympathetic guidance, with the ordinary social and economic motives intact, you have the adjustment of machinery to the penological principle of reformation seen nowhere else in the world.[62]

Again, this experiment has shown that the penological principle of punishment for the purpose of deterring others from the commission of crime has distinct limitations. Deterrent it doubtless is. When these people first come into the settlement, without question they do not wish to come. The threat of bringing others into the settlement in certain cases doubtless helps to keep them straight on the outside. Nevertheless, after a certain part of the reformatory process has gone on, deterrence is no longer needed; they are glad to stay, and, as we have seen, many of them do not wish to leave. If any such situation as that existed in our country, the hard-boiled *a priori*, man-on-the-street penologist would cry to high heaven against such laxity.

From all the evidence I have been able to obtain, these principles were not set out with in the beginning. They have appeared as the result of experiments on the spot. However, let us assume that they have been borrowed by Englishmen from other lands. It remains, nevertheless, that they have practiced them to an extent far beyond that anywhere else on earth.

The contrast between this system and the Indian jail is well stated by one of the men at the head of one of the settlements:

The man, mentioned above, who has spent twenty-two years in jail, is a model prisoner, so long as his thinking and deciding are done

---

[61] *Report of the Administration of Criminal Tribes in the Punjab for the year ending December, 1920*, p. 4.
[62] *Ibid., 1926*, p. 5.

for him, but our attempt to give him liberty to manage his own affairs led him into trouble at once. In the jail his life is abnormal in many respects. There are no women and children and family life. If they have families the men are separated from them for the term of their sentences. They do not earn wages on a competitive system as in a village, with its stimulus to individual effort and initiative. Each man is assigned a task, which runs from one-third to one-fifth of what the normal man in the village would have to do to earn his livelihood, and thus the criminal in the jail is set a false standard, economically, if he ever attempts to be an honest laborer outside the jail. The amount, materials, and quality of his food are determined by law, and the industrious prisoner and the slacker who just accomplishes his stint fare alike. His hours of labor, every moment of his day and night are determined by other wills than his own. Is it any wonder that when he is released from the control the reaction is to the excess of license and crime? [63]

Contrast with the man mentioned above another, not quite so old, whom I picked up a few days ago at the Allur Settlement to show me his work out on the fields. He was the first man confined in our K. R. S. a year ago because of drunkenness under special temptation. I do not think he will ever drink again. I hope not. He has a wife and children, to each of whom as well as himself an acre of irrigated land in the swamp has been assigned. He has a yoke of fine bullocks, a cart and tools for his field work, holds Settlement patta for his house site, and is a hard worker, with about 400 rupees in sight from the crops he is now cutting.[64]

RESULTS OF THE CRIMINAL TRIBES SETTLEMENT PLAN

Rather than attempt to interpret the results and achievements of the operation of the Criminal Tribes Act, it will be better to give the verdicts of those who have the information at firsthand. Such a decidedly optimistic note prevails throughout these opinions that one is led to wonder a trifle whether what is said represents the actual situation or what is still only in the process of becoming. The marked agreement among them, however, leaves no doubt that the improvement in the criminal tribesmen has been nothing short of revolutionary.

[63] *The Annual Report of the Erukala Industrial Settlement for 1924,* Kavali Repairment Settlement, pp. 12, 13.
[64] *Ibid.,* pp. 13, 14.

Almost all district reports express satisfaction at the results achieved so far through the provision of the Criminal Tribes Act. It is admitted on all hands that it has had a salutary effect in checking the evil propensities of a large number of professional criminals, and has engendered respect for law and order.[65]

The results of this great experiment have passed all expectations even in the short time which has elapsed since the inception of the scheme. The nuisance of the Wandering Criminal Tribes has ceased to exist and it is obvious that there has been an appreciable decrease in crime reported and unreported. The inmates of Settlements for whom it has become a practical impossibility to indulge in crime make no secret of the fact that they used to live mainly by crime. The condition of the inmates of the Settlements has been completely revolutionized. Instead of the cringing, debased, and demoralized criminals who ate carrion, drank, or drugged themselves heavily and professed to live by begging, they are now decently clad, eat wholesome food, and wear an air of self-respect. Escapes still occur occasionally from Settlements, but on the whole the inmates have given up the idea of remaining away from Settlements. The children, instead of sneaking away at the least pretext and starting to beg from passers-by, have now other things to attend to and prefer to win a prize in a fair competition at games. The inmates have settled down to a peaceful life, enjoy sports on holidays, and celebrate their marriages and festivals in a manner befitting a civilized population.[66]

The one obvious result of the enforcement of Act III of 1911 on criminal tribesmen still outside the settlements has been that the settled criminal tribesmen, most of whom had begging and pilfering for their sole occupations, have taken to some sort of occupation, though in most cases still merely ostensible, and the nomads have begun to settle down instead of roaming from place to place.[67]

Most reckless types of men and gangs have been received in this Settlement (reformatory settlement) from time to time and it is a matter of satisfaction that besides drilling the hopeful criminal tribesmen into discipline and befitting them for milder treatment in other Settlements, the institution has been successful in completely curing them of their lust of crime, some of the worst offenders among the criminal tribes known as incorrigibles and the

[65] Report on the Administration of Criminal Tribes in the Punjab for the year ending December, 1926, p. 4.

[66] A Note on the Administration of Criminal Tribes in the Punjab, 1917 to 1919, by Hari Singh, p. 10.

[67] Report on the Administration of Criminal Tribes in the Punjab for the year ending December, 1920, p. 3.

most notorious leaders of burglars and dacoits are now among the most useful and reliable workers in the Settlements.[68]

The results attained have, however, more than repaid all the trouble taken by the staff. Indeed, I must confess that the reformation effected in the settlements is even beyond my expectation. Not only have so many men, women, and children, who used to live mainly by crime, been prevented from following the evil pursuits, not only has their mode of living entirely changed, not only has the younger generation been brought under healthy influence, but, what is more important, a considerable number of hardened criminals known as incorrigibles have turned over a completely new leaf and instead of being leaders of gangs of burglars and robbers are today earning an honest livelihood in the settlements and driving others to increase their earnings by the sweat of the brow and thereby setting a most useful example to the less reformed. Such men have been encouraged by favorable treatment. The inmates of settlements are getting accustomed to hard work, the prejudice against their employment in mills, factories, etc., is dying out, and their mode of living has become so much cleaner. Cases of breach of discipline are fewer. Ill-begotten accumulations of previous years come to light occasionally and are invested profitably in the Savings Bank or in Postal Cash Certificates. Attempts are being made at starting Co-operative Credit Societies, etc.[69]

In the early days, especially in the Punjab, those in charge of the settlements were very enthusiastic about the results. Some of the statements quoted above are from those early days. As time went on, however, it became apparent that while the registration and restriction in villages of the criminal tribes had wrought some important changes, the results desired did not always appear. As in everything else with accomplishment new objectives appear, so here. Furthermore, those interested in the plan of solving the problems of the criminal tribesmen began to think they ought to have objective instead of subjective standards in judging of the success of the experiment. The earlier judgment of results was subjective on the basis of common observation, reports of police officials, etc. In more recent times some of the criminal tribes' officials in local governments have endeavored to measure the success of

[68] *A Note on the Administration of Criminal Tribes in the Punjab, 1917 to 1919,* p. 5.
[69] *Ibid.,* 1919, p. 2.

the plan by comparing crime rates in districts before this plan was put into operation effectively with those since.   Let us look at a few of these attempts and then evaluate them.   The criminal tribes administration in the Punjab in 1919 cited the fact that before 1917 the percentage of total convictions of the total registered male population was 10.8.   In 1917 it fell to 2.3, and in 1918 to 1.6, and in 1919 it had risen to 3.1, but in 1920 it fell to 2.3.[70]

Those who report these figures, however, do not point out that those were the years of the War when many of the criminal tribesmen as well as other Indians were in the army, when prices were high, and when economic need in general was somewhat lessened.   In 1920 in the Punjab the usual phenomena following a war appeared.   The total reported crimes rose from 40,192 in 1919 to 40,747 in 1920.   However, the number of burglaries, the class of crime in which criminal tribes mostly indulge, fell from 15,061 to 14,453.   This was true in spite of the bad economic conditions prevailing in the province that year.   No special active crime on the part of the criminal tribesmen was reported by the district officers.[71] However, it is possible that since the worst criminals are taken out of the villages and placed in settlements, it is natural that there should be a diminution in criminality.   Moreover, the figures from one year to another, even in the same local government, are not comparable, not only because of economic changes but by reason of the fact that the policy with regard to exempting men from registration has fluctuated.   In 1922 in the Punjab the number of people registered in 1917 had been reduced by 13,261.   Some of these people who were exempted doubtless resorted to crime again.

As the result of the rather careful selection of the worst characters and the careful supervision of those registered by the police, only the bolder and more resourceful criminals remain at large.   It has been found that even a member of

[70] Report on the Administration of Criminal Tribes in the Punjab for the year ending December, 1919, p. 7; Ibid., 1920, pp. 2, 10, 11.
[71] Ibid., 1920, p. 11.

a notified criminal tribe may operate under the patronage of a local notable who is more or less of a sleeping partner in crime and is ready to protect his protégé in trouble. Evidently graft and influence work in the courts of India as well as in this country.[72]

Another method used to show improvement is to cite the convictions under the Indian Penal Code, which fell in 1926 in the Punjab from 142 to 130. However, the numbers convicted under the Criminal Procedure Code and under the Criminal Tribes Act rose that year from 24 and 169 to 38 and 274 respectively. This rise is explained as due to more rigid application of these laws to absconders. The rise under the Criminal Procedure Code is thought not to be due to the criminal tribes, because from the police records their complicity has been suspected in less than 1 per cent of the untraced cases. In 1916, prior to the inauguration of the scheme in the Punjab, the number of convictions obtained against the members of the notified criminal tribes was 1349 and of these 974 were under the Indian Penal Code. Ten years later the number of total convictions was less than one third, and the number of those under the Indian Penal Code was less than one-seventh of the number in 1916.[73]

Such figures seem to make out a good case. The report points out, however, that the amount of crime committed by members of criminal tribes who were not registered remains considerable in the Punjab. In 1926 in the same province only 28 persons were convicted under the Indian Penal Code out of 3498 males in settlements. However, the administration believes that half of those in the settlements are still apt to commit crime if allowed opportunities to do so.[74]

In Bombay the administration is not quite so optimistic. In 1923 it was necessary to send 189 persons to prison from the settlements, a proof that the work of reformation was not complete. The administration adds that for permanent suc-

[72] *Ibid.*, 1926, p. 4.
[73] *Report on the Administration of Criminal Tribes in the Punjab for the year ending December, 1926*, p. 3.
[74] *Ibid.*, 1926, pp. 6, 7.

cess they are looking to the education of the children and the removal to the special reformatory settlement at Bijapur of such persons as refuse to reform and who lead their fellows into commission of crime. While striking results cannot be expected too soon, it is the belief of the administration that steady and gradual improvement in the methods of dealing with these people will inevitably lead to a general decrease in their offenses.[75]

In 1924 in the Bombay Presidency only 1 per cent were absconding.[76] Occasionally the reformation of a tribe seems to be fairly complete. The following report indicates gratifying results in one of the criminal tribes:

The reformation of this tribe (Jagiranis) is highly gratifying. There can be no doubt that their former depredations and crimes were the result of poverty and debt combined with the grasping avarice of the money-lenders. Now they have land and a co-operative Credit Society to advance money, to purchase seeds and agricultural implements, they are content to cultivate it knowing it to be for their own advantage. Not only this, they know that the land will not be taken from them on any petty pretext and that every chance will be given them to make good. This sympathetic attitude of the local police officers has done much in the way of their reformation.[77]

However, the Bombay administration says that it is impossible from figures to show whether the conduct of the criminal tribes is improving or not. No such statistics are at present available.

On the whole the impression gained from the reports is that those in charge of it and the governments themselves concerned feel quite certain that the experiment is making progress. Its effective working is dependent upon close co-operation between the police departments, the criminal tribes settlement officers, and the district magistrates. There are many indications that this co-operation is not perfect. Furthermore,

[75] *Report on the Working of the Criminal Tribes Act in the Bombay Presidency,* 1922, pp. 7, 8; *Ibid., 1923,* p. 5.
[76] *Ibid., 1924,* p. 7.
[77] *Police Report of the Bombay Presidency, including Sind and Railways, 1924.* Bombay, 1925; *Report on the Working of the Criminal Tribes Act for the year 1924 in Sind,* p. 3.

throughout this experiment many changes have been made in the hope of improving the technique of handling these very serious criminals. There seems to be no question that in the case of the children who have lived in the settlements and have been educated there, most of them have gone out to well-paid positions and are doing well. That is also true of some of the adults in the settlements. It will take a number of years yet, however, to demonstrate completely whether the experiment is a complete or only a relative success.

BIBLIOGRAPHY

A Note on the Administration of the Criminal Tribes, Punjab, 1917 to 1919, by Hari Singh, Lahore, 1920.

Act No. VI of 1924, passed by the Indian Legislature.

Bombay Criminal Tribes Settlement Rules, 1926, Bombay, 1926.

India, Edited by D. R. Bhandarkar, Part II of Vol. CXLV, *Annals of the American Academy of Political and Social Science*, Philadelphia, Sept., 1929.

India in 1924–25, by L. F. Rushbrook Williams, Calcutta, 1925.

India in 1925–26, by J. Coatman, Calcutta, 1926.

Indian Jails Committee, Report of the, 1919–20, Simla, 1920.

Kavali Repairment Settlement, The, being the Annual Report of the Erukala Industrial Settlement for 1924, Madras, 1925.

Police Report of the Bombay Presidency including Sind and the Railways for the Year 1921, Bombay, 1922; *Ibid., for the Year 1922*; *Ibid., for the Year 1923*; *Ibid., for the Year 1924*; *Ibid., for the Year 1925*.

Report of the Working of the Criminal Tribes Act in the Bombay Presidency for the Year 1922, Bombay, 1923; *Ibid., 1924*; *Ibid., 1925*; *Ibid., 1926*; *Ibid., 1927*.

Report of the Administration of the Criminal Tribes in the Punjab for the Year 1918, Lahore, 1919; *Ibid., 1919*; *Ibid., 1923*; *Ibid., 1924*; *Ibid., 1925*; *Ibid., 1926*.

Saunders, Albert J., "Reclaiming Criminals in Sholapur, India," *Sociology and Social Research*, Vol. XII, No. 1, September-October, 1927, pp. 61–64.

Tucker, F. Booth, *Criminocurology, or the Indian Crim and What to do with Him, being a Review of the Work of the Salvation Army among the Prisoners, Habituals and Criminal Tribes of India*. Simla, 1916.

CHAPTER VI

WITZWIL, THE SWISS CORRECTIONAL COLONY

Two small nations of Europe have been innovators in the correctional treatment of delinquents. In different directions and by dissimilar methods Belgium and Switzerland have pioneered experiments of the greatest significance. The similarities and differences I shall discuss later. We are here concerned with the Swiss experiment.

Switzerland in May inspires in the visitor at once wonder, languid enjoyment of its fresh beauty, and awe at its rugged mountains. Clothed in fresh, new green to the snowline, the mountains are capped far down with their white winter hoods. The blue lakes reflect the green trees and the snow caps. In the valleys the frugal Swiss peasant is busy on his land. Villages with comfortable and well-kept houses and farm buildings nestle in the fat valleys. Here none of the febrile hurry of our American cities is to be discovered. Few movies flaunt their scandalous or sentimental advertisements before the eyes of children and youth. The automobile is still only for the wealthy—or the tourist. Many pedestrians are still seen along the highways. The ox cart has a place of honor; the horse cart is frequent.

Can there be criminals among this peaceful, frugal, hardworking, but unhurried people? Yes, there are criminals in Switzerland.

What does she do with those who, in sight of awe-inspiring mountains, cobalt lakes, and the simple life of this almost model democracy, break the laws? Some of them she puts in prisons—made in America a hundred years ago, with some slight European improvements—others she sends to reformatory institutions, many of them as machine-like as most of ours, but she has one interesting institution for delinquents which is unique.   It is Witzwil.

You are probably in Bern, the capital city of the Swiss Confederation.   Possibly from the summit of Rigi-Kulm or Pilatus, your eyes have taken in the panorama of peaks in the Bernese Alps, of Mount Blanc, and then have looked down upon cities lying beside lakes which mirror mountain and cloud. You take a train on the Bern-Neuenburg Railway, and after a short hour's ride, alight at Ins.   Down from the hills you have come to a level plain.   At Ins you are on the edge of what was once a great swamp.   A motor car sent from the colony at Witzwil, only two miles away, meets you by appointment. You discover that the driver is a convict in the colony.   You are driven over a good road through fields in which gangs of men are planting potatoes or doing other work upon the land belonging to the correctional colony known as Witzwil. There Herr O. Kellerhals, or perhaps his son, Hans Kellerhals, meets you and takes you in charge for a visit to the institution.

The Juras are above you; stretching away to the south is the Neuenburger Sea, or Lake.   Here all about is a peat moor redeemed by the hand and art of man.   In the redemption of a swamp, the redemption of Swiss vagrants, petty criminals, alcoholics, and ne'er-do-wells was the main object.   If ever you will see it on earth, here you will see the realization of Emerson's famous aphorism that "an institution is but the lengthened shadow of a man."   The institution is Witzwil; the man, O. Kellerhals.

THE ORIGIN AND DEVELOPMENT OF THE CORRECTIONAL IDEA IN SWITZERLAND

The history of any idea, while of the utmost interest, is always difficult.   Why, like so many good ideas, did it not die at birth or in early infancy?   How shall we explain that while in other countries the same ideas had existed, it remained for Switzerland to show in practical form how the idea could be realized?

In 1855, in a public meeting of a society, the first suggestion was made in Switzerland for an intercantonal correctional institution. The discussion of this scheme continued for some time but without results.

In 1863, Dubs, later a Swiss senator, raised the question whether the young offenders should be kept with older and more hardened criminals. It is possible that the question arose in the minds of these Swiss leaders because of what they had heard had taken place in the United States of America. At the beginning of the nineteenth century, New York built the first house of refuge in the United States. For the first time young offenders were thus taken out of the institutions for adults. It was opened on January 1, 1825. Other states soon followed, among them Massachusetts and Pennsylvania. Knowledge of these early houses of refuge for young offenders was carried back to Europe by men who had been sent to the United States to study the new prison system which had originated in this country. De Beaumont and De Tocqueville, sent by the French Government, made their reports in the late twenties on the penitentiary system in the United States. In this book are accounts of these houses of refuge. A little later, Dr. Julius, of Prussia, visited the United States for the same purpose and wrote an elaborate report. Mr. Crawford came over from England in the late thirties, when it became apparent that England would have to take some steps to supplant her penal transportation system, and wrote a two-volume report. Doubtless some of these reports came to the attention of Swiss readers.

Furthermore, in 1876 the Elmira Reformatory, which had been authorized by law in 1869, was opened. This had wide publicity both in Europe and America and stimulated thought as to the importance of isolating young offenders from the hardened criminals.

In 1893, after it had become apparent that the intercantonal scheme had fallen through, Canton Aargau established a reformatory school known as Aarburg. The previous year Canton Bern opened a reformatory school called Trachselwald.

In this institution were received two classes: (a) Young people from sixteen to twenty years whose imprisonment was desired by the administration; (b) judicially sentenced youths from sixteen to twenty so far as positive circumstances did not require their incarceration in another institution. The pupils in this institution were divided into four groups for education and correction. Here is the first effort to put into practice what Switzerland had heard was going on in America.[1] All of these developments, however, were primarily aimed to take care of the young offender apart from the older and more hardened.

How did the colony idea originate, especially the farm colony? At the International Prison Congress of Vienna in 1895, and at the later one in 1905 held at Budapest, the problem of the employment of prisoners on the soil was discussed. The latter movement, without a doubt, was motivated by the dissatisfaction of penologists and some prison officials with the results of the prison system. Close confinement in prison was seen to be inimical to health, and when large bodies of men are gathered together in close proximity, severe discipline seems to be necessary. In these circumstances the question arose, Why not get the men out on the land?

All of these movements and discussions form the background of the founding of Witzwil. The immediate occasion of its origin, however, was a conjunction of two sets of circumstances in Canton Bern, Switzerland. One was the failure of a company which attempted to establish on the drained land near the southeastern part of the Neuenburger Lake an agricultural colony. These lands had been drained by the water-control system finished in 1870 to control the waters from the Jura Mountains. When the agricultural colony failed, Canton Bern bought from the owners, in 1891, about 2000 acres of this land. The other and more immediate circumstance was that about this time the necessity became apparent of removing the prison, then occupying the site of the present post office

<hr>

[1] Kellerhals, O., "Die Erziehung der jugendlichen Rechtsbrecher," *Zeitschrift Pro Juventute*, Heft 7, 1926, pp. 1, 2.

in Bern, to some other situation.   This led the magistrates to resolve to remove the less hardened criminals to an agricultural colony on this available land.   Earlier attempts in this direction in Switzerland—that is, of placing prisoners upon land—had turned out to the satisfaction of the magistrates.   In the St. Johannsen institution since 1886 there had existed a prison with agricultural projects for the prisoners.   With this institution at St. Johannsen, Witzwil was joined and from there was administered until 1895, when Witzwil became independent.   In the meantime necessary buildings had been constructed.   On May 1, 1895, the administrator took over the institution with a bookkeeper and thirteen other employees, and eighty prisoners.[2]

DESCRIPTION OF THE COLONY

The colony is located at the southeastern end of the Neuenburger Lake near the borders of the Cantons Bern, Waadt, Freiburg, and Neuenburg.   Toward the south is the canal. Toward the north and east are the villages of Gampelen and Ins. Toward the west is the lake.

The whole area is traversed by two roads and a network of roads for field wagons.   There is a railroad connection six kilometers long at Gampelen with the Bern-Neuenburg Railway.   The Ins station is also near.   There is a good auto road to Ins.

The Extent and Character of the Land.   At present the extent of the domain is about 2400 acres.   Besides that up in the mountains the institution has command over enough land to pasture about 300 head of cattle.   More than four-fifths of the land is peat land.   The peat is from twenty centimeters to three meters deep.

The chemical constitution of the land consists of from two to three per cent nitrogen, two to four per cent lime, traces of phosphoric acid, and prussiate of potassium.

The land is well watered so that every kind of moor culture

<hr />

[2] *Strafanstalt Witzwil, ein Beispiel von Innenkolonization durch die Arbeit von Gefangenen und Arbeitslosen,* Ins, 1925, pp. 1, 2.

is possible. However, the land naturally is sour. Care must be taken to dike back the water from the lake and canal. At the present time the whole plot has been carefully drained.

The canal is navigable for three kilometers along the estate so that barges may be run up the canal from the lake and used for the transport of products.

Because of its depth, peat is dug and was sold to Neuenburg and other communities until the increasing use of coal crippled the traffic. During the War the peat industry grew to the amount of 100,000 francs per year. However, with the close of the War and the increasing amount of coal available, little peat is now dug for sale. It is, however, used in the institution for fuel.

The uncultivated moor land is in danger of fire in dry weather. In 1885, 400 acres, and in 1893, 100 acres of turf land were burned out. Where it has been burned out it is not so fertile as the other land.

Products Raised on this Land. Fruit trees do not flourish because of the wind. However, it is the belief of the authorities that when other trees have grown up as wind-breaks, fruit trees can very profitably be developed. In the beginning, false hopes were held as to the fertility of the land. It was thought at first that with virgin ground no fertilizer would be needed, but it was soon found that plant food was lacking in the soil. For the truck gardening manure is needed. The city of Bern has a department of garbage disposal which sends the institution several carloads of garbage a week. To produce manure, cattle are necessary and their manure must be collected. Hence the cattle are stall-fed except those sent into the mountains, and the manure is put upon the ground. They even collect the liquid from the stalls and put that upon the land. Furthermore, it has been found that the land produces more if sub-irrigation is provided. At first open irrigation was tried, but without good results.

Cost of the Colony. The first cost was 792,000 francs. 50,000 more were paid for the inventory. About 1,000,000

WITZWIL PENAL COLONY, SWITZERLAND. HANS KELLERHALS, DEPUTY SUPERINTENDENT

Railroad Station

General Appearance of the Moorland before Development

WITZWIL PENAL COLONY, SWITZERLAND

francs more were spent by Canton Bern for buildings, for additional land, and for pasture land in the mountains.

During the first five years the colony, with eighty prisoners, needed about 30,000 francs per year as an extra allowance. Later this allowance from the state needed per year for necessary buildings and construction was about 100,000 francs. However, during the War the income rose to unexpected heights. In 1918, 800,000 francs were earned by the institution. This surplus was placed in reserve for improvements and new construction. Today there is in the state treasury remaining about 1,700,000 francs, approximately as much as the state invested in the estate, including the pasture land in the mountains and the amount invested in the buildings. For drainage, streets, and railway buildings no state funds were used. The cost of these was paid out of the earnings of the institution. From 1921 to 1925 Witzwil had to deliver to the state about 613,326 francs as rent and taxes out of its income. Today the entire estate is worth at least 5,000,000 francs. From 1895 to 1924 a total of 5,894,940 francs in value was earned from the animal products, 10,340,771 francs from the products of the land, or a total of 16,235,711 francs.[3]

Employees and Inmates. In 1928 the total number of employees in this institution was 74. Two of these employees, the director and the bookkeeper, have spent thirty-two years of service with the institution. Of the other employees, one has spent thirty-one years, one twenty-eight years, one twenty-five years, one twenty-three years, three twenty-two years, two twenty-one years, three nineteen years, etc. All but five of these employees are men. During the course of the year, fifteen of these employees were beginners. The long-continued service of so many of the employees indicates admirable administrative procedure on the part of those in charge. If one may judge from the reports, when an employee leaves it is like the breaking up of a family. The loyalty and devotion of most of these old employees reflect the spirit of the institution and without question explain much of its admirable work.

[3] *Ibid.*, pp. 2–15.

The number of inmates in the institution varies from year to year, but normally runs between four and five hundred. On January 1, 1928, there were 430 in the institution and on December 31st of that year there were 453. The highest number in the institution during that year, 460, was on February 10th. The smallest number, 383, was on September 17th. The average number during the year was 427. 208 of these were in the institution for the first time and 313 were repeaters. Through this institution flows a continuous stream of prisoners. Thus in 1928, 521 were admitted and 498 dismissed.

The religious confession of the 521 who entered was: 408 Protestant, 111 Catholic, and 2 Jewish. The marital status of the 521 was: 332 single, 110 married, 27 widowed, 52 divorced. 492 of them were born in wedlock and 29 were illegitimate.

Most of them spoke German—368, while 141 spoke French, 11 Italian, and 1 Armenian. Canton Bern furnished 338 of these 521. 164 were from other cantons, while 17 were foreigners, and 2 were men without a country.

The educational status of these 521 entering the institution in 1928 shows a similar situation to the prisoners of our own country. Only 17 had finished high school, 74 secondary school, 426 only primary school, and 4 were illiterate.

The occupation of these entrants shows a large proportion from the unskilled classes. Only 7 were from what might be called the professional classes; 28 were from the skilled artisan class; 217 from what might be called in our country the factory workers, and 233 were day laborers, ordinary laborers, farm laborers, and other unskilled workers. Only 2 of these had any property, 519 were propertyless.

The swift movement of the population in and out of the institution is explained by the fact that the large proportion of the inmates have but short sentences. Thus, 213 in 1928 had up to a six months' sentence; 203 from six to twelve months; 86 from one to two years; 8 over two years, and 11 received what we should call an indeterminate sentence.[4] During the year the number of days spent by the inmates in the institution

[4] *Jahresbericht der Strafanstalt Witzwil für 1928*, Witzwil, 1929, pp. 2–5.

amounted to 156,144. Of these, 26,323 were not spent in labor by certain of the inmates. New inmates, for example, lose some days' work. 331 days were spent in punishment; 1710 days in sickness, while 22,320 days are accounted for by holidays. Of the 156,144 days spent by the inmates in the institution in 1928, 129,821 were spent at work, or a little more than four-fifths of the entire time. More than one-half of this time was spent in agricultural labor and in the care of live stock.

One must not get the idea, however, that in the eyes of the administration this institution is merely a work institution carried on for profit. The difficulty of resolving the two contrasted purposes of profit and of preparing these men to go out into life again has not been entirely solved. Herr Kellerhals, the superintendent, frankly admits the difficulty of coordinating these two purposes. He must make the institution pay and at the same time he must use the activities of the institution for the purpose of preparing these men for a free life. In order to make a profit he must not neglect the proper feeding of the inmates; he must look after their education to prepare them for the practical exigencies of a free life on their discharge. He must teach them to love work who formerly had not loved it. That work must be profitable and contributory to the purposes of the institution. Yet withal, consideration must be given to the natural inclinations of the inmates and to the opportunities that will face them when they go out. Therefore, the activities in which they are engaged in the institution must fit them for the day of their discharge.

There is a portion of the institution set aside for discharged prisoners where efforts are made to adjust them to a free life and provide for them until they get a free position. On a part of the domain at Nusshof there is a labor-house for old men, often drunkards, which attempts to provide them care and reformation. This house is always over-full, yet in 1928, so small is it, only 9009 days were served there by the inmates. The administration hopes to see this colony enlarged. In 1928 the inmates earned 6905 francs. The institution furnished them their clothes, shoes, and washing.[5]

The Discipline of the Institution. As much attention is given to the conduct of the inmates of the institution as is given to producing economic efficiency. Regulations are carefully laid down both for the employees and for the prisoners. Printed in the institution's print shop are three sets of instructions, one for the employees, one for the work-leaders, and one for the prisoners, concerning their rooms, cells, and their general conduct.

In the instructions for the employees, it is made clear that all of the employees are under the control of the Director and his representative. They are immediately responsible, however, to their other superiors, such as work-leaders, supervisors, guards, etc. They are personally responsible for the minute fulfillment of all functions which are laid upon them by the regulations as well as by special instructions. They must replace all objects which are trusted to their care whether for their own use or for the prisoners under their supervision.

The employees have direct supervision over the prisoners. They must see that the prisoners live up to the house regulations, the time schedule, and that they do their work in accordance with orders.

No supervisor is allowed to punish a prisoner in any way. Corporal punishment is strictly forbidden, as is also rough and undignified talk and especially any mention of the prisoner's crime and of the penalty. Any misconduct on the part of the prisoners must be reported to the superior officer. No reports concerning the prisoner's behavior shall be given to relatives.

At the first ringing of the bell in the morning the employees go to their places of work, and get the necessary instructions for their daily tasks from their superiors. After the second ringing of the bell the prisoners appear, with the exception of the monitors of the rooms, who come last, after they have seen to it that nobody is left in the open rooms or cells. After the employee who has charge of a certain number of prisoners

---

[5] *Ibid.,* p. 11.

makes sure that all the men under his care are present, he marches them by twos to the courtyard or to the workroom. In the courtyard the men who are to be given tools have them distributed by the employee with the help of one or two assistants. Every group then under the leadership of the employee goes to its appointed tasks. The foreman and supervisor take part in the work assigned to their group, thus there are no idle employees in Witzwil. It is their duty to keep the prisoners at work and to give the instructions briefly but clearly and with tact. Reports are made by these employees concerning the conduct and efficiency of the prisoners entrusted to their care. After the working time is finished each half day, they march back to the building in the same way as they came. The tools are deposited at definite places and the group is marched into the prison in the same way it came out. Ten minutes are allowed at the end of each half day to get these men into their cells or the dining and living room. The employee has entire responsibility until each man is in his appointed place.

As has been indicated, there are two men with each group, the foreman and the supervisor, or what we should call guard. It is the guard's duty to see that none of these men escapes. He also teaches the inexperienced workers and must serve as an example of diligence to his group.

While there is no rule of silence in the institution, there is a rule that during working hours quiet must be maintained. Mischief of any kind is punished as disorderly conduct, whether done at work or during periods of rest. In case of misconduct the prisoner is admonished by the employee. If this warning is without result the guilty party is brought to the office of the superintendent. The house master then shuts him in a cell after he has been thoroughly examined by the superintendent. A report on the case must be given at once to the Director. Rules provide that every employee is entitled to use necessary measures against a prisoner for his own security.

In case of attempted escape, one or more employees must follow the fleeing prisoner at once while the supervisor brings back the other prisoners to the building and, if necessary, shuts them up in their cells. The Director must be informed at once by telephone or messenger. If on investigation the attempted escape is due to lack of caution or negligence of an employee, he is punished. He may be imprisoned or fined or eventually dismissed.

On the other hand, it is the duty of the employees to see that the prisoners get their share of food, both in quantity and quality, according to the number of people sharing it. They must also see that no bread is wasted, that the dishes are well taken care of, and that the food remnants that are left over from the meal are brought back into the kitchen.

Employees are required to keep themselves clean, to look after the cleanliness of the house, the dishes, and the clothes of the prisoners.

Each week the prisoner is entitled to a shave and frequently to a haircut. It is the duty of the guard or supervisor to see that the men under his care are conducted to the barber shop where they are not only shaved but have their shoes cleaned and oiled. Quiet must be preserved in this shop. Smoking and bartering of victuals, tobacco, etc., are not allowed among prisoners. Employees are not permitted to smoke during working hours. The employees also have the responsibility of seeing that on Saturday evenings the cells and living rooms are clean.

A prisoner may obtain audience with the Director by appointment. He must also make his appointment to see the doctor except in cases of emergency.

Employees are cautioned to be careful about their keys. They have the responsibility of seeing that all doors are properly locked and other precautions taken to prevent escape.

Very strict requirements are laid upon the employees as to their own personal conduct. Indecent language, cursing, and vulgar talk are to be avoided. Neither they nor their families are permitted to receive any gifts, presents, or loans from the prisoners or from the prisoners' relatives or acquaintances. They may not buy from or sell to prisoners. Without permission they cannot order work to be done on their own account. They are required safely to take care of any objects which belong to the prisoners. Both they and their families are forbidden to trade with goods produced in the institution.

Furthermore, upon the employees rests the responsibility of keeping the tools in good order and seeing that they are properly repaired.

During working hours employees are not allowed to leave the institution without permission; tardiness and absence are excused only because of special accidents or sickness. Each employe is required to work every fourth Sunday and during the week following in what is called supervising service.

These minute regulations on the conduct of the employees and their duties have grown out of experience and have been made necessary by the increased number of prisoners in the institution.

The Institution Guards. Special regulations are in force concerning the guards who look after the buildings and the men Saturday afternoons, Sundays, and other holidays. These are the so-called house regulations of the institution. This service begins on Saturday afternoon and lasts until the next Saturday by the same group of guards. Thus the employees take turns at this work. These guards are under the supervision and orders of the chief guard (Hutchef).

The duties of these institution guards are the opening and shutting of cells and rooms, the distribution of meals, supervision during recess inside and outside the institution, looking after the cleaning, bathing, shaving, etc., guard duty during the night, and doing whatever other work is necessary on Saturday afternoons and Sundays, such as cleaning the courtyards, getting vegetables, etc.

The Hutchef assigns the various kinds of work to each of the various guards, such as the cleaning of the yards, mowing the lawns, etc. He also assigns the proper number of assistants to help in this kind of work. Another crew takes charge of the change of clothing, supervises the cleaning of the cells, the clothes, the shoes, and looks after the shaving and hair-cutting of the inmates.

Every Saturday night there is a thorough inspection of the cells. If there is not time then, on Sunday morning. Every guard has to inspect all the cells of which he is in charge and any other rooms under his care. The Hutchef is charged with the responsibility of seeing that these underlings do their work properly. Those prisoners who are not housed in the main institution take care of all these kinds of work themselves under the supervision of the man in charge of the particular building or camp in which they live. In short, the responsibility of the Hutchef is to see that all buildings are properly taken care of in their physical arrangement, as well as the proper physical care of the prisoners.

These prison guards also have the responsibility of seeing that their prisoners attend church, lectures, and other similar meetings.

Another crew has charge of the opening and shutting of the cells and other rooms in the morning, afternoon, and evening. They also supervise the feeding of the prisoners. One of the guards with the necessary assistants takes charge of the kitchen crew for a week and sees that the food is properly and promptly prepared.

These prison guards under the supervision of the Hutchef also are responsible for quiet during the recess period especially on Saturdays, Sundays, and at night. The Hutchef also, at least once a week, must inspect the kitchen and the stables and other outside places to see that they are in good condition.

After a week's service of this sort, every married employee is entitled to a free week day while those who are not married have a free half day or whole free day after two such weeks. In short, the institution on Sundays and holidays is immediately controlled by this chief guard or Hutchef.[6]

The Foremen. The foremen also have printed for them special instructions relating to their duties. These foremen, who

[6] "Hutordnung für die Angestellten der Strafanstalt Witzwil" in *Règlement für die Angestellten der Strafanstalt Witzwil vom 15, Februar 1926.*

are in active charge of the men while they are at work, are the immediate superiors of the supervising guards and of men who are in immediate charge of gangs doing a specific kind of work. Their business is to supervise not only the activity of the groups and services especially under their guard, but lend a hand in assisting and ordering what shall be done when quick instructions are necessary. These foremen report any misdemeanor in the industrial activities and the functioning of the institution at the morning report each day. They also, at the weekly meetings of the particular group, discuss important events and point out problems and how they may be met for the improvement of the service or of the economic conduct of the institution. They have special duties with reference to the newly arrived employees in teaching them their duties and to report to the Director flaws in character which would make the new employee unfit for service. These new employees are taken on for service only on probation. These foremen stand next to the superintendent or his representative in authority, and in the absence of the Director or his representative they carry the responsibility. The foreman who is oldest in point of service or who is especially appointed for that purpose by the Director is the superior of the other foremen and gives instructions to them at any time. The chief foreman has general oversight over the agricultural and industrial activities of the institution and makes a report each week to the superintendent on the state of affairs.

Thus it is apparent that the institution is carefully organized from top to bottom both for guarding the prisoners and for carrying on the activities of the institution. The responsibility is placed in gradations from top to bottom among the employees so that there is no question as to where the authority rests.

Wages of Employees. The pay of these employees is also graded from top to bottom, in accordance with the position which he occupies and the efficiency which he shows. There is a carefully graded scale of wages or salaries which at the most, to our way of thinking, is not very large. According to the published scale the highest salary paid below the superintendent and his deputy is 3300 Swiss francs, which means only a little more than $800 per year. Some of those with the higher salary also receive some extras in the way of maintenance. The lower paid groups receive free dwellings for themselves and their families, laundry, fuel, and light.

Rules for the Prisoners. Regulations are also worked out for the government of the prisoners in their cells and rooms. Every prisoner is given the following pieces of furniture: 1 bed, 1 straw mattress, 1 pillow, from 2 to 3 blankets, 1 rug, 1 pitcher for water, 1 wash basin, 1 saucer for soap, 1 pail, 1 mop, 1 cleaning rag, 1 bedside table, 1 table (only in the cells), 1 electric bulb, 1 salt cellar, 1 calendar, 1 spittoon, 1 bucket with cover. It is the responsibility of the prisoner when he moves into his cell to see that this inventory is complete. Any damages which occur have to be reported to the guard of his hall. Books, bread bags, and other objects are not allowed in the cell except after special permission. In case other things than those in his inventory are found there he will be punished. Prisoners are not allowed to keep in their cells or rooms, mice, birds, or any other kind of animals.

The responsibility is upon the prisoner to keep his cell always clean. Every morning he must dust it with a mop and every Saturday he must wash it. He is forbidden to treat it with oil, petroleum, or anything of the kind. Every Saturday all the furniture, windows, doors, and walls are to be cleaned thoroughly. Modern sanitary provisions are not found in this institution, for the famous old night bucket still prevails there; however, it is strictly required that it be emptied every morning and evening as well as at noon, if it has been used, and must be flushed out thoroughly.

Regulations go even further. Without permission, nothing in the equipment of the cell can be changed, pieces of furniture cannot be moved around. Prisoners are not permitted to fix boards or shelves in the cells. They may have pictures, but only decent ones are allowed, and the parts of the walls covered with pictures must be cleaned periodically. Otherwise, the pictures will be taken away.   The electric lights must be put out when the prisoner leaves and change of bulbs is forbidden.   Beds must be kept in order by attention every morning.   No one is allowed to trade things from his cell for those of another man in another cell.   Every Saturday night, in some cases also on Wednesday, the bed clothing also is changed.   Prisoners are not permitted to climb to the cell windows to talk with neighbors or outsiders.   The prisoners must be quiet in the cells and rooms; they are forbidden to sing, whistle, scream, or make any other noise.

If the prisoner does not feel well enough to go to work he reports this to the guardian of his hall and goes back into his cell.

The prisoner who wishes to talk with the Director sends word through the guardian of his hall and on up through the other ranks to the Director.   It is apparent from these rules and regulations that rather strict control is exercised over the prisoners in the institution.

As I observed the men at work, however, I saw no evidence of such severe repression as I have seen in institutions in our own country.   If I had not known that the institution was a prison, I should not have been aware, from the conduct of the men, that they were not ordinary laborers carrying on the activities of the place.   Here was a group of men out in the fields planting potatoes.   So far as I could observe they went about their business very much like a group of hired men.   In a building was a group of older men cutting the potatoes ready for planting.   Conversation was going on that would go on among any group of men except that there was no laughing or loud talking.   The men are given to understand that they are there to work and to obey orders in the interest of the sobriety and the industrial activity of the institution.   There was not the quietness of the tomb which is to be seen in some of our institutions, nor was there any of the hilarity which I saw in one of our Southern prisons and which may be seen at recreation periods in almost any of them.   I would say, therefore, that the repression in Witzwil is present, but not severe.   Everything, so far as I could tell, went forward with orderliness and efficiency as on a well-regulated farm, and in the shops as in a well-regulated factory.

Education in Witzwil. Witzwil endeavors to provide educational facilities for those who desire it and who give promise of being helped thereby. In addition to the religious services which may be counted as educational, the regular instructional activities consist of (1) regular school hours, (2) the evening courses, (3) lectures. The first of these is for young people deficient in their elementary education. In 1928 the day school numbered only 15 scholars. The evening course during the winter of 1928-29 offered courses in German, English, French, Italian, bookkeeping, agriculture, stenography, and singing. Each year from December to March there is also a series of lectures on various subjects. The institution publishes a monthly paper called *Unser Blatt.* The print shop also does the other necessary printing for the institution. All the yearly reports, record and report forms, etc., are printed here.

The Industries of the Institution. The institution is primarily an agricultural institution. The non-agricultural industries carried on in Witzwil are only such as contribute to the necessities of the place. Those who have trades when they come in are as far as possible kept at such trades. During 1928, 33 different industrial activities were listed in the report. However, when one looks over the number of days spent by inmates in each of these, it is clear that the main emphasis in the institution is on agriculture and occupations necessary to agriculture, while the iron-working, wagon-making, carpenter work, etc., would require but few people constantly at work in order to keep the institution going. None of the products of the shops enter the market. They are only for the purpose of assisting in carrying on the other work of the institution.

Furthermore, the efficiency of the management is shown by the fact that the prisoners work in the shops only when something must be made which is needed in the farming operations or when the weather will not permit work outside. The main business of the institution is farming; the shops are auxiliary

FIELD GANG, PENAL COLONY, WITZWIL, SWITZERLAND

PASTURE LANDS OF THE WITZWIL COLONY IN THE KIELY ALPS

Closer View Shows Some of the Buildings

to that purpose. Yet in this way by planning the work beforehand it is possible to have the men at work all the time instead of sitting idly in their rooms in bad weather and in winter. The institution is just a large, well-managed farm.

The volume of business at Witzwil is one measure of the effectiveness of the administration. As the visitor passes around the various parts of the domain he notices that every one is busy. The agricultural and garden products go to all parts of Switzerland. During the growing season every one possible is worked upon the land, or in the pastures with the cattle. My visit to Witzwil was in the month of May. Out in the fields were groups of men preparing the ground for potatoes and other crops. Here and there a group of men were planting potatoes, while in one of the buildings in the institution a group of older or weaker men were at work cutting potatoes for planting. Around the barns men were busy with the cattle and hogs, others were out in the gardens cultivating the garden truck, still others gathering it to be packed into baskets and prepared for market, while down in the shops were a number of men making or repairing wagons and doing carpenter work necessary for the institution. Everywhere was activity; no one was idle.

Because of the necessity of drainage work to control the supply of water upon the land, men are used in the winter to develop drainage systems and water control. Also in the winter the street sweepings from Bern are spread over the land to fertilize it.

The Alpine Colony. Up in the Kiley Alps a number of men keep the cattle in the pastures. From twelve to thirty prisoners stay up there the year round. In 1928 for the second time the establishment in the Kiley Alps was kept open throughout the year. The colony is directed by a superintendent assisted by one or more overseers and the number of prisoners appropriate to the needs. The number of employees is increased during the summer when the cattle and sheep have to be looked after. One of these takes over the responsibility of caring for the cattle in pasture and in the stalls. The maintenance of the establishment is the work of the prisoners. A number of small buildings, among them a bake-house and wash-house, serve as winter quarters. The storehouses are there also. From this center in the summer the kitchens on the higher peaks are supplied. The necessities of the colony are sent from Witzwil to a station called Oey part way up the mountain and from there transported in carts to headquarters.

The maintenance of discipline in this colony has offered no particular difficulty since the experiment has been going. The improved arrangements in the colony assisted in carrying out the proper household management so customary in the parent institution at Witzwil. Greater freedom of movement is allowed in the colony, but the members of the colony must, on their part, make some sacrifices and forego some of their rights.

The experiment shows greatly improved health on the part of the prisoners. Upon young, sickly, and weak-lunged people the healthful effect of the life in the high altitude is astonishing. Those who at first can hardly get their breath in going up to the colony after a few weeks do not feel any exertion in climbing. Their appetite improves, they sleep well, their troubles leave them, and they acquire a new outlook on life. While a correctional institution cannot be a sanatorium, it can give those likely to develop tuberculosis healthy work in a favorable place and a chance to escape what might develop in other circumstances. In this way Switzerland escapes the necessity of providing a special institution for tubercular prisoners which has had to be developed in some of our state prisons at considerable expense to the tax-payers.

In addition to a certain number of prisoners who looked after the cattle and sheep through the summer of 1928, many other prisoners were sent thither to construct stables for the winter and to do other construction work for the colony. With the increased number of cattle pastured and fed there cheese warehouses have to be constructed, methods of providing water for the stall-fed cattle must be devised, and many other provisions made for the larger use of this Alpine colony.

Construction work on a water system which will bring down from the high mountains sufficient water for the stock it is hoped may also provide power for electric lighting and power.

Here again the administration has combined the economic and the correctional motives in a most unusual way. Development of the live stock industry of the institution becomes possible on land which is very cheap. At the same time there is developed a phase of the correctional program which improves both the health and the outlook of the prisoners.[7]

Herr Kellerhals has established a small agricultural research station in the institution. A young agriculturist devotes himself to research upon the particular problems to be met with in this moor land. Already they have learned that they must enrich the land with more potash, while other results are beginning to appear.

One of the problems Herr Kellerhals has is the sale of the surplus products of the institution. When I was there what seemed like a large number of baskets of vegetables were being shipped to people in various cities of Switzerland. Yet wider markets for quality products are necessary in order to bring in greater profit.

Various experiments of different kinds show unlike results. Rye and wheat do well, sugar beets not so well. Vegetables are most important for the weaker prisoners can handle them. As in every penal and correctional institution, the number of weaklings here is large. The institution needs hothouses in order to have a supply of vegetables going to market all the year and to have steady work for the men. Most of the vegetables, of course, are used in the institution. Yet a surplus is now produced and a greater is possible.

Cattle, sheep, hogs, horses, and chickens are raised. One of the great industries, of course, is milk with its cheese products.

Diversity of Agriculture. The variety of products raised and the extent to which each is cultivated will perhaps best be shown by the following table:

---

[7] *Jahresbericht der Strafanstalt Witzwil für 1928.* Witzwil, 1929, pp. 30–35.

1928 Cultivated meadow land   660 acres (Jucharten)
       Rye   430 acres
       Wheat   125 "
       Oats   141 "
       Summer rye and wheat   21 "
       Winter barley   10 "
       Summer barley   10 "
              Total acres in grain   737 "
       Corn for silo   22 "
       Sunflowers for silo   2 "
       Potatoes   454 "
       Sugar beets   212 "
       Beets, cabbage, and other
          roots   9 "
       Rape   10 "
       Rape sown with grain   7 "
       Vegetables   80 "
              Total root crop and
                 vegetables   765 "
       Fiber crop   3 "
       Leased crop land   62 "
              Total   cultivated
                 land   2251 "
       Turf pits   22 "
       Forest   75 "
       Straw land by the lake   212 "
       Roads and streets   80 "
       Canals   50 "
       Building   grounds   and
          railway right of way   50 "
              Total acres in the
                 domain   2740 "

On this land in 1928 were raised the following crops:

Hay and emd (2d crop)	1,041,000 kilograms
Grain	325,000 sheaves
Potatoes	3,990,000 kg.
Sugar beets	3,056,000 kg.
Beets and cabbages	300,000 kg.
Grapes	120,000 kg.

On the 31st of December, 1928, Witzwil's inventory showed the following live stock:

Cattle	658	Chickens	299
Horses	62	Ducks	90
Hogs	607	Geese	30
Sheep	340	Turkeys	12

Finances of the Institution. The inventory value of this stock for 1928 was 310,273.5 francs. Yet during 1928 the institution received:

	Francs
For cattle	117,503.4
For swine	95,401.55
For milk	50,479.7
For other agricultural products	824,032.05 [8]

The annual financial statement for 1928 shows the following sums paid by the institution to the State.[9]

	Francs
House rent	41,000
Ground rent	91,000
Tax for pasture	1,384.5
Taxes on the Witzwil domain	8,758.95
Pécule for discharged prisoners	29,420.2

BALANCE SHEET

Receipts:

	Francs
Industries	66,078.45
Agriculture	596,126.31
Board	51,271.8
Total	713,476.56

Expenditures:

	Francs
Administration	72,434.92
Education and religious services	12,740.2
Food	213,120.55
Attendance	197,856.79
House rent	39,240.35
Total	535,392.81

Business gain or profit	178,083.75
Inventory increase	8,171.05
Net gain	169,912.7

[8] *Ibid.*, pp. 28–30.   [9] *Ibid.*, p. 36.

The colony at Witzwil carries accident and death insurance for the employees, and has established a fund to cover that. This fund on the 31st of December, 1928, had in it 155,830.80 francs.

This statement speaks for itself. In spite of the uncertainty of weather and of the number of inmates in the institution, in spite of the difficulty of so managing the 400 odd inmates as to make each one's work count, and to provide development of each person in preparation for his discharge, the institution each year makes a profit. When I was there in 1927, Mr. Hans Kellerhals assured me that in the thirty-three years since its establishment, the institution had repaid the government every cent it has invested in it, and in the state treasury was over 5,000,000 francs of pure profit.

Conclusion. Thirty-three years have passed since this adventure in penology. The snow-capped Jura Mountains then looked down upon a Swiss lake surrounded by a vast moor land. There from time immemorial it had stood, useless to man. The majestic mountains sent down, spring after spring, their floods of waters into the Neuenburger See. Spring after spring the floods poured their surplus waters over the desolate face of the moor. Then came the attempt of the company to develop this land into an agricultural tract. The attempt failed. Then the sturdy Swiss people decided to take it over and attempt to make out of it a place where its prisoners could be trained for life and usefulness. Through those thirty-three years, step by step the moor has been redeemed, the flood waters have been kept back, the land has been drained, buildings have risen to house the prisoners, and this tract of desolation has blossomed into fruitfulness. It is the product of one man of vision and resourcefulness backed by the Swiss people. Year after year a stream of 500 men has flowed through its gates, been taught to work, and contributed, under the guidance of the superintendent, to their maintenance. Both land and men have been redeemed. The state is richer for the adventure. Nothing so clearly demonstrates what can be done with the right leadership in the handling of useless ground and useless men.

Could not some of our states learn a lesson from Switzerland in the handling of prisoners? Most of our states have sufficient land, and good land. They have lands to reforest, bricks to be made for buildings needed. They have the prisoners, in many states lying in idleness in the prisons, and in most states, idle by the thousands in jails, degenerating physically and morally. Have we met the leadership of little Switzerland? "Aye, there's the rub."

BIBLIOGRAPHY

Fetter, "Witzwil, A Successful Penal Farm," *The Survey*, February 4, 1911, pp. 760–767.
Dawson, *The Vagrancy Problem*, London, 1910, Chapter VIII.
Kelley, *The Elimination of the Tramp*, New York, 1908, Chapter IV.
Jahresbericht der Strafanstalt Witzwil für 1925, Witzwil, 1926.
Jahresbericht der Strafanstalt Witzwil für 1926, Witzwil, 1927.
Jahresbericht der Strafanstalt Witzwil für 1927, Witzwil, 1928.
Jahresbericht der Strafanstalt Witzwil für 1928, Witzwil, 1929.
Règlement für die Angestellten der Strafanstalt Witzwil vom 15, Februar, 1926, Witzwil (No date).
Kellerhals, O., *Strafanstalt Witzwil, Ein Beispiel von Innenkolonization durch die Arbeit von Gefangenen und Arbeitslosen*, Ins, 1925.
Kellerhals, Hans, *Die Erziehung der jugendlichen Rechtsbrecher*, Separatabdruck aus der Zeitschrift Pro Juventute, Heft 7, 1926.
Kellerhals, O., *Strafvollzug in Verbindung mit Landeskulturarbeit*, Separatabdruck aus der Verhandlungen des Schweizer, Vereins für Straf-Gefängniswesen und Schutzaufsicht, Neue Folge, Heft 5.
Kellerhals, O., *Die Einheitsstrafe*, Separatabdruck aus "Verhandlungen des Schweizerischen Vereins für Straf-Gefängniswesen und Schutzaufsicht." Heft 3, 1923.*

* (Evidently the last two are reprints from the same publication. I have reproduced them just as they were printed.)

CHAPTER VII

BELGIUM'S ADVENTURES IN REDEEMING MEN

IT is not strange that throughout history it has been the small country or countries which may be described as being in the social pioneer belt which have tried out new experiments and devised new methods for the socialization of her criminals. Even in the days of John Howard, it was in Holland and Belgium that he found the best institutions for the treatment of criminals. Today Switzerland, Holland, and Belgium are the experiment stations of Europe in this field, unless one includes the new prisons of Russia which I have not studied; if they be included, you have there also a pioneer social belt, since the government of Russia is an entirely new experiment in every way. As we have seen, in the Philippines and in India also we have a pioneer social belt by reason of the necessity of organizing a new social relationship—in the one by reason of the conquest of the Philippines by the United States and in the other by reason of the reorganization of political and social life in the Indian Empire under the British Government.

BELGIUM'S HISTORY IN PENAL PRACTICE

In the latter part of the eighteenth century, when prison reform was in the air in all western Europe, Count Vilain XIV created the *Maison de Force* at Ghent in 1775. This institution was visited by John Howard on his first visit. In it he saw a new kind of prison from which many lessons might be learned.[1] Whether or not, as suggested by a recent Belgian

---

[1] Howard, *State of Prisons*, Warrington, 1777, pp. 140–144.

penologist,[2] the description of this institution in Ghent provided the founders of Auburn Prison in New York State with
their idea of separate confinement of each man at night and
work in common during the day, it is true that that was exactly the way in which the institution at Ghent was managed.   This institution was in striking contrast with the other
Belgian prisons of those times.

The separate or Pennsylvania system of prisons was introduced about 1845 by the director of prisons, Dubectraux,
who became inspector-general of prisons about 1830.   As the
result of his fifteen years of work previous to the time of the
establishment of the cellular system, and doubtless also of the
discussions which were being carried on in America and Europe
as to the respective merits of the Pennsylvania and the Auburn
systems, he became convinced of the superiority of the cellular
system and put it into operation throughout all the prisons of
Belgium.   The cellular or separate system became a dogma
which by 1904 had shown itself, from the statistics, as producing more recidivism than the old Auburn system which it
had displaced.[3]

Following the World War, when Belgium's institutions were
again taken charge of by the Belgian Government, a number
of practical prison reforms were introduced.   These reforms
had two phases: (1) Proposed changes in many of the laws
relating to the treatment of prisoners.   A report has been
made on these proposed changes and the suggestions are now
under consideration.   (2) In the meantime, however, the
administrative reforms have gone forward and have been quite
largely accomplished.

The proposed legal changes represent an endeavor to bring
penal theory as expressed in the law into accordance with the
findings of science as to the differences between individual
prisoners.   They contemplate different treatment for (1) ab-
normals (dements, mental defectives); (2) recidivists; (3)
young delinquents.

The administrative reforms realized in large part at the

[2] Delierneux, *Prisons Nouvelles; Lois Nouvelles* (ms.), p. 1.
[3] *Ibid.*, pp. 3–5.

present time include the following: (a) Individual study and classification of delinquents by what is called the penitentiary anthropological service. This was created by Mr. Vandervelde in 1920. It included the psychiatric examination. Belgium is divided into seven regions in each of which is a penitentiary anthoropological laboratory in the most important prison of each region. Every person condemned to more than three months' imprisonment is examined in one of these laboratories as a routine matter. Thus the normal prisoners are separated from (a) the abnormal, (b) the tubercular, (c) the venereal, (d) the nervously unstable, (e) the dope addict, alcoholics, etc. Each one of these various classes is then sent to the institution adapted to its special treatment. Thus the tuberculars are sent to the prison sanatorium, the venereals to the section of the prison set apart for them, the epileptics and hysterical to the special institution for them, and the young normal delinquents to the prison schools.

The creation of these special institutions has all been planned for. The following have been created: (1) Prison schools for young delinquents; (2) ordinary industrial prisons for normal prisoners who are believed to be corrigible; (3) cellular prisons for recidivists, the undisciplined, the incorrigible, and the vicious, which are the old cellular prisons in existence since 1845; (4) the penitentiary hospital located at Ghent; (5) the prison sanatorium located at Merxplas; (6) the section for venereals in each of the principal prisons; (7) prisons for the nervously unstable, including epileptics and hystero-epileptics at Merxplas; and (8) asylum for the criminal insane, and those who have been accused of crime who are irresponsible for one reason or another, located at Tournai. The colony institutions are contemplated in the system but have not yet been provided: (1) Sanatoria for alcoholics and dope addicts, (2) a prison asylum for degenerates and feeble-minded, (3) a special section in already existing institutions for kleptomaniacs, for foolish and for sexual maniacs.

The first new institution to be created in the sense of the reform intended is the penitentiary establishment at Merxplas. This establishment comprises a number of institutions as follows: (1) a prison agricultural school for young delinquents, (2) a prison for condemned epileptics and hystero-epileptics, (3) a prison sanatorium for condemned tuberculars, (4) a prison asylum for the feeble-minded. Three of these are in existence and the fourth will be created as soon as the budget permits.[4]

A word perhaps should be said about each of these institutions at Merxplas. The prison sanatorium for the tubercular is the first one of its kind ever established on the Continent and perhaps in the world. It is a large establishment where 210 tuberculars may be taken care of at a time. It is equipped in modern fashion and provides modern care for the tubercular. Since it is a new institution, time enough has not yet elapsed to enable us to appraise its results.

In the prison for the nervously unstable are placed the epileptics and hystero-epileptics, for the most part profoundly defective, perverted, dangerous, and condemned to severe punishment, and who constitute in the ordinary sense the elements of trouble and disorder. By thus separating them from the normal prisoners, better care can be given to those prisoners suffering from profound disorders, and at the same time better conditions can be provided for the normal prisoners by themselves. Furthermore the normal prisoners are not exposed to the danger of moral degeneration. Among them are many epileptics who became such because of the injuries received on the head during the War. Among them are many recidivists who should not be lightly discharged into society.

Of vastly greater social importance and much more helpful from the standpoint of treatment are the young delinquents. For them Belgium has provided two institutions—an industrial prison school at Ghent and an agricultural prison school at Merxplas. In these institutions the purpose is, not punishment, but moral regeneration and social readaptation. Those in charge of these institutions in Belgium hold to the view that for the most part these young delinquents are more the victims

---

[4] Delierneux (ms.).

of defective heredity, of bad surroundings in the home and in the community, than of inherent evil.

It is because the Belgian authorities realize that the majority of young delinquents are the victims of social conditions over which they have no control, that Mr. Vandervelde, then Minister of Justice, in 1921 established the prison schools. In these institutions are placed young delinquents from the ages of sixteen to twenty-one years; eventually it is hoped that the age may be extended from twenty-one years to thirty. The institution at Ghent employs these young prisoners in industrial activities, while the one at Merxplas engages them in agriculture and allied professions.

The selection of these inmates takes place in the penitentiary anthropological laboratories noted above, where the dangerous, mental-deficient, and the sexual pervert are eliminated. Then from those remaining are selected the ones to go before what we should call a vocational guidance commission to ascertain their special aptitudes, the profession or trade, if any, which they followed before coming to the institution, so as to know whether to send them to Ghent or to Merxplas.

In these prison schools a new spirit and purpose reign. The old separate cellular system is given up, the purpose is clearly held in mind that these young people gone awry must be regenerated, and that instead of an atmosphere of continual defiance, of more or less automatism and of apathy, there must be an atmosphere of energy, of confidence, and of life. Consequently they refuse to try to handle a large number of delinquents in these prison schools. Their theory is that with a smaller number they can give better individual treatment according to the psychic make-up of the individual, his past history, and of the conditions which brought him into trouble. The régime is one of education, not of repression. The education is conceived as vocational, intellectual, physical, and social.

Work is considered as a primordial factor of social readjustment. The authorities believe that labor is indispensable in order to give the young delinquents a trade, so that they may earn an honest livelihood upon discharge. As the authorities look upon it, work has a double purpose—to give them a trade in the first place, that they may be kept from idleness which engenders so much perversity; in the second place, in order that they may make some money, part of which will be saved for them to go out with, part to aid their necessitous parents or to indemnify, in a certain measure, their victims.

The teaching in the trade is practical rather than theoretical. Each trade is taught by a specialist and each of these teachers serves as a companion in the work of the young convict and teaches by example as well as by precept.

The work is carried on in common in parties of from ten to fifteen as in the agricultural colony at Merxplas. Each of these companies go to the fields, to the farm, gardens, or to the workshop with the instructor. A discipline of silence is strictly enforced. M. Delierneux says that a great part of these boys understand that silence is a measure intended for their own good and submit voluntarily.

For the last few years at the prison agricultural school at Merxplas, they have sent the boys out about the farm on their honor. Among those prisoners, one was found who had been condemned to twenty years of forced labor. They work at all the various kinds of tasks to be found upon a farm. For the first two years of the experiment there was not a single escape. It is believed that this working upon their honor teaches them to control their own actions, and has a decided regenerative effect upon them. This relaxed discipline seems to have made a great impression upon these young delinquents. One sign of this is that they have organized themselves into what they call the circle of "the broken chain," a sort of self-government association. The second article of its constitution is as follows: "The circle has for its purpose (1) to make morally and socially free all the students of the prison school, and more especially the members of the circle; (2) to aid the members of the circle to assist mutually in the work of their moral and social regeneration; (3) to develop in each of the students three points of view—social, intellectual, and physical; (4) to collaborate with the prison school which has for its purpose our social readaptation (*notre réclassement*); (5) to provide each of the members a means of spending usefully their leisure time." M. Delierneux says that as a result of this treatment the inmates do not consider the officers purely as their chiefs but also as their friends and as their guides. They have confidence in the officers, solicit their advice, and try heartily to put the advice into practice.

Every officer who comes in contact with these inmates has the duty of carefully studying them from his particular point of view and making a report to the director. The social history of the young man is secured from the community in which he lived, from the priest and the doctor and from other persons who know about him. These various reports from the different members of the personnel and the social record are studied carefully by the director. He notes the differences in these documents and the points on which they agree. At the weekly meeting of the personnel, these various observations are discussed and if possible a common agreement as to the nature of the man and as to his difficulties, etc., is arrived at. A plan is then made for each one. These various things are made a matter of record so that each person who deals with the individual may review the record and have a case history of the boy with whom he is dealing. The first stage of this study of the individual lasts from fifteen days to three weeks. During the early days, the newcomer to the prison school is sent into solitary confinement; then he goes to classes and to conferences where he may be observed. Then, unless his attitude is unpromising, he enters the prison school and remains provisionally in what they call the category of observation.

The prison school comprises four categories of inmates: (a) Les Meilleurs; (b) Les Bons; (c) Ceux en Observation ou d'Epreuve; (d) Les Pervers ou de Punition. Thus there are four grades in the classification of these men. The passing from one grade to another takes place upon the basis of points earned in various activities; for example, each month four points are given for good conduct, four points for neatness, four points for manifestation of the spirit of economy, four points for the employment of the time passed in the cell, eight points on the close observance of silence, eight points on the application in school, eight points on application to work and sixteen points on general improvement, a total possible of fifty-six points.   A boy earning fourteen points or less goes into the fourth division, cited above as Les Pervers, or de Punition.   If he earns from fifteen to twenty-eight points he is placed in the third division called above "those under observation," or officially "d'Epreuve."   If he earns between twenty-nine and forty-two points he is placed in the second division called "Les Bons," or if he has from forty-three to fifty-six points in his favor, he is placed in the first division, that of "Les Meilleurs."

These points are decided upon by a commission composed of the chiefs of the workshop, the man in charge of the quarters where they live, the instructors, and of the director-adjutant. The advancement from one category to another, however, is not given on one's making the required number of marks in one month; the advancement takes place only after he has obtained that number for three successive months.   A man in the third division, "d'Epreuve" or "en Observation," who for three successive months does not make at least fifteen points, goes back into the fourth category, "de Punition."   Moreover, in this punishment division are placed those from any other category who are guilty of grave breach of discipline or of serious moral fault.   Those in this last division are deprived of the use of the canteen; they may not receive letters or visits save in exceptional circumstances, they are excluded from the musical and choral activities; they are not allowed to participate in recreation nor in organized games on Sunday. Anyone in this punishment category who does not for three successive months improve, is considered unworthy of the prison school and is sent back to an ordinary prison for the rest of his term.   Those in the observation division, "d'Epreuve," have the privilege of the canteen with the exception of two articles, tobacco and chocolate.   They have the right of correspondence with their parents and may receive visits, however, strictly limited. They may not participate in recreation and organized games in common. As they advance from the lowest category to the highest, additional privileges are given, to stimulate their improvement. Moreover, distinctive signs or symbols are worn on the collar and upon the sleeve, indicating the particular class to which each one belongs. Regular school classes are carried on for these young men. These classes occur every day of the week except Saturday from ten o'clock to midday. There are three classes, one composed of the illiterates and those who have not learned to read well. They are divided into two divisions, the Flemish and the Walloons or Dutch. The second class comprises the Walloon inmates and the instruction is given in French. They are divided into two subdivisions. The third comprises the Flemish and the instruction is given in the Flemish language. This class also has two subdivisions.[5]

In addition there is a good library of from thirteen to fourteen hundred volumes and a special library of two hundred twenty-five volumes containing books and manuals on the various trades and technologies taught in the prison schools. The distribution of books takes place once a week.

In addition there are various religious services conducted by representatives of the different cults such as is usual in the American penal and correctional institutions.

Regular physical exercises and military drills are carried on twice a week. Musical exercises, both vocal and instrumental, are carried on three times a week with selected inmates.

Plays and games are held especially for those in the categories "Les Bons" and "Les Meilleurs." A journal is published for the prisoners. Fine medical service is supplied. Particular attention is given to prepare them for what we call in this country after-care (*réclassement*).

Perhaps the most important arrangement in the whole scheme is the individual attention given each man in the course

[5] *Notice sur la Prison—École Industrielle a Gand*, Saint-Gilles, 1927, p. 10.

of his treatment. The scheme is organized to guarantee that the inmate may not feel that he is merely submitting to punishment but that he is learning how to live. Every effort is made gradually to lead him not only to escape discipline but to govern himself. In those of the two higher classes, "Les Bons" and "Les Meilleurs," an increasing confidence is placed, and upon them increasing responsibility is gradually imposed. The rights of the men in these categories increase as well as their duties. Greater liberty is given with the hope that they will learn to use it without abuse. The attempt at moral regeneration includes work, which demands as much of the personnel as of the inmates. Conferences are held between them regularly in which the officials endeavor by a face-to-face talk to show the students the difficulties of life, and give them directions how to evade or how to surmount those difficulties. Visits are made by the personnel to the inmates individually in the cell, in which they try to help the inmates to get a new point of view. The official aims to help the inmate in his moral struggle, to counsel and to guide him. His difficulties are discussed, his points of view gone over, and his hopes encouraged. These conferences are looked upon as an opportunity to treat these inmates as men, not as prisoners or even as suspects. An appeal is made constantly to their *amour propre* and to their dignity. They are followed as they go out in order to help them in what they call re-classing themselves; that is, restoring themselves to society.

Up to the present time, the results of this program have been good. Of those who have been out of the prison school more than six months, ninety per cent are regularly engaged in labor and have conducted themselves honestly and with dignity as shown by the official reports received from those who have supervised them. The present management recognizes that this is a preliminary result and that more and better follow-up work must be devised, such as exists in Holland, in England, and in America with young delinquents. The present administration hopes to see this amateur work develop and a law enacted which will provide the indeterminate sentence.[6]

This system of prison schools comprising the industrial institution at Ghent and the agricultural school at Merxplas, is an experiment quite different in many respects from that to be found in any young men's reformatory in this country. It deserves study and careful watching, it means one step in advance of anything that has been done here. This advance is marked in the first place by the separation of those who are to be trained for trades and those who are trained for agriculture. It is marked also by the special study which is given to the incoming inmates by every device known to modern science. Again it is marked by individual treatment, such as is rare even in our best reformatories in this country. Finally, it emphasizes once more the importance of having first class, understanding men at the head of such institutions who see that mere mechanical treatment *en masse* cannot perform the task of readjusting these young men, victims of their heredity and their circumstances, to a normal social life. Here is to be seen an experiment, an adventure in the endeavor to reconstruct distorted personalities, an adventure in which is combined all that science has to teach as to personality with all that the art of personal adjustment can contribute to this great task.

Beyond this adventure with youth are the endeavors described above to classify the various prisoners and place them in separate institutions designed to meet their needs. This is of the utmost significance for the United States where we have been dallying with the matter. In no state have we gone as far with adults as has Belgium. At the present time in our prisons, those afflicted with venereal disease are usually in with

---

[6] I am deeply indebted to M. Delierneux, the director-adjutant of the prison school at Merxplas, for much of this information. My conversations with him, and the papers and the unpublished manuscript which he gave me, have given me an insight into the spirit of the present administration much better than the published report. His father is the director of all the institutions at Merxplas. Delierneux had a very distressing experience as a prisoner of war under the Germans and his experience during that period led him to take an active stand against the cellular imprisonment.

the other prisoners.   We have isolated the insane criminals in some states.   New York has endeavored to segregate some of the feeble-minded delinquents, but where is there a single state in the United States which has attempted to segregate the epileptics and the hystericals in a special institution? Where have we, aside from some of our Southern states, separated and done a good job with the tubercular criminal? To be sure, New York has a special prison for the tubercular, but she uses it also for others.   Belgium's adventure can well be watched with great care and profound interest.

THE COLONY FOR VAGRANTS AT MERXPLAS

Let us turn now to another of Belgium's adventures in redeeming men, an adventure which is not new but which seems to be little known in this country.

Belgium's experiment with beggars and vagrants developed in the European atmosphere of a repressive program which goes back three centuries.   The struggle of England with vagrants and beggars is well known.   Neither in England nor on the Continent was repression ever successful.   On the Continent, however, much more than in Britain, private societies took up the matter when legal repression had failed in the endeavor to solve the problem.   Finally, out of these experiments grew unique measures in Holland and Belgium.   In Belgium the experiments resulted in the state colony at Merxplas.

In Belgium the treatment of vagrants and beggars is not looked upon as part of the prison system but of the poor-relief system.   Nevertheless, it was organized and yet remains under the Minister of Justice.   To Americans with a history of *laissez faire* treatment of the beggar and the vagrant, this may seem harsh but is based upon a long experience of profound significance.

History of the Colony.   In 1793 when Belgium was still connected with Holland, the decree of October 15 made vagrancy and begging misdemeanors punishable by a house of correction sentence of one year.   Vagrants on the second, and beggars on the third, conviction could be transported.[7] The law of July 5, 1808, provided for the detention of beggars in *maisons de force* (houses of correction).[8] The penal code of October 12, 1810, applied this provision to loafers generally. However, the public mind was not ready for the severity of these acts and consequently the law was relaxed in 1848 with a consequent increase of vagrancy and begging.

Certain observers viewing the results of these experiments were not satisfied. Among them was Prince Frederick of Nassau. In 1823, strongly under the influence of the theories of Fourier, Owen, and other communists of the time, he conceived the idea of gathering needy families on the frontiers of what are now Holland and Belgium, and creating there a beggars' city which would serve to colonize the wild country and act as a link to bring the two peoples of Belgium and Holland together. The revolution, however, of 1830, which separated Belgium and Holland, upset these humanitarian plans. Moreover, the colonies which grew out of this early attempt were somewhat of a failure by reason of the error in taking men from the cities without any preparation and apprenticeship and putting them at agricultural work.[9]

As the result of the growing numbers of beggars and vagrants, a severe law passed in 1866 imposed heavier penalties on loafers. In this law, vagrancy was punished more severely than begging. Following this law, in 1870 the Belgian Government bought the land at Merxplas from the Holland Benevolent Societies. In Belgium at this time there existed only the Dépôts de Mendicité created by Napoleon in the provinces. The administration of these various Dépôts differed from one department to another; there was no homogeneity. The cost grew progressively. Consequently, after buying the land in 1870, Belgium established one central station at Merxplas. When colonists were first sent to the institution, the length of

[7] Dawson, *The Vagrancy Problem*, London, 1910, p. 104.

[8] *Ibid.*, p. 104.

[9] Van Schelle, "A City of Vagabonds," *American Journal of Sociology*, July, 1910, p. 2.

term was from fifteen days to six months, but it was soon per-
ceived that it was always the same individuals who returned
to the colony.[10]

In 1891 (November 27) a law was passed taking away from
these offenses their penal character in order to insure indefinite
detention of beggars and vagrants, and organizing the various
agencies into a unified system. This law deals with the beggar, the vagrant, or the loafer in a series of three kinds of institutions: (1) Beggars' Depots (*dépôts de mendicité*); (2)
Houses of Refuge (*maisons de refuge*); and (3) Reformatory
Schools (*écoles de bienfaisance*).[11] The first two are called
colonies. The regulations describe them as *colonies de bienfaisance*.[12]

Organization of the Colony. The colony is under the immediate administration of the Minister of Justice. It is inspected regularly by (1) the inspector-general; (2) the controller of construction; (3) the controller of accounts of the
establishments of bienfaisance of the state.

Moreover, committees named by the king inspect and over-
see the institutions. There are ten members on the committee for Hoogstraeten, Wortel, and Merxplas. There are
six for the colony at Reckheim.[13]

Purpose of these Institutions. Begging, loafing, and vagrancy in Belgium are not penal offenses. The whole scheme
is set up on the theory that it is the duty of the state to prevent the degeneration of these people, from whom criminals
are recruited, to take them in hand, see that they are given
work, and as far as possible, that they are trained to become
useful citizens.

The houses of refuge mentioned in the law are exclusively
devoted to the confinement of persons whom the judicial authorities place at the disposal of the government to be confined there, and of persons whose confinement is requested by

---

[10] *Ibid.*, pp. 2–10.
[11] Dawson, *op. cit.*, p. 105.
[12] *Colonies de Bienfaisance de l'État; Règlement Général*, Bruxelles, 1907, p. 2.
[13] *Ibid.*, pp. 1, 2.

the commune. The law, curiously, states that persons over eighteen years of age whose confinement in a house of refuge has been applied for by the authority of the commune shall be admitted when they present themselves voluntarily provided with a copy of the order of the burgomaster and alderman authorizing their admission. That is to say, these Beggars' Depots are intended to be places to which people who cannot find work on the outside shall be provided work by the state. When confinement has been requested by a communal authority, the cost of maintenance is charged to the commune.

The law also provides that persons under twenty-one years of age confined in these depots shall be entirely separated from inmates above that age. The able-bodied must be kept at work. They receive daily wages except when they are withdrawn as a matter of discipline. The Minister of Justice fixes for the several classes in which the inmates are placed, and according to the labor at which they are employed, the rate of wages and the amount of reserve which shall serve as a leaving fund. The leaving fund is paid partly in cash and partly in clothes and tools. In spite of the fact that the inmates supposedly are there voluntarily, they may be subjected to solitary confinement.

Moreover, persons confined in the houses of refuge are set free when their leaving fund reaches the amount fixed by the Minister of Justice for the several classes in which the inmates are placed and according to the trade they follow. In practice this leaving fund amounts to about three dollars. Persons confined in the houses of refuge may not be kept more than a year gainst their will.

A subdivision of the house of refuge at Hoogstraeten and Wortel is for the non able-bodied.

The Depot of Mendicity, which is at Merxplas, is for those who are found begging or in a state of vagrancy. *Souteneurs* are treated as vagrants. Any person found begging may be arrested and brought before the police tribunal. They may be sent to the Depot of Mendicity for at least two years and not more than seven years, if they are able-bodied, and if instead of working for their living they depend upon charity, or are professional beggars, or are persons who from idleness, drunkenness, or immorality live in a state of vagrancy or are *souteneurs*, or procurers.

Moreover, the correctional court may put at the disposal of the government to be confined in the Depot of Mendicity for not less than a year nor more than seven years, after the completion of their punishment, vagrants and beggars whom they sentenced to imprisonment of less than a year for a breach of the penal law. Thus the Depot of Mendicity serves also as a post-imprisonment institution.

The cost of maintaining persons confined in the Depot of Mendicity under a decision of the judicial authorities, is borne equally by the commune of their settlement, the state, and the province from which they come.[14]

The personnel of both these institutions, the Beggars' Depots and the Depots of Mendicity, is numerous according to our standards. The functions of each of the personnel is definitely described.[15]

Classification in the Colony. In general the colonists are classified according to their age, their morality, their antecedents, the duration of their term, etc. In addition, in each of the institutions they are classified as follows:

(a) Inmates of *Dépôts de Mendicité*. In Section One are persons eighteen to twenty-one years old who do not have to undergo a special kind of punishment. In Section Two are the sick capable of a certain amount of work. In Section Three are the sick incapable of any labor. In Section Four are the persons of more than twenty-one years entering for the first time the Depot of Mendicity, who do not have a grave judicial history. In Section Five are recidivists who have escaped. In Section Six are individuals sentenced for incendiarism or the destruction of trees, or those who have at-

---

[14] The Act of November 27, 1891, will be found in Appendix 3, Dawson, *The Vagrancy Problem*, London, 1910.
[15] *Colonies de Bienfaisance de l'État: Règlement Général.* Bruxelles, 1907, Regulations 15–91.

tempted incendiarism during their sojourn in the colony. In Section Seven are the procurers, those individuals who have suffered one or more sentences for grave offenses against morals, and those whose immorality is notoriously recognized. In Section Eight are dangerous or undisciplined convicts, individuals accused of crime or misdemeanor, or who have to undergo a sentence of imprisonment and who have been transferred from the prison by judicial authority. In Section Nine are those sentenced and not included in the above categories.

(b) Inmates of the houses of refuge. These are divided into three sections. (1) The first section consists of those who are between eighteen and twenty-one years who are not required to be punished by a special measure. (2) The older inmates. (3) In this section are included dangerous or undisciplined inmates. These individuals are not guilty of crime or of misdemeanors. In this section are also included those who have finished a prison sentence and who have been transferred by the judicial authorities to the institution.

So far as classification is concerned, without question the endeavor has been made to keep separate the classes who could do injury to each other. Practically all of the old and infirm are in the subordinate station of Hoogstraeten which is a subdepartment of the Beggars' Depot at Wortel.

Very careful regulations are set down concerning the food, clothing, the state of the bedding, the baking, the laundry, the lighting and the heating of the rooms, hygiene, order and neatness of the institution, the buildings, and the furniture, religious services, medical services, and the guarding of those in the institution.

Visits to the establishments are closely regulated. No stranger may visit the institution without the authorization of the Minister of Justice. Schools are established for the instruction of the children of the personnel. Canteens are provided where the inmates may buy certain articles, especially supplementary food.[16]

Very careful regulations are also laid down with regard to

[16] *Ibid.*, Regulations 98–199.

discipline. The surveillance is close and the discipline rather rigid. Visits and correspondence are closely regulated. The circulation of money in the colony is strictly forbidden. The rule of silence prevails in these institutions.

Punishments include, according to the gravity of the circumstances, the withholding of wages, the deprivation of labor, of lectures, of the canteen, of visits, of correspondence and other favors accorded to the inmates not under discipline. They include also putting upon bread and water, sending to the ordinary cell, to the solitary cell, or internment in the special section. Placing in a solitary cell or, as we say, a punishment cell, is given only as a discipline for grave fault, or when the other punishments are not effective. The number of days to be spent in a punishment cell or upon bread and water is closely guarded by placing the responsibility upon the director and the physician to see that the inmates are not kept long enough under that régime to impair the health. Recidivists may be punished with double penalties inflicted for the first breach of discipline. The discipline of these institutions follows very closely those practised in the reformatories and prisons of this country.

Labor and Salary. Work is organized both in the Depot of Mendicity and in the House of Refuge for the purpose of preventing idleness in any of the able-bodied colonists. What we should call the foreman in all work must labor with the colonists and not merely direct them. This provision we have seen in operation at the Swiss colony at Witzwil. It means, of course, increased product and it serves to dignify the labor in which the colonists are engaged.

In assigning the colonists to different kinds of work, account is taken of the trade which he has followed before. Those colonists who do not have any trade and who do not take to agricultural labor are employed in domestic services, in building earth-works of various kinds, and in common labor. Flying labor brigades may be created for clearing land at a distance.

The colonists are employed principally in types of work on

state account chiefly those which accord with the purposes of
these colonies. However, the products of the workshops
which are not used by the state are sold on the market. Moreover, it is permitted that certain of the colonists who are not
needed for the work available in the colony may be contracted
out to private entrepreneurs. These contracts are subject to
the previous approbation of the Minister of Justice. Thus it
will be seen that the internal policy of the colony is to keep
every able-bodied person at work.

Wage Payments to the Colonists. Wages are allowed to
the colonists according to a scale annually set by the Minister
of Justice according to the suggestions of the principal director. A part of this wage forms the leaving fund for the
colonists. Damage to finished goods or to raw materials which
is due to the negligence or the bad will of the colonists must
be paid for by the colonist out of his wages. The wages actually paid are very small when compared with that of the free
workman. This is made so on purpose, because it is desirable
that the colonists should not be able to earn as much in the institution as they earn outside.[17]

The Discharge of Colonists. Colonists are liberated at the
expiration of the term for which they have been sentenced or
earlier if the Minister of Justice judges it useless to prolong
their stay. Whenever possible, they are sent back to the
community from which they came with information concerning their institutional history in the hope that they may find
replacement in society in that community.

Escape. The director takes all measures necessary to recapture escaped inmates. He advises the state's attorney of
the community of their habitual residence or the place of their
presumed destination and also the burgomaster of that community of their escape. A report also is made to the Minister
of Justice and to the burgomaster of the commune of the place
where the man lives. Colonists may be transferred to other
institutions under judicial orders. Insane colonists are transferred to asylums.[18]

[17] *Ibid.*, Regulations 253–270.   [18] *Ibid.*, Regulations 280–289.

The prevention of beggary and vagrancy is the oustanding social aim of these colonies. That this plan succeeds in that purpose fairly well is witnessed by the fact that one can scarcely find a beggar on the streets in the cities of Belgium. Anyone found begging or even loafing about or wandering from one place to another is at once taken up and sent to the colony. If he is well, he is put to work; if he is sick, he is placed in one of the divisions of the colony where he is properly taken care of. No excuse is given him to go about begging for his living. Every effort is made to stimulate industry, to make him feel that he is able to make his own way, and to provide him, so far as possible, with a trade or a vocation in which he can earn an honest living.

Perhaps we should turn now to a brief description of the colony as we saw it.

The train from Brussels landed us at Antwerp early one morning. A bit of dickering with a taxi driver led to an agreement to take us to Merxplas some thirty miles away. Out past one of the forts of Antwerp destroyed by the Germans in their early advance towards Paris in the World War we whirled into the open country over roads which are not since the War, the best in the world. Through a great flat plain we rode, passing numerous villages on the way. A dinky steam, narrow-gauge railway ran beside the roadway, formerly the only way to reach Merxplas from Antwerp. A hotel stands at the entrance, a hotel belonging to the colony at which friends of inmates and visitors to the institution stay. We drove on to the main office between rows of fine trees so often seen in France and Belgium.

Here at the office we met our first obstacle. Did we perhaps have a permit from the Minister of Justice at Brussels? No, we had neglected to attend to that minor detail, but we had our passes from the French Bureau des Prisons admitting us to certain French prisons. He would see the director-adjutant. Happily the adjutant was the son of the director and a man of understanding. With delicate politeness, he overlooked the lack of credentials and made arrangements for us to see the institution. We were savants who had come all the way around the world to see Merxplas, Belgium's famous hobo and petty criminal colony; we should not be turned away.

We soon learned that here had grown up also a new correctional institution, La Prison-Ecole industrielle for youths sixteen to twenty-one years of age, engaged chiefly in agriculture.

This institution for vagrants was described by Von Schelle in the *American Journal of Sociology* almost twenty years ago. Since that time, however, as a matter of fact since the War, a part of the building of the Depot of Mendicity has been taken over by the prison school. As we noted before, at Hoogstraeten is that division of the colony which receives only vagrants who have been taken up for the first time.. Many of them are sick and infirm and therefore cannot do much work. There the attempt is to reconstruct them and to get them jobs so that they may support themselves. At Merxplas are the workshops and the farm colony for the more serious cases. Six hundred were employed in the workshops and a hundred on the farm when we were there in 1928. This is less than half the number who were to be found there in 1910. At Merxplas, as we have seen, there are several subdivisions of these. One of these divisions is for old men who cannot work. Here you have an institution which is really a home for the aged vagrant.

Again, they have a hospital or infirmary filled chiefly with old men.

There are about 2800 acres of land in the entire plot used for the colony for vagrants and the prison school. The vagrancy colony cultivates only about 400 acres. The boys in the prison school cultivate about 200 acres. Much of the other land is swamp and woods.

In the workshop a large number of different trades are carried on, such as blacksmithing, machine work of various sorts, electrical engineering, weaving, tailoring, at which they make uniforms for the black soldiers in the Congo; wooden shoes, weaving of cloth and rugs, making buttons from shells, making gas for the use of the institution, carpentry and cabinet work. The head of the central electric system is one of the inmates of the boys' school. The industries, except for the small funds paid by the community from which the men are sent, is self-supporting. The national government makes no appropriation. The buildings have all been built of brick made by the inmates themselves. Even the plans of the buildings have been worked out by some of the men who have been inmates. Decoration of the chapel and the plans for it have been done by the men themselves. Care of the buildings, grounds, stock, lawns, fences, and roads is given by the inmates. From the standpoint of an industrial colony it has been very successful. On the other hand, since only about 400 acres are worked by the vagrants themselves, it would seem that the agricultural work has not developed as well as the industrial. This is probably due to the fact that most of those who are taken up as vagrants and beggars have not been trained to farm work. Nevertheless, when I was there in 1928, they had 268 sheep, 156 cows, 22 horses, 60 oxen, and between 100 and 200 hogs. They give the inmates some of the milk, the officers also get some; from the rest butter is made. They do not butcher any of their own hogs or cattle for meat; they import sausage from America for the vagrants to eat.

THE EVALUATION OF THE COLONIES FROM THE POINT OF VIEW OF AN AMERICAN

The original idea of placing the colony for vagrants and beggars at Merxplas was to provide a great deal of outdoor work in clearing the land and preparing it for farming. As we have seen, experience has forced them to make it chiefly an industrial colony. This change of ideal was probably due to the fact that so many of the vagrants were from the cities and were not accustomed to farming, partly to the perception gained from experience that an industrial colony was more profitable in money than a farm colony, and partly also from the notion that if these men are to be prepared to go back into civil life and become useful citizens they must have some kind of a trade. Since a large part of the people of Belgium are engaged in industry of one sort or another, that again was a reason why industry should be followed rather than agriculture alone.

The comparative failure of these colonies to develop farm work as contrasted with the colony at Witzwil, Switzerland, and in our colonies here in the United States is especially noteworthy. Probably this is due to the industrial situation in Belgium.

The size of the colony has very greatly decreased since the War. Whereas in 1907, 1279 men were engaged in farming, and 1970 in industry, the number has shrunk for the whole colony and the proportion of men in industry has increased.[19]

This colony has indeed solved the problem of begging and loafing in Belgium. While the colony is not self-supporting, nevertheless, it probably costs the people of Belgium less to support these beggars and vagrants in the colony than it would cost them if they were at large. Moreover, it has put under social control these masses of shiftless and useless men, most of whom are addicted to drink and from whom the army of criminals are constantly recruited. Therefore society has been protected in more ways than one.

The high hopes held out when it was established of curing these vagrants and beggars have not been realized, either in the colony at Wortel for sick and incapable beggars nor at the Dépôt de Mendicité at Merxplas where the able-bodied and the more hardened and criminal-like vagrants are to be found. Even of those who go to Wortel from half to two-thirds are recidivists. A part of that is due to the fact that they can get out so easily. As already explained, escape is not very difficult; they may leave at any time that they have three dollars accumulated in their savings, and while the maximum term of detention in this colony is a year, the average stay is only two or three months. At Merxplas between 80 and 90 per cent of the inmates are recidivists. From the standpoint of reformation, therefore, the experiment has not been a great suc-

[19] Dawson, *op. cit.*, p. 113. Kelly, *The Elimination of the Tramp*, New York, 1908.

cess. However, it does keep the number who are in the institution off the streets while the control is made light so that they can go out and possibly find a job. The theory back of that practice has not been approved by that experience. If they had a system of parole and an indeterminate sentence in the colony until it was quite certain that they could be replaced in society with some hope of success, the constant sending back of people who have been in again and again might be obviated.

The Belgian colonies provide a splendid illustration of what can be done with poor material under skilled direction, in producing economic and social value. Every building on this formerly waste land is a product of the inmates; practically every tool used, the wagons, the roads across the estate, the drainage ditches—all have been made by the inmates. A great variety of trades, chiefly hand work, to be sure, in order to provide employment, are taught.[20]

One of the points of contrast with Witzwil and the colonies in some of the states of the United States is that of the ease of escape. There are no walls, and as there is only a small number of guards, during certain times of the year, large numbers of the inmates do take "French leave." It must be remembered that most of these are not under penal law; they are committed to this institution as we commit people to poorhouses. If they get a job they are not brought back and the order for their capture is suspended by the Minister of Justice. If they are brought back, liberty is restricted and privileges are lessened. A former director of the institution believes that the ease of escape is a sort of safety valve which makes discipline in the institution very much easier.

Most of the work on the estate is done by hand both in the shops and in the fields. The plowing, of course, is done with oxen and horses and the amount of spade culture is reduced thereby. The reason for hand work, however, is to give work to as many as possible. With the large number that were formerly in these colonies, that was necessary. Without question, however, it does reduce the output. This policy also

[20] Kelly, *op. cit.*, p. 19.

helps to keep down wages paid to the inmates and increases the cost of the support of the institution.

In addition to the contrast just noted between this colony and the colony at Witzwil, Switzerland, on the one hand, and that of the District of Columbia, known as the workhouse, at Lorton, Va., and the state farm for misdemeanants at Putnamville, Ind., on the other, are the following differences: In the Belgian colony, there is a very much better classification of the inmates. The law and the regulations require that the young shall be kept separate from the older, more hardened persons. The more vicious must be separated from those who are less vicious. The nine classifications under the regulations in Merxplas and the three classifications at Wortel indicate the extent to which the Belgian colonies have carried the process of classification.

Our judgment of the value of this will doubtless depend upon how much stress we lay upon the classification principle. Doubtless so long as large numbers of these men are kept at night in dormitories instead of separate cells, the principle of classification has a value to prevent corruption of the less hardened.

Another outstanding contrast as between the Belgian colonies on the one hand, and the other farm colonies I have mentioned, is the greater development of industry. At Merxplas and even at Wortel the main emphasis is upon work in the shop. At Witzwil, Switzerland, the tendency is just the opposite. There, as we have seen, the industries are entirely subordinate to the farming operations. That is true in Indiana and at Lorton, Va.

These Belgian colonies, while not a part of the penal system of Belgium, are of the very greatest importance and significance. They have given to the world an example of how the beggar and the vagrant can be controlled. This lesson is especially pertinent to the present situation in the United States. The tramp problem has never been seriously tackled in this country. Belgium has shown us one way in which to control the problem. Switzerland has given us another illustration.

From these two countries America can learn lessons of the greatest value.

———————

BIBLIOGRAPHY

Carlile, Wilson, *The Continental Outcast: Land Colonies and Poor Relief*, London, 1906.

Colonies de Bienfaisance de l'État à Merxplas, Réponse au Questionnaire de Mr. le Consul de la République de l'Uruguay. (Mimeographed sheets.)

Colonies de Bienfaisance, de l'État: Règlement Général. Ministère de la Justice, Bruxelles, 1907.

Dawson, W. H., *The Vagrancy Problem*, London, 1910.

Delbastee, F., "Prison Reform in Europe: I. Belgium," *The Survey*, November 4, 1922, pp. 888, 889.

Delierneux, A., *Prisons nouvelles: Lois nouvelles.* (Ms. given author by M. Deliernieux on visit to Merxplas, 1928.)

Delierneux, A., *Luttre contre le Vagabondage.* Extrait de la *Revue de Droit Pénal et de Criminologie*, Louvain, Janvier, 1929.

Encyclopedia of the Social Sciences, Art. "Begging," Vol. II.

Kelly, Edmond, *The Elimination of the Tramp*, New York, 1908.

Notice sur la Prison-École industrielle à Gand, Saint-Gilles, 1925; Same, 1927.

Van Rast, J., *Organization du Dépôt de Mendicité à Merxplas-son Evolution.* Extrait de la *Revue de Droit Pénal et de Criminologie*, Louvain, Janvier, 1929.

Van Schelle, "A City of Vagabonds," *American Journal of Sociology*, July, 1910.

CHAPTER VIII

PENOLOGICAL EXPERIMENTS IN ENGLAND

THE prison system itself was originally an experiment, tried out first in America as a substitute for such primary methods of punishment as execution, mutilation, flogging, burning, and other corporal punishments. It was carried to England after the Revolutionary War had closed the American colonies to English transportation.[1] England adopted in the beginning one particular type of American prison, the so-called Pennsylvania System. In the thirties of the last century this appealed to European students of the American prison system as the best type. The English adoption of this Pennsylvania or separate confinement system explains many survivals which we find in the English prison system today. For example, such things as separate confinement for the first period of imprisonment, serving food in the cells of the prisoners, instead of in a common dining room, and work in the cells—so far as these measures are carried out in the modern British prison system—are survivals of that old system borrowed from America.

In a sense the various methods of treating the criminals in Great Britain, as almost everywhere else in modern times, were begun as experiments. The penal transportation system, which for many more than a hundred years was the characteristic method of treating criminals in Great Britain, developed out of the old system of exile which has its roots in the far distant past.

England also used the hulks for a time following the close of the Revolutionary War before she had developed her penal

[1] For further details, see Gillin, *Criminology and Penology*, New York, 1926, Chapter xviii.

transportation to Australia. They continued to be used as collecting centers after the penal transportation system to Australia had developed. They were a signal failure.

Following the objections of the Australian free settlers to the transportation of such large numbers of penal convicts to that country and the attacks upon the system by numerous leaders of thought in England, among them Jeremy Bentham, the penitentiary system was borrowed from the United States and with some modifications became a competitor of the penal transportation system to Australia. Milbank Prison was started under the agitation of Jeremy Bentham in the early nineteenth century, and as penal transportation became more and more objectionable, the penitentiary system finally became the main reliance of England for the treatment of her convicts. In 1877 the local prisons of England and Wales were put under the control of the Home Office and ultimately under the same board as that which had control of the convict prisons. The local prisons then became the resort to which the government turned for the punishment of those who were not sentenced to penal servitude.

Gradually England developed a classification system which has been her great contribution to penal practice. This system of classifying the different convicts was adapted from the experiment of Colonel Maconochie who had charge of the convicts at Norfolk Island near Australia. It is based upon a system of marks. Later Colonel Maconochie tried it out in the Birmingham prison of which he was governor. Sir Joshua Jebb adopted it in the prisons of England, working out what was known as the progressive stage system according to which men were classified in the different groups with increasing liberty as they went up through the different stages. This system was borrowed by Crofton, who was in charge of prisoners in Ireland, and became known as the Irish System. From that time to the present England has experimented with classification inside each prison and also as between prisons. Greater details of the present system of classification will be given later.

Another experiment which England developed out of the Australian penal transportation system was the ticket-of-leave plan or what she calls at the present time release on license. The latter part of certain men's sentences was spent in society at large under the supervision of the police. This system was borrowed in 1876 by the founders of Elmira Reformatory and was called parole. England still uses this system for certain classes of her prisoners.

Later on, after probation had been developed in America, England took that plan over and is now using it to a considerable extent.

Thus it will be seen that the modern British prison system has developed as the result of certain experiments for a period of more than a hundred years.

THE PRESENT PRISON SYSTEM IN ENGLAND AND WALES

As a background for the discussion of experiments now going on in the English prisons, the present system in England and Wales should be briefly described.

Number and Kinds of Institutions. In 1926 there were thirty-one local prisons with a daily average of 7840 inmates in England and Wales. These are what remain of the old local prisons. Gradually over recent years the number of local prisons has been decreasing because of the very rapid decrease in the number of prisoners sent to institutions in England.

In addition there are five convict prisons, four for men and one for women, with an average number of inmates for the year 1925–1926 of 1339. It will be noticed that this number is small as compared with the number of prisoners in most of our state prisons in the United States, and very much smaller than the numbers usually to be found in our federal prisons. These are for those who have committed the more serious crimes and have been sentenced to what is called in England "penal servitude."

England has two institutions for what she has called "preventive detention," one for men and one for women. The average number of inmates for 1925–26 for both of these institutions was 162.   The institution for men is a separate institution, while that for women is a separate department of another institution.

In addition to these institutions for delinquents, England and Wales have four Borstal institutions, three for men and one for women, with an average number of inmates for the year 1925–26 of 1108.   These Borstal institutions are a cross between an American juvenile reformatory and an adult reformatory.

With the opening of this century crime has decreased very much in England.   Furthermore, with the extension of probation and what we call parole, the need of so many local prisons has diminished.   Consequently between 1900 and 1926, twenty-six local prisons have been closed.   England has discovered what America may some time learn—that if a system is properly integrated, there is no need for so many institutions for the confinement of delinquents as we have at the present time.

Classification.   No nation in the world has developed to a like degree classification of prisoners.   Some understanding of how this process of classification grew will make clear the present system.   Beginning with Maconochie's experiments at Norfolk Island, step by step the classification of different types of prisoners has gone on until today England has the most minute classification of its prisoners to be found anywhere.

Since 1877 when the unification of the prison system of England took place and the local prisons were put under the control of the Home Office, the Home Secretary has had the power to classify both within the prison and by prisons.[2]   Up to 1895 this power was sparingly used except to keep first offenders and juveniles away from the habituals.[3]

In convict prisons the inmates have been divided into the star class and the habituals since 1879.   The star class consisted of those convicted for the first time.   A similar classification was introduced into the local prisons in 1896–1897.

[2] Hobhouse and Brockway, *English Prisons Today*, London, 1922, p. 214.
[3] *Ibid.*, p. 214.

The prison act of 1898 provided for the introduction of the first and second divisions for first offenders of hitherto good character. That is, this law attempted to divide even first offenders into different classes. That law gave the magistrates power to make this classification on the basis of what they knew about the individual when he was sentenced. The prison administration had nothing to do with it. However, the magistrates paid little attention to this provision in the law. Consequently when the prison administration saw the importance of such classification they had to accomplish it by administrative orders.

Furthermore, gradually there has grown up in the law, partly as the result of the survival of old ideas, the classification according to such categories as "Sentenced to Hard Labor," "Court Martial," "Debtors," and "Penal Servitude." In other words, you have a double classification in the law, one based upon pre-existing laws and the other based upon a new theory. The classification "To Hard Labor" was an attempt to classify according to the severity of the sentence, based upon the gravity of the crime. So with "Penal Servitude." "Court Martial," however, was provided for offenders against military law. The sentence of "Debtors" was intended only for those who could not pay their fines. They were supposed to be treated much more leniently. These various classifications based upon different principles confused the matter and made the classification, according to any one principle, very difficult. Consequently, these classifications have failed, in part, of their intention. They have failed because they have been carried on chiefly within the institution. Observation has shown that because there are so few in the first and second divisions in each local prison, as a practical matter it is impossible to grant the greater privileges which the law provides for those in the first division or those in the star class.[4] In practice, however, these struggles at securing a classification of prisoners have resulted, at least in part, in separating juveniles and first offenders.[5] As a result of this confusion in an endeavor to classify within the

[4] *Ibid.*, p. 216.   [5] *Ibid.*, p. 216.

institution, the authorities have seen that classification, to be effective, must be by institutions. Here the process of development has been slow because of expense. Recently, however, the attempt has been made to bring that about. Avowedly it is an experiment and the results must wait upon careful study. *Classification by Institutions.* In recent years the attempt to classify the prisoners in separate institutions, each intended for a different class, as well as to classify them within the institutions on the basis of the star class, first and second division and habituals has led to the setting aside of certain institutions for specific types of prisoners. For example, Wakefield receives the longer sentenced local prisoners with the intention of giving them industrial training.[6] To Wakefield, therefore, are sent men who have been sentenced to six months or more. Short-term prisoners are eliminated. However, men convicted for the first time and men with previous convictions alike must be received. They are trained, however, in separate classes, each with its own system of progressive stages.

Another local prison, Wormwood Scrubs, is reserved for men who have not been in prison before. With full recognition that the classification has now been carried as far as it is possible within the limits of the establishment, the prison authorities are determined to extend the principle further by classifying prisoners in different prisons. One of the difficulties that has had to be faced is the expense of journeys from a distant part of the country to a particular prison intended for that kind of individual. Wormwood Scrubs, on the other hand, has been set apart for men who have not been in prison before. The object here is to enable the training to be carried on in a better spirit by eliminating so far as possible the prison atmosphere. Repression does not need to be so severe when you have only first offenders. At both Wakefield and Wormwood Scrubs a vigorous scheme of training, physical, industrial, mental, and moral, is the rule. The prisoner has an active day of fifteen hours, nine of which at Wakefield and eight at

[6] *Report of the Commissioners of Prisons and Directors of Convict Prisons,* 1923–1924, p. 16.

Wormwood Scrubs, are spent in the industrial shops. The attempt is made in both to develop responsibility by imposing trust and encouraging the men in every possible way. At neither is the system perfect. At Wakefield the scheme is hampered by the presence of recidivists, while at Wormwood Scrubs you have a number of short-sentence prisoners who have to be treated as a separate body in order that they may not impede the training of the others.

The authorities feel that the net results at Wakefield are encouraging. For example, out of 628 men discharged from that institution since the new system was introduced, only 15.6 per cent have been reconvicted. These 628 included 334 star class; that is, prisoners of respectable antecedents or convicted for the first time, and out of these 334 only 24 have been reconvicted.[7] The results at Wormwood Scrubs have not yet been established.

With the development of mental hygiene in England and knowledge concerning the close relationships between mental conditions and criminality, it has been found desirable to segregate the weak-minded from the other prisoners. England has a law which provides that those which are certifiably insane or certifiably feeble-minded—that is, those who come under the definitions laid down by the law as certifiable—are to be treated as insane and sent to the proper institutions for those people; but the prison authorities have found prisoners who, while not certifiable, still do not fit in well with the other prisoners in the ordinary local and convict prisons. It is one of the pressing problems to know what to do with these men under the present law. The authorities in their reports are constantly urging that the law be changed so that those who are not at present certifiable may be taken out of the prisons or dealt with separately from the ordinary prisoners. Hence, about 1924 the prison commissioners made arrangements to collect these uncertifiable, weak-minded prisoners in certain of the local prisons. The local prisons of Liverpool and Wands-

[7] *Ibid.*, 1925–26, p. 19.

worth are such centers for the collection of uncertifiable, weak-minded prisoners.[8]

Experience in the Borstal institutions has now gone far enough to raise the question of the importance of the careful study of these boys and girls before they enter the institution, consequently there has been established in the local prison of Wandsworth, in London, within the walls of that institution but separate from the other parts of the prison, a reception prison for the Borstal boys, who are there studied physically, mentally, and socially, in order better to adapt their training to treatment. Furthermore, classification within the three Borstal institutions for boys and between the three institutions, enables the officials at this receiving institution at Wandsworth to send the boys to the place where proper training can be given.[9] Furthermore, this institution at Wandsworth is used as a place of remand for the boys who are awaiting trial or who have been sent there by the courts for investigation. The purpose of it is to provide a special institution for young offenders where a scientific study can be made to determine, if possible, the chief causes of their anti-social conduct and the best lines of treatment. The social workers have prolonged interviews with the lad and also investigate his history, visit his home in all cases where they can do so. There is only one drawback in this institution, and that is that it is not only used for this scientific study on the basis of which the lads are distributed to the various Borstal institutions, but it is also used for the incarceration of those who receive short sentences of imprisonment.[10] One other regressive step has been taken at this institution. In the early days of the experiment each lad was

---

[8] *Ibid.*, 1925–26, pp. 46, 50.

[9] Formerly this reception class was in the Borstal institution at Feltham. It was transferred to Wandsworth because the Feltham staff had many other duties to perform and were somewhat overtaxed. Furthermore Wandsworth was more central and by using it as a reception institution for the lads, some saving could be made in travelling expenses. Experienced medical officials are available there for the work of mental and physical diagnosis. Social workers are used to secure the social history on the basis of which a determination is made of the capacity for education and training and for weeding out those of unstable or of questionable mentality. *Ibid.*, 1922–1923, p. 29.

[10] *Ibid.*, 1923–24, p. 23.

given individual mental tests. This process with the large numbers proved to be too lengthy and exacting. Furthermore, the lads were detained rather too long in the institution before being transferred to the Borstal institutions. Group testing, therefore, has been substituted with individual mental examinations in the case of those only who failed to reach a certain standard in the group test.[11]

In the Borstal institutions, parole has been introduced by which promising boys who have been in the institution a certain length of time are allowed to go out on license.

What shall be done with those Borstal boys who are left out on parole and break it? That was a problem with which the authorities struggled after the establishment of the Borstal institutions, which even yet is not entirely settled. If they were sent back into the Borstal institution, that was not satisfactory; if they were put into an ordinary prison, that was equally unsatisfactory. Consequently, the commissioners provided a special department at Wormwood Scrubs for these boys. This department is also used for a few of the boys in the Borstal institutions who have to be transferred from those institutions because of persistent misconduct. In this department a regular system of review with a view to re-license is in operation. Say the commissioners, "We are opposed to prolonged periods of detention under revoked license in surroundings which are necessarily those of the prison, in spite of all that can be done in the way of visiting, teaching, gymnastics, etc. At the same time the failure has to be taught a lesson. The practice is to examine and consider each lad on reception and to settle a provisional period for which he shall be detained, which in no case exceeds six months, and may be less. Periodical reviews are held subsequently and the date of re-license is governed by the lad's progress."[12] This system provides further classification of the Borstal boys, but is not very satisfactory by reason of the fact that it is not a separate institution but a part of a local prison.

Among the boys' Borstal institutions there is further classifi-

[11] *Ibid.*, 1924–25, pp. 21–22.   [12] *Ibid.*, 1923–24, p. 68.

cation. Feltham is reserved for lads who have been in prison, but who have incurred only fines or who have broken probation and whose lives have hitherto been spent at home, and for those who are mentally backward and unstable. At Portland those are received who have failed at industrial and reformatory schools and have already been away from home for prolonged periods. The third Borstal institution at Borstal receives those who fall between those sent to Feltham and Portland.[18]

Dartmoor Prison is used chiefly for habitual offenders from among those sentenced to penal servitude. It is not possible, however, to have all the habitual offenders here, consequently the classification on that basis is not strictly carried out by institutions.[14]

Present Classification Within the Prisons. While a similar classification obtains within both the local prisons and the convict prisons, there are some differences which have developed in the two sets of institutions. As already observed, classification developed first in the convict prisons and later was applied to the local prisons.

In the local prisons, the following classifications obtain:

(a) *The Star Class.* This class is so named because of the red stars which are worn on the sleeves of the coat. The star class consists of those prisoners not previously convicted and not clearly of the habitual type of criminal. While the star class has existed in convict prisons since 1879, it was not introduced into the local prisons of England until 1896–1897. Star prisoners are selected by the police representatives of the courts after making an investigation and furnishing a report on the character and antecedents of the prisoners who have not been previously convicted, whose previous offense has been of a trivial character, or who have been convicted several years before. When no information is procurable, the governor may at his discretion class them as stars. The doubtful cases are submitted to the registrar of habitual criminals with the description form and a finger print. The results of the inquiry are submitted to the visiting magistrate who is sup-

[18] *Ibid.*, 1923–24, p. 26.   [14] *Ibid.*, 1923–24, p. 26.

posed to give the decision in the matter. These inmates are not supposed to have any privileges or differential treatment, the purpose being merely segregation. They are supposed to be located in cells where they cannot come in contact with prisoners of other classes and must sit in chapel and take exercises separately.[15] In actual practice there is some difficulty in carrying out this classification for the purpose intended. While first offenders are awaiting this investigation they frequently mingle with habituals, and in many prisons it is reported that it is the custom to class them among the habituals after sentence while the claim that they have not been previously convicted is being investigated. Furthermore, these inmates are not strictly separated. Often they are employed at domestic service in the prison, in the bath-house and chapel, at cleaning, etc., occupations which frequently bring them in contact with other prisoners. It is the general impression that the early hopes of this system have not been realized.[16]

(b) *First Division.* The commonest offense for which people are assigned to this class is non-compliance with the elementary education act. The prisoners in this class are supposed to have special privileges. The numbers, however, are very small and, therefore, the purpose of the division is not realized to any great extent. Under the regulations, the first-division prisoner as compared with one in the third division is supposed to be kept apart from other classes of prisoners. He may also, if he has the means to pay for them, have his own clothing, and such books, newspapers, or other means of occupation as are not considered to be objectionable by the authorities. He also has privileges of a visit once every two weeks for a quarter of an hour by three friends and may write and receive one letter each fortnight. Moreover, he is not required to work, but may be permitted, if practicable, to follow his trade or profession, receiving the whole of his earnings, providing he is not maintained at the expense of the prison. He may have his own food supplied and a limited

---

[15] Hobhouse and Brockway, *op. cit.,* pp. 214, 224, 225.
[16] *Ibid.,* p. 226.

quantity of beer or wine; if he can pay for it, he may occupy a specially furnished room or cell; he may have the use of private furniture and utensils suitable to his ordinary habits and he may also have the services of another prisoner to clean his cell and wash up his crockery, if he has the means to pay for it. These first-division prisoners have been called the aristocrats of the prison world.[17]   In actual practice, however, because of the small number of first-division prisoners there are serious deprivations.   He has almost no chance to communicate with his fellows and is in almost perpetual confinement within his cell or other parts of the prison.[18]

The third division in these local prisons includes all of the others apparently habitual.   This division contains the greatest number of prisoners.   If one takes the aggregate number in both the second and third division, only a small proportion remain in the star class and the first division.

What have been the results of this attempted classification within the local prisons?   Because of the small numbers in the star and the first division classes, it has not always been possible to carry out the purposes of these classifications.   Furthermore, in an investigation carried on by the Prison Enquiry Committee about 1920, the testimony seemed to indicate that the attempt to separate the various classes had largely failed. So long as the different classes are kept in the same building, illicit communication is possible under almost any conditions between landings, between the various wings of the prison, between the prison and the hospital, or in the same workshop. It is this consciousness of the failure of classification within the institution that has led the prison authorities to attempt to classify by different institutions.   Such a plan, however, has not been feasible up to the present time.   Nevertheless, it must be admitted from the testimony offered, classification within the institution has protected somewhat the members of the star class and the young offenders.[19]

In Convict Prisons.   In convict prisons are confined those sentenced to penal servitude.   These prisoners are supposed

[17] *Ibid.*, pp. 220–21.   [18] *Ibid.*, p. 222.   [19] *Ibid.*, p. 216.

to be those who have committed the more serious offenses. In these institutions there are three classes, the star, the intermediate, and the recidivist. Here again the star class is intended for those who, while they have committed very serious crimes and therefore are sentenced to penal servitude, are not clearly habitual criminals. It is intended for first offenders, as in the local prisons.[20]

The intermediate class consists of the large body of those between the star class who have not been previously convicted of a crime on the one hand, and the recidivists on the other. This three-fold grouping was not introduced into the English prisons until 1903 and 1904. Up to that time there had been only two classes, the star and the recidivists. The introduction of the intermediate class was intended to separate into a class by themselves those who were not up to the star-class qualifications and were not as bad as the recidivists. However, with the decreasing number of prisons the convict prisoners scattered among five different institutions with an average of only about three hundred in each, it has sometimes proved to be impossible to carry on the work of the institutions and keep the intermediates and the recidivists apart. There seems to be a fair degree of separation of the star class from the recidivists. The most important difference, however, in the treatment of the three classes is the longer period of the initial separate confinement to which the recidivists are liable. The practice has been until recently to send the male intermediates and the recidivists who are fit for hard labor to Dartmoor or Portland.[21] The treatment, however, of the intermediates and the recidivists after the first three months seems to be practically the same.

A man sentenced to penal servitude in the convict prisons up to 1899 served a preliminary period of solitary confinement of nine months. Then this period was reduced to six months. In 1905 the period was varied with the class of prisoner, the stars being required to serve three months, the intermediates six months, and the recidivists nine months. Finally in 1911

[20] *Ibid.*, p. 214. [21] *Ibid.*, p. 318.

Mr. Churchill reduced the period to three months for recidivists, and one month for stars and intermediates. This preliminary period was served in the local prisons, and after that was finished these men were sent to the convict prisons. However, this definite period has been somewhat modified since that time. Often only a few days are spent in preliminary separate confinement, even by recidivists. Immediately on arriving at the convict prison they begin to work in association.[22]

Since the War great changes have taken place in the conduct of the prison system, and the young convict has been given unusual thought. The young convict as a problem, however, has not yet been solved. The reduction in the number of convict establishments has increased the difficulties, but the prison authorities are giving attention to the matter. Before the War young men whose antecedents were such as to exclude them from the star class were usually classified as intermediates and were frequently placed in that class on the ground of their age, even though their previous records might have logically ranked them with the recidivists. For a time Portland was the prison for these intermediates; since Portland has been changed into a Borstal institution, the young intermediates have had to go to Parkhurst and Dartmoor. The Prison Commissioners themselves admit that in these institutions the separation from the older convicts, while it has been attempted, has been found ineffective. They urge that a separate institution should be established for these young convicts.[23]

The third class of prisoners in convict institutions is composed of the recidivists. Into this class are supposed to be placed all habitual criminals, especially the older ones.

The progressive stage system applies to the inmates of the convict prisons. This system was introduced very early in the history of the English prison system by Sir Joshua Jebb, as

[22] *Ibid.*, p. 319.
[23] *Report of The Commissioners of Prisons and The Directors of Convict Prisons,* 1924–25, p. 24.

a result of Maconochie's experiments in Australia. It is based upon a system of marks and advancements from the first to the fourth stage, with gradual relaxation of the discipline and an increase of freedom. It reached its greatest expansion in Ireland under Crofton. At the present time in the convict prisons of England it is much like the classification system in many American prisons and is used as a means of securing good conduct and industry. In the convict prisons there are four stages: (1) ordinary, (2) probation, (3) superior, and (4) special.[24]

The standing orders which provide for these four stages were introduced in 1920–21. After two years of the ordinary stage, if the convict has earned 4380 marks with good conduct and industry, at the discretion of the governor he may pass into the probation stage. In the probation stage he may be brought out of the cells in the evening on certain days in the week and may take part in the readings, recitations, lectures, etc., which are organized for the superior stage. After one year and the accumulation of 2920 marks in the probation stage, he is advanced to the superior stage. His dress is of a different pattern. He is allowed certain privileges as to shaving and hair-cutting. He may have a looking-glass and a washstand. The star class men in the probation stage, however, are given these special privileges after six months and the attainment of 1460 marks. In the probation stage, recreation classes are conducted two or three evenings a week. Readings, recitations, lectures, discussions, and music may be arranged. Games, such as chess, draughts, and dominos are allowed. Moreover, during the summer months those in this stage are permitted to walk or sit in the grounds of the prison garden. When prisoners are advanced to the superior stage, they are encouraged to contribute by their own efforts to the formation of clubs and classes, for the organization of debates and discussions on prescribed subjects, or they may co-operate with the officers of the prison in organizing musical entertain-

[24] *Ibid.*, pp. 21–24; Hobhouse and Brockway, *English Prisons Today*, pp. 217 ff., 333.

ments.   Moreover, it is in the superior stage that the convict may by exemplary conduct earn a remission of three days if he remains in the stage for any period less than six months, and of seven days if he remains in the stage for any period of six months or over.   After a convict has served four years of his sentence and has accumulated 11,680 marks with exemplary conduct, he will pass into the special stage.   In this last stage he is subject to the rules laid down for the long-sentence division.   He is allowed to purchase a weekly journal or newspaper and have pipe and tobacco.   Smoking is allowed him during the dinner hour and for those entitled to association in the evening after supper.   Furthermore, the visits and the writing and receiving of letters depend upon the stage which one has reached.   It is apparent that entrance into the higher stages does not begin until one has spent two years in the institution.[25]

In addition to these four stages for the ordinary prisoner, there is a special class for juvenile adults.   That is, all prisoners under twenty-one are placed in this special class.   A few, however, are in this class who are even over thirty.   These belong logically to the intermediate stage, but are separate from the other intermediates.   They are kept at Parkhurst and Dartmoor.   This special stage can be entered by three-year stars at the end of two years, by four-year stars at the end of two years and nine months, and by five-year stars and by intermediates at the end of three years and six months, by six-year convicts of all classes at the end of four years, and by those serving more than six years at twelve months before the date of their discharge.   Those in this special class have the benefits of the ordinary fourth stage with some further priveleges.[26]

All of these arrangements pertain to the ordinary division of convicts.   In 1905 a long-sentence division was created for selected convicts sentenced to ten years or more.   Ten years later the division was extended to include men sentenced to

[25] Hobhouse and Brockway, *op. cit.*, pp. 333–34.
[26] *Ibid.*, p. 330; *Report of the Commissioners of Prisons and the Directors of Convict Prisons,* 1924–25, p. 24.

eight years or more. These inmates are eligible when they have served a term of five years. But something more than good conduct and industry are necessary to secure admission. The convicts in this division are separated from the rest, wear special uniforms of light gray, are permitted to talk during a period each day, and earn a gratuity of one penny per day for themselves.[27]

The convict prison at Parkhurst contains separate departments for the diseased, imbecile, mentally deficient, and the aged.[28] I was very much interested, when visiting Parkhurst, to observe the special department of the prison set apart for the old men. Here were about seventy-five or eighty old convicts no longer able to do much work, who live by themselves, take care of the grounds, and have many privileges not accorded to the ordinary convict.

This rather long survey of the attempt made by the authorities of England to separate different classes of convicts according to various principles, represents the most thoroughgoing attempt at classification and segregation made anywhere in the world. The purpose behind it originally was partly to deter from crime and partly to enable the authorities to individualize the treatment of prisoners. In spite of the detailed attempts at classification it is a question as to whether this system of England, aside from the juveniles and the star class, is of very great benefit. If England, with her numerous institutions all under one control and the small number of prisoners, cannot succeed, it is a question whether it is possible in an American state with a smaller number of institutions to carry out successfuly the segregation of convicts by classes. If we ever come to the place where we shall have convicts segregated in a large number of small institutions, it might be possible. Doubtless we shall some day move in that direction. Furthermore, there is another difficulty in the English system, viz., that the classification has been according to no one single principle. Should men be segregated according to the kind of crime they commit, according to the length of

[27] Hobhouse and Brockway, *op. cit.*, p. 330.   [28] *Ibid.*, pp. 226–227.

sentence given them, according to conduct and industry in prison, or according to some other single principle? At the present time confusion exists in the classification system of England because no single principle obtains throughout. Furthermore, it is a question on the part of some English students of the problem as to whether, from the point of view of treatment such as will fit prisoners for ordinary life, specialized segregation is of value beyond a certain point.

These students suggest that unless for special treatment separation is necessary, the limitation of association of persons to those of the same peculiar or degraded type may be positively harmful.[29] While the Prison Commissioners seem to think that the convict-stage system works fairly well, their reports also raise a question especially with reference to the problem of the young convict, and express the opinion that these men require an entirely separate establishment, governed by a man of vigorous personality, to give them a new set of ideas and an active life of hard training.[30]

ADVENTURES . IN . PENOLOGY . IN . ENGLAND

With the present organization of the prison system in England thus clearly in mind, let us turn to a consideration of some of the adventures in the treatment of criminals being made at the present time in England. Some of these are new experiments being tried out in the endeavor better to adapt the prison system to the needs of the men under their control.

Meals in Association. Historically with the separate system prevailing in England in order to carry out the determination to prevent prisoners from contaminating each other, meals were taken in the cell. At the present time in eighteen prisons, star class and second division prisoners are permitted to dine in association.[31]

Separate Institutions for Young Prisoners. In the endeavor

---

[29] Hobhouse and Brockway, *op. cit.*, p. 217.

[30] *Report of the Commissioners of Prisons and the Directors of Convict Prisons,* 1924–25, p. 23–24.

[31] *Report of the Commissioners of Prisons and the Directors of Convict Prisons,* 1924–25, p. 20.

to segregate entirely young prisoners from the older and more hardened, the authorities have been experimenting for some time with the placing of young intermediates and juvenile adults in a separate institution.   These were formerly sent to Portland.   However, since that has become a new Borstal institution, they are now sent to separate departments at Parkhurst and Dartmoor.   The experiment, however, has convinced the prison authorities that an entirely separate institution is necessary.[32]

The Progressive Stage System.   Experiments with the progressive stage system are still going on.   As we have seen, in its simple form it was introduced early in the last century by Sir Joshua Jebb.   With the increase in the experiments in classification, the progressive stage system is now confined entirely to the convict prisons, and has been supplemented by all kinds of divisions and classifications.   The authorities, however, have not given up the idea that it is essentially good and are experimenting with it to make it still more effective.[33]

Preventive Detention.   One of the most interesting innovations introduced into the prison system of England in the last quarter of a century is what is known as "preventive detention."   This experiment was inaugurated in 1909, under the Prevention of Crimes Act, passed in 1908.   Under this law any person sentenced to penal servitude may have added to the ordinary sentence for that crime an additional period of preventive detention following the expiration of his sentence of penal servitude, provided that the jury has found evidence that since he reached the age of sixteen years he had at least three times previously been convicted of crime, and that he is still leading a persistently dishonest and criminal life, or that he had already been found to be an habitual criminal and had been sentenced to preventive detention before, provided also that the consent of the director of public proscution had been obtained to this charge being made, and finally that due notice

---

[32] *Ibid.*, p. 24.

[33] Hobhouse and Brockway, *op. cit.*, p. 325; *Report of the Commissioners of Prisons and the Directors of Convict Prisons, 1924–25*, p. 23.

has been given the courts and the offender of the evidence upon which the charge is founded. The period of preventive detention must not exceed ten years nor be less than five. There is provision also that the Secretary of State for Home Affairs may at any time discharge on license such a preventive detention prisoner, and that the license may be revoked at any time if the prisoner escapes from supervision or commits any breach of the conditions of the parole.[34]

The purpose of this particular device is not to deal with habitual criminals who are such by reason of mental defects, but the hardened or professional criminals sound in mind, often highly skilled, and who deliberately prefer a life of crime. The experiment was based upon the experience that these habitual criminals are not deterred from a life of crime by giving them the maximum sentence prescribed by law for their crime. When the law was under discussion in Parliament, there was a body of opinion that held that such men ought to be detained indefinitely, until they could prove to the authorities that they had changed their way of life. However, a majority opinion prevailed which limited the term of detention to ten years.

The prisoners at Camp Hill, as the preventive detention institution is called, are divided into three grades—ordinary, special, and disciplinary. Inmates start in the ordinary grade and may at once by their work at one of the prison industries earn a gratuity up to a maximum amount of three pence per day. Half of this small sum a prisoner may spend at the canteen. After every six months he is eligible for a certificate obtainable by good conduct and industry. When he has received four of these he is advanced to the special grade. He recieves a good-conduct stripe which carries some important new privileges and a special gratuity of five shillings. After the first six months he has meals in association; after twelve months he may enjoy evening recreations in association; after eighteen months he may have an allotment of ground on which

[34] Hobhouse and Brockway, op. cit., p. 441.

to raise produce which he sells to the prison at market prices. In the special grade he may receive additional letters and visits, an increased tobacco ration, a daily paper instead of a weekly, and other privileges. Also after he reaches the special grade he has that most important privilege, admission to the "parole lines." The parole lines is the term used to designate a block of sixteen cabins lying in a garden outside the main prison walls. Each man on the parole line is given one of these cabins which opens upon a veranda, contains a bed-sitting room, a scullery-kitchen, and a water closet. The prisoners have their own latchkeys, a small gas stove, and a few cooking utensils in which they can prepare food purchased from the canteens or raised upon their allotment. After a certain hour these prisoners, like those in the cells, are obliged to be in their cabins, lights out. However, they have their meals separate from the rest and their own association room. They are less strictly super-vised than the others. Hence it is apparent that the parole lines provide an intermediate condition for those in the special grade between custody and discharge. It is intended as a preparation for return to ordinary life, something like Crof-ton's "intermediate stage."

On the other hand, the man reduced to the disciplinary grade for personal misconduct or because he is known to be exercising a bad influence upon others, really reverts to penal-servitude conditions. He is strictly under the silence rule from which the other grades are relieved. Many of his privileges are withdrawn.

I saw Camp Hill after I had just been through the old Park-hurst Prison. The two institutions adjoin each other. Park-hurst is down on the bottom of the hill, while Camp Hill oc-cupies a location at the top. There is no connection between the two, however. Parkhurst is one of the older prisons, and, as already indicated, has a conglomeration of various types of convicts. Camp Hill is the newest prison for convicts in England. Its cell blocks are small, each accommodating only a small number of men. The shops provide employment at various trades. In many respects the contrast between the two institutions is very great. Aside from the men who are working outside of the walls of Parkhurst, clearing land, doing some farming, and building officers' quarters, the régime inside, aside from the treatment given the old men in their special department, seems to be rather severe, although I understand very much less so than it was before the War. In Camp Hill, privileges are allowed not accorded to the convicts in any other prison. I asked the officer who took me about why this was, since these are supposed to be the most hardened criminals. He replied that the discipline had to be softened here to keep the men from revolting. Here they were hopelessly incarcerated for at least another five years and possibly ten years after they had served three years in penal servitude. What seems to an American a curious anomaly is that the most lenient treatment is given to the most hardened criminals.

Early in the history of Camp Hill under the leadership of a decidedly liberal governor the institution seemed to give better results in reformation than any of the other institutions. Hobhouse and Brockway, on the basis of reports up to 1919, showed that over fifty-three per cent had, on the whole been of good conduct after their discharge, while sixty-eight per cent had incurred no further conviction.[35] However, the reports of the Commissioners of Prisons and Directors of Convict Prisons in recent years indicate that the reformatory influence of Camp Hill upon the men incarcerated there is rather small. The chaplain in 1925-26 states that in only two instances had he noticed any effect of a reformative character.[36] In recent years regulations have been put into effect which prevent the issuing of tickets-of-leave, or parole, to men in Camp Hill, and, therefore, requiring them to spend more time in the institution than had been the case earlier. This modification of the practice was based upon a study of 402 discharges on licenses from Camp Hill from the opening of the institution in 1912 to June 1924. Of these 25 were discharged

[35] Hobhouse and Brockway, op. cit., p. 459.
[36] Report of the Commissioners of Prisons and the Directors of Convict Prisons, 1925–26, p. 55.

on license the second time, so that actually 377 men were discharged. The subsequent history of these men was as follows: No unsatisfactory report received of 127 men (however, 28 of these had died); unsatisfactory, but license not revoked, 3; unsatisfactory and license revoked, 49; reconvicted, 198. Of the 99 men living of whom no unsatisfactory report had been received, 57 had not been heard of since 1921; 52 of these were over forty-five years of age when released. Hence out of 377 only 42 were known to be living a satisfactory social life.[37] The Prison Commissioners, therefore, are rather pessimistic about the reformatory effects of preventive detention. They do, however, express the opinion that preventive detention protects society from these habitual criminals.[38]

Preventive detention differs from the indeterminate sentence in a number of respects. It comes only after penal servitude has been tried out and failed at least four times. It provides liberality of treatment after a man has undergone the repressive measures of penal servitude rather than before. It originated as a method whereby a man who is supposed to be an habitual and irreformable could be kept away from society for a longer period than the penal-servitude sentence permitted. It is a measure very much more like the sentence for habitual criminals in some of the states of the United States than like the indeterminate sentence to be found here. It is not as severe as the life sentence under the Baumes laws of New York after the fourth conviction for felony, or similar laws in a few other states. Its chief value, therefore, up to the present has been to preserve society from the depredations of men who have been convicted of serious crimes for at least four times. It is a movement toward the indefinite sentence, but is based upon quite a different theory.

Preventive detention has been imitated in a number of the British possessions and dominions, especially in the Orient. They are experimenting with it there, especially in Ceylon, but are not yet convinced of its efficiency. Whether preventive detention and the severe life sentences after the fourth con-

[37] *Ibid.*, 1923–24, p. 22.   [38] *Ibid.*, 1924–25, p. 54.

viction for felony in some of the United States serve any useful purpose aside from the protection of society is a question which cannot be answered on the basis of present experience. Whether the one of these is superior to the other must also await further study.

Humanizing Prison Life. Another adventure in the improvement of the English prison system is the attitude displayed by the Prison Commissioners through the officers of the various prisons toward the prisoners. Such severe critics of the Prison Commissioners as Hobhouse and Brockway had noticed this change of attitude in 1922.[39] In addition to the experiments described above, movements in the direction of showing a more humane attitude toward the prisoners, introduced by the Prison Commissioners and the prison officials, is the attempt to improve the educational work in the local prisons; increasing the numbers of lectures available to the men; the practice of holding occasional evening debates, which in 1922 and 1923 had been extended to more than half the local prisons; the introduction of concerts and good music given regularly in the local prisons, although limited to one a month in 1922 and 1923; the starting of clubs for educational and recreational purposes in the local prisons; the establishment of a league of honor among the prisoners at Nottingham and at Dorchester; the tendency to place more responsibility upon certain classes of prisoners; the introduction of men visitors in the local prisons in order to prepare the prisoner for discharge; the co-ordination of the work of the visitors, including the information they get about the man and his social circumstances, with the work of the aid societies for discharged prisoners; the introduction of new special classes for young men over twenty-one and under twenty-five, permission to shave at least two or three times a week and allowing men to have their own razors and shaving brushes sent in if they desire; provision for visits of relatives to a larger degree, and in the smaller prisons allowing these visits to take place in an ordinary room instead of in the old-fashioned visiting boxes; the

---

[39] Hobhouse and Brockway, *op. cit.*, p. 465.

condition of the clothing and cell furniture at some of the local prisons; allowing star and second division prisoners to dine together at one or two prisons; increasing the number of letters allowed; the development of honor parties besides the red band prisoners, who are trusted to work individually without supervision, one of which honor parties is to be seen in most of the local prisons; the introduction of a system of patrolling among the men rather than continuous supervision by stationing officers at points on raised platforms to watch the men, and thus placing more trust in the men themselves than under the old system; removing the officers from raised seats facing the prisoners in chapel and moving them to the back and sides of the prison chapel; increasing the hours of associated labor; the attempt to limit the work day of the associated prisoners to a minimum of eight hours, thus far introduced into a few of the local prisons; the attempt to establish at least one good or fairly good industry in every prison so as to abolish as much as possible the reproach of the small prisons where the sedentary work of sewing mail bags was for a long time the only regular form of employment besides the kitchen and the laundry; devising as rapidly as possible better forms of work to be performed in the cell—all of these are adventures which show the desire to mitigate the circumstances of life in the local prisons and to make them better fit the inmates for discharge.

In the convict prisons the officers received authority from the Secretary of State to suspend, as an experiment, the period of separate confinement which had hitherto been enforced at the beginning of every convict's sentence. Originally this separate confinement took place partly in the local prisons at the place of conviction before transfer and partly in the convict prisons after transfer. In 1922 and 1923 the Secretary of State authorized the prison commission to give up this preliminary separate confinement, to the advantage of the man's physical and mental health until such time as the necessary revision of the statutory rules could be obtained. At Camp Hill, the preventive detention institution, the "honor party" system was introduced in the early years of this decade and was further extended. The purpose of this system was to put the men at work without continuous supervision.[40] In 1923 and 1924, educational classes for adults were held in the evening in all save four of the local prisons. An educational adviser to the governor who organized and supervised the work had by that time been appointed in every local prison except Brixton, Ipswich, and Shepton Mallet.[41] By 1925–26, 9000 prisoners had attended these adult-educational classes.[42]

After-Care of Discharged Prisoners. Probably in no country in the world has as much attention been given to the after-care of discharged prisoners as in England. The work is done by private organizations or societies for discharged prisoners, with a central organization of all these societies that has the whole matter in charge. The government subsidizes these organizations in order to enable them to accomplish their work. In 1925–26 and for a number of years previous thereto the treasury gave a special grant of £1000 sterling which was carefully distributed to the various local discharged prisoners' aid societies, after consultation with the representatives of the central discharged prisoners' aid society. In addition, the local prison societies collected a total of £12,056 for this work. Admittedly this is quite insufficient for the needs of the work. These local aid societies in 1925–26 assisted 56 per cent of 40,568 convicted men who were discharged from prison. Of this 56 per cent, 30 per cent were suitably placed in employment. In addition, out of 1839 lads who were discharged during the year, 925 were placed at work. For those discharged from the Borstal institutions there is a special Borstal association to aid them upon their discharge. 567 lads and 56 girls were discharged in 1925–26 from these institutions to the care of the association. On the 31st of March, 1926, 347 of the boys and 30 of the girls had been at liberty for at least three months. The association had by that time placed 322 of the boys and 24 of the girls. In addition, at the end of the

---

[40] *Report of the Commissioners of Prisons and the Directors of Convict Prisons,* 1922–23, pp. 17–28.
[41] *Ibid.,* 1923–24, p. 17.   [42] *Ibid.,* 1925–26, pp. 220–21.

year the association still had under its supervision more than 500 boys and girls released during previous years. The commissioners seem to think that this work is very much worth while. They cite the fact that during the year 1923, 519 boys and 96 girls had been discharged to this association. At the end of two years of liberty, 65 per cent of the boys and 73 per cent of the girls had not again come in conflict with the law. The central association for the aid of discharged convicts takes charge of those discharged from the convict prisons. During the year 1925–26, 565 men were discharged from penal servitude to the care of the central association. Of this number, 374 were repeaters. Employment was found by the association for 190, substantial assistance was given in other ways to 272, and limited assistance to 43. No figures are provided showing the results of this work.[43]

I found attention given to this matter in a number of the English colonies and dominions. After-care work by private associations is also carried on in Japan to a limited extent. Nowhere, however, is this care found in like proportion as in England. Here is an adventure in the treatment of criminals which might well be followed by other countries. While we have discharged prisoners' associations under various names in several states of the United States, after-care in this country is not developed to any such extent as in England, nor are any such adequate provisions made as are made through the prison visitors to bring about close and intimate contact between the prisoner and the association, both before he is discharged and afterwards. The prison visitors provide a great deal of information that enables the societies to do their work in a very much better way than they could without such information.

Outdoor Work. One thing which strikes the visitor to English prisons is the very small amount of outdoor work provided for the inmates. A departmental committee in 1895 called attention to this matter, and Hobhouse and Brockway again in 1922 pointed out the value of outdoor work for cer-

---

[43] *Report of the Commissioners of Prisons and the Directors of Convict Prisons,* 1924–25, p. 26; *Ibid.,* 1925–26, p. 22.

tain classes of prisoners, and the very small extent to which outdoor work is used in the English prisons.   The prison commissioners of England do not have very much land on which to
experiment.   However, in 1924–25 and again in 1925–26 a
small party of long-term prisoners from Maidstone was sent to
Camp Hill, the site of the preventive detention prison, to clear
a forest and do other outdoor work.   The commissioners report very favorable results on the men's health and general
welfare.   The prison authorities look upon this extension of
outdoor work as an experiment and hope to be able to increase
the amount.[44]   The extent to which outdoor work, moreover,
is practiced in the English prisons, both local and convict, is
very small as compared with the amount found in the United
States, in India, and in the Philippines.   Up to date, the English prisons have been largely industrial prisons.   Some of the
inmates, however, complain that the sedentary occupations
which they follow in the English prisons unfit them for hard
outdoor work.   It would seem that prison farms are not impossible in connection with the English prisons.

Collecting Centers for Prisoners about to be Discharged.
In the endeavor to segregate young prisoners, more and more
the prison authorities have provided that certain of the local
prisons shall serve as collecting centers for the young prisoners.   In 1925–26 there were five of these institutions, one
each at Bedford, Bristol, Durham, Liverpool, and Wandsworth.
These institutions are used for collecting the young men from
the prisons from which they are about to be discharged in order
that the prisoners' aid societies may have access to each one
before he goes out, and thus be able to deal with them more
effectively.[45]

Borstal Institutions.   Borstal institutions in England were
established in 1909 to serve as intermediate institutions between
the juvenile reformatories and the prisons.   They were recommended by the departmental committee of 1895, but the first

[44] *Report of the Commissioners of Prisons and the Directors of Convict Prisons,*
1925–26, p. 22.
[45] *Ibid.,* 1925–26, p. 23.

unit was not opened until 1909, when the old Borstal prison was taken over and transformed into an institution for young offenders between the ages of sixteen and twenty-one. In the course of the experiment, the original Borstal institution was over-crowded. Hence two other institutions for boys, one at Feltham and the other at Portland, have been turned into institutions for Borstal boys, while the old prison at Aylesbury and the women's inebriate institution at the same place were taken over as the Borstal Institution for Girls.[46] The Portland institution is an old convict prison made over, and the one at Feltham is a former industrial school.

This experiment differs somewhat from our American reformatories both for juveniles and for adults in that it includes individuals only between the ages of sixteen and twenty-one. Furthermore, instead of being committed on an indefinite sentence, as they are in our adult reformatories and until twenty-one in our juvenile reformatories, boys sent to Borstal institutions are sent for a maximum of three years and a minimum of two. However, it is provided that after six months of Borstal under certain conditions the inmates may be licensed to freedom under the care of the Borstal Association, which provides after-care for all those on license and all those discharged from the institution. If they are on license they are under supervision to the Borstal Association for one year beyond the three-year sentence.

The classification system worked out in the prisons is applied even with greater care in the Borstal institutions. For the boys at least there are what might be called seven grades. However, within the institution itself there are five. When a boy is sentenced to Borstal, he goes into the reception prison for Borstal boys at Wandsworth Prison in London, as I have described above. There after careful examination as to his mental and physical condition, his social history, etc., he is sent to the Borstal institution which is best suited to his needs. When he enters the Borstal institution, he enters into the first, or ordinary stage. Here he stays three months or longer if

[46] Hobhouse and Brockway, *op. cit.*, pp. 410–435.

his conduct does not warrant promotion. Then he goes into the second grade again for three months, and so on in each case. The fourth grade is called the probation grade. Here he is given much liberty. At the top there is a special grade where even greater liberty is allowed. If he goes out on license and does not do well he is returned not to the Borstal institution from which he came, but to Wormwood Scrubs, which has a special department for boys that have failed on parole.

When I visited the institution at Borstal I found that the old prison buildings had been entirely replaced by modern buildings. To be sure there is still a wall around the institution, and the boy is met at the gate by a warder. However, there are four different homes or cottages, each holding about 100 boys, with a house father and a matron. Each house is divided into eight sections, with a monitor, a senior boy, at the head of each. A good deal of self-government has been introduced here. In one of the cottages there are dormitories for sleeping, each of the sections having a partitioned-off space to themselves. In the other homes each boy has his own cell. These look more like prisons. The present governor believes in the mixture of private cells and dormitories.

Moreover, the present administration has endeavored to introduce competition in games, in standings, in condition of cells and sections, between the sections in the same house and also between the different houses.

Each boy works eight hours and attends classes two hours in the evening. Besides this there is time for recreation, dramatics, athletic matches, etc. Cups are offered in these contests for which the different groups work.

In addition to these homes, there are industrial shops for production and training. All the work is productive, but such trades are chosen as will be useful on the outside. Carefully selected instructors are employed, some of them Oxford and Cambridge men.

There are about 400 boys in this institution at Borstal. They do all their own building and practically all the repair work about the institution. By good conduct a boy can get out in fifteen months and is then placed by the Borstal Association.

The spirit of the place seemed to me to be good. The governor makes a good impression. He says he is frankly interested in making better boys. However, he admits failure in some cases. He is an educator and not a mere prison man. He says that morals are taught by example and attitudes rather than by formal teaching.

In connection with the institution, there is a 300 acre farm of poor chalk soil. The farming operations, however, are on a small scale. There are only 6 horses, 14 cows, some pigs, sheep, and chickens. The present governor believes that the wall around the institution is unnecessary.

There are some punishment cells in Borstal, but they are seldom used. The punishment workshop is used instead where the few boys who need punishment break stone. Each punishment cell in the workshop is open to the outer air, but there are walls dividing it from the next one and in this open cell a boy being punished is put to work breaking stone in an iron pot set into the ground, with an iron stomper or crusher. It is hard work and uninteresting.

Frankly the Borstal institutions are an experiment in which changes are being made which are believed to be improvements on the basis of experience in the past. One of the difficulties felt in connection with the institutions is the lack of proper industrial work.

In connection with the institution, the attempt is made to introduce self-control. Those in the special grade, for example, are given great liberty after they have taken a solemn promise to the governor to control themselves. In 1925–26, 24 of the lads in the special grade were allowed to attend the Municipal Technical School in the evening. Groups of the higher grade boys go out for long walks with a leader and seldom make use of their opportunities to escape. For a number of years now large groups have been sent from the several Borstal institutions to camp. In 1925, 82 went from Borstal, 105 from Feltham, 131 from Portland, and 14 girls from

Aylesbury.   These constituted the special grade in each institution.   The camps are very successful.   The expense for
holding these camps was contributed by private individuals.

Recently in Portland at least the old method of segregating
the ordinary grade and the intermediate A has been given up
and instead the newcomer has been plunged straight into the
life of the house.   The experiment seems to be promising.

Again at Portland a feature of the educational course has
been the establishment of a discharge class into which were put
all the boys who were within two months of the time of leaving.[47]   The evaluation of this important experiment will be
given later.

Education.   In recent years in the English prisons the adventure has been made of trying to educate the inmates.
Great numbers of them are poorly educated and some of
them are quite illiterate.

The present elementary educational system is conducted by
a mixed system of teachers.   Twenty-three officers of the
prison service employed in clerical work within the prisons
are teaching the younger prisoners and illiterates for a few hours
each week.   In addition, a number of paid certificated teachers
are teaching English classes.   In 1925–26 there were 12 of these.

In these cases the inspectors of the Board of Education visit
and report on their work.   The first class of teachers is made
up of volunteers who are giving their assistance without pay.
In 1925–26 there were 58 of these.

In that year not everyone in the prison was permitted to take
these classes.   Generally speaking, a sentence of three months
was regarded as a minimum for anyone who was permitted to
attend these elementary educational classes.

Adult education classes are also held in the prisons.   In
recent years the numbers in the classes have increased.   In
1925–26, 9000 individual prisoners attended these classes.
To the governors of the local prisons prominent educators are

---

[47] *Report of the Commissioners of Prisons and the Directors of Convict Prisons,*
1925–26, p. 53.   See also Hobhouse and Brockway, *op. cit.,* Chapter xxvi, and
Brockway, *A New Way with Crime,* Chapter viii.

attached as educational advisers. For the third time in January 1926 the educational advisers and the teachers at the local prisons held an annual meeting at the Home Office where the problems of education in the prisons were discussed. Whatever may be the value of these educational experiments, there is no question that the prison commissioners have been endeavoring to introduce and expand educational classes within the prison.[48] The development of educational work in certain of the prisons at least seem to have shown good results. Some of the after-care workers have noticed the improvement since educational measures have been introduced. One is reported as saying that the men have been more responsive and easier to deal with on discharge than any body of ex-prisoners in his experience. He adds, "I believe the educational program is largely responsible for the difference in the mentality of the men on discharge."[49]

Prison Visiting. Incidental reference has been made to an adventure which is altogether alien to our American prisons. A system of visitors has been organized at the local prisons which has the greatest significance. Volunteers from outside the prisons, from Rotary Clubs and such other organizations, are secured each to pay regular visits to ten or twelve different prisoners in the institution. This was introduced as an experiment at only certain prisons at first, but has proved to be so helpful that all the local prisons now have their bodies of visitors. In 1925–26 there were a total of 578 of these visitors to the local prisons, 465 men and 113 women. The authorities state that the work of preparing the prisoner for discharge ought to be commenced on the day when he enters. These visitors collect information about him, his prospects, and his home circumstances. No one is so well qualified as these visitors to supply these particulars to the aid societies, who handle the men on discharge. As the result of this close interrelation between the visitors and the discharged prisoners' aid

---

[48] *Report of the Commissioners of Prisons and the Directors of Convict Prisons,* 1925–26, pp. 19, 20.
[49] *Ibid.,* p. 49.

societies, the prison commissioners have brought it to pass that these visitors are often members of the executive committee of the aid society at the local prison.

Not only is the prison visitor of enormous importance to the aid society, but through him the prisoner who has been shut away from society is made conscious of the fact that society has not forgotten him. From the outside there regularly comes to see him a person who is interested in him. As says one of the reports, "A most powerful and lasting impression is made on a prisoner's mind by the fact, which he often realizes only slowly and after a preliminary period of suspicion, that society, which he has hitherto looked upon as hard and hostile, actually contains people who give up their time and take much trouble to come to the prison to befriend and assist him, without being paid." [50]

This is an adventure in human relationship which deserves a serious watching by prison authorities in every country. In the past, prisons have taken the attitude that almost every tie which binds a man to society on the outside should be broken. Perhaps that is true with reference to the social ties to which he has been accustomed, especially the habitual criminal. Here, however, is an attempt to introduce members of society who represent altogether different ideals and attitudes; this system attempts to build up ties of personal association between the outside and the inside of the prison which will be constructive and helpful.

The Growing Reformatory Purposes of Punishment. Remember that the original purpose of imprisonment was punishment. A man had committed so much injury and therefore he must pay for it with so much pain, pain induced by the deprivation of liberty and privileges, by hard work and other repressive measures. Gradually, however, as one reads the reports of the prison commissioners, he can see growing the emphasis upon the reformatory purpose of punishment. Again and again the commissioners emphasize that in the local

[50] *Report of the Commissioners of Prisons and the Directors of Convict Prisons,* 1922–23, p. 22; *Ibid.*, 1923–24, p. 19; *Ibid.*, 1924–25, p. 19; *Ibid.*, 1925–26, p. 20.

prisons at least as well as in the Borstal institutions the purpose is for the reformation of the criminal so that when he goes out he will be a law-abiding member of society. True, the commissioners have not always adjusted the treatment of the prisoners to this end. Nevertheless, it is hopeful that the authorities take that point of view, for that is the ideal toward which they strive. There is no question that in time they will come to see the inconsistency between the ideal and the measures often taken to deal with the men and will make the latter conform to the former. Many of these changes which have been introduced into the English prisons, even the local prisons and the convict prisons as well as those for the young and first offenders, stress this point. The difficulty recognized by the prison commissioners is the presence of short-term inmates upon whom educational and even personal influence counts for little.[51]

English Prison and Judicial Statistics. To a student of criminal statistics in the United States, the collection and publication of statistics in England seem almost marvellous. They are not as extensive as before the War, probably due to the expense of printing. Nevertheless they provide means of judging of the efficiency of the system and the trend of affairs much more accurately than any of our criminal statistics in the United States.

Psychiatric Service. In recent years England has also introduced the practice of mental examination of criminals. It is not universal and depends upon the intelligence of the court. It is pointed out by the medical officials of the prison and by the commission that the majority of courts adopt this practice of mental examination in *prima facie* cases. They do this by remanding prisoners to prison for observation and report. It is purely in the experimental stage, and the work it places upon the prison officials, especially the medical officers, is very great. The medical member of the prison commissioners states that a medical examination of all prisoners before adjudication of their cases is impossible, as large numbers are not

[51] *Ibid.,* 1925–26, p. 17.

remanded to prison at all by the judges, but all of those who are remanded or committed for trial, whether the report is asked for or not, have their mental state investigated. Moreover, in the prisons it is the practice of this official that prisoners charged with certain offenses which experience has shown may be associated with diseased mentality, are placed under observation for mental investigation. Furthermore, as intimated before, the prison commissioners have appointed certain of the prisons as the center for uncertifiable mental cases. That is not ideal because special institutions for these cases are needed, nevertheless it means a great advance.

Recently also the prison medical officers have been intelligently applying the Mental Deficiency Act of 1913 to the inmates of their institutions or those remanded for investigation. This has resulted in a permanent diminution of the prison population estimated by the Medical Commissioner as possibly 200 daily. Consequently the certifiably feeble-minded are being drained out of the English prisons into institutions for that particular class of care. The Medical Commissioner suggests that a logical extension of a similar measure to those persons who are to some degree unbalanced or feeble-minded though not certifiable under the lunacy or mental deficiency acts, either by some form of indeterminate sentence or permanent segregation in some form of special institution or farm colony, would in his opinion lead to the elimination from the unsuitable environment of the prison a large part of the weak-minded and habitual petty offenders.[52]

THE EVALUATION OF THESE EXPERIMENTS

Contrasted with the condition in the United States, England's present prison system has since 1877 been a unified system. This is possible in England, as it is not possible with forty-eight states, each controlling its own prison system, in the United States. This experiment, however, has now gone on long enough to show the advantages of a unified system. The local jails are a part of the prison system. Each performs

[52] *Ibid.*, 1925–26, pp. 32, 33.

a certain function in the whole scheme. It enables classification of prisoners by institutions to a certain extent, and thus enables one more step to be taken toward the individual treatment of the prisoners.

In the United States, however, most of our states have not unified their own prison scheme. Most of the jails are county institutions or city institutions with only very limited supervision by state boards and with practically no functionalization of the jails at the hands of the state authorities. England has here made an experiment which may be studied with a good deal of profit by the American commonwealths.

Not only has England unified her prison system, but she has taken them out of politics. The Commissioners of Prisons and the Directors of Convict Prisons are parts of the great English civil service system. True, they are under the Home Secretary's office. He changes with every change in the cabinet. The Commissioners, however, are appointed for life and thus provide continuity of policy not possible where a board changes with every change in the political administration of the state. In some of the United States the problem of taking the prisons out of politics has been solved in another way, but on the whole we cannot say that it has been as successful as has the English civil service system. In most of our states the governor has a good deal to do with the appointment of the board which has charge of the prisons. Furthermore, the officers of the prisons in England are also a part of the great civil service system. In contrast to the situation frequently to be found in our states, they are not disturbed at the fall of any British cabinet.

England's prison industries constitute one of the weakest points in her system. She has experimented here less than almost any other country. Her labor unions are strong and they have forbidden contract labor long ago. The prisons were limited to providing articles for the state and had to resort principally to the making of mail bags. As a result, her prison labor neither pays from the financial point of view, nor does it teach men a trade which they may follow after they go out.

Her system of discipline seems to be one of rather severe repression.   In spite of the experiments in softening the discipline, in providing debates, concerts, etc., for those in the upper grades, in spite of the reduction of the probationary period of solitary confinement, England's prison system has suffered from the tradition of the old separate system with which she started out.   Here the United States, by following the Auburn plan in most of our prisons, has not had to break away from a theory and a tradition which in England gave form to the very structure of the prison buildings and fastened itself for a long period of time upon the attitude of mind of the prison commissioners and the prison officials.   The silent system is no more rigidly carried out there than it is in many prisons in this country.   Nevertheless, dining in association is a new innovaton, and working in association is a special prvilege in many of the English prisons.

England's minute classification, both within each prison and as between prisons, is perhaps one of her most outstanding experiments.   Here she has set the pace for the world.   While it is not an entire success, enough favorable progress has been made to indicate that the plan is sound and should be carried out as rapidly as possible to its logical conclusion.   Classification in our American prisons would solve many difficulties.   If in any of our state prisons the prisoners difficult to handle could be separated from the mass of prisoners, and put in a separate institution, discipline could be very much relaxed for those who give no trouble.   The rule of silence could easily be dispensed with, greater privileges could be accorded to those who are not troublesome, and whatever stern repressive measures are necessary would not be visited upon the difficult and the easy to handle alike, but only upon the trouble-makers.

Furthermore, our American prisons could well learn the advantages of having more numerous institutions with smaller numbers in each.   Even with her numerous prisons, the present prison commissioners and some of the officers feel that the numbers in the English prisons are too large.   They are of the opinion that not more than 300 men should be in any one institution. Some of our Southern states with their prison farms have already learned that lesson. For example, in Mississippi, with their dozen or more camps on a great area of land, they are able to classify prisoners somewhat and to reduce the number under the control of any one set of officers.

Like many other modern states, England has at last recognized the insane criminal, and the criminal having a mental defect so serious that under the law it is certifiable. These men are moved to institutions for the insane and for the mental defectives. However, her definitions of insanity and of mental defects are much behind the finding of her prison officials. The presence in the prisons of many uncertifiable insane and mental defectives creates a problem for the prison management. She has an institution for the certifiable insane at Broadmoor and for her certifiable feeble-minded at Rampton.[53] In every report, however, the officials complain of the large number of uncertifiable insane in the institutions, and urge a modification of the law with respect to certifiability.

England's Borstal system for young offenders between sixteen and twenty-one seems to mark a decided advance over that of most other countries in the treatment of this class of young offenders. In spite of the fact that a number of her Borstal institutions are old prisons, and therefore not adequately adapted to their purpose, the adventures made recently in dividing the inmates of each institution into small numbers, each with its own house, and organizing them into social groups that are more or less self-governing, is decidedly promising.

England's system of after-care is a subsidized private system. The various private associations for discharged prisoners connected with each local prison and also the central association for the convict prisons have made a record of which all the world can well take account. It is a question, of course, whether the state itself should not provide this after-care in a regularly organized unit of service provided for under the law.

[53] *Report of the Commissioners of Prisons and the Directors of Convict Prisons, 1924–25, p. 15.*

However, the present step is an intermediate experimental one which has shown the importance of looking after the prisoner after he is discharged at the gate. No society has discharged its full responsibility to a man whom it has incarcerated in a prison unless it takes some responsibility for his care on discharge.

Likewise, the organization of visitors who make it a practice to enter the prisons and confer with the inmates keeps intact the social bond with the outside world which theoretically is very desirable. The usefulness of the information which these visitors obtain by conferences with the boys and girls to get acquainted with their family history and the social circumstances which led them to crime, are beginnings of what is done in some of the courts in the various states of this country. The question arises as to whether it should not be extended and be a regular part of the court's function.

England borrowed the probation system from the United States. Almost every report of the prison commissioners has something in it criticising the present probation system. It is not sufficiently officered to make it adequate. There, as here, what is needed is to develop the system so that the probation officers need not carry too large a load and to improve their quality.

As one looks at the statistics of the English prison population and notices the steady decrease that has taken place in the last twenty-five years, the question naturally arises as to whether the English prison system or something else accounts for this decrease. It is perhaps the most outstanding country, in the decrease of its prison population, in the world. Doubtless her system of criminal procedure has something to do with the matter, the nature of her population perhaps more; but even so, one might not be beside the mark in suggesting that the English prison system has something to do with the whole question. The fact that comes out in the statistics in the reports of the prison commissioners shows that there is a very large number of men who are not improved by their prison experience. That is true of all countries. Recidivism is a very striking and stubborn fact which must not be overlooked. It constitutes a challenge to the present methods of handling criminals which has not yet been fully solved. Whether it is the prison system that is lacking here, or whether it is the whole social situation in society which drives men back again and again to the prison, is a question which cannot be answered without more adequate study.

On the whole, one comes away from studying the English prison system with the feeling that, with all of its drawbacks, it represents one of the great adventures of the modern world in the treatment of men who have not shown themselves to be amenable to the ordinary methods of social control. Many more steps must be taken, both inside the prison and without, before the problem of handling the poorly adapted individual is solved so as to readjust him to the social conditions under which man must live, in order that he may be a useful member of society.

BIBLIOGRAPHY

B–2–15, *Amon the Broad Arrow Men,* London, 1924.

Brockway, *A New Way With Crime,* London, 1928.

Devon, *The Criminal and the Community,* London, 1911.

Gillin, *Criminology and Penology,* New York, 1926, pp. 408–413.

Hobhouse, *An English Prison from Within,* London, 1919.

Hobhouse and Brockway, *English Prisons Today,* London, 1919.

Reports of the Commissioners of Prisons and the Directors of Convict Prisons issued annually.

Ruggles-Brice, *The English Prison System,* London, 1921.

Topping, *Canadian Penal Institutions,* Toronto, 1929. (For the Canadian Penal System.)

CHAPTER IX

SOME SOUTHERN PRISON SYSTEMS IN THE UNITED STATES

COMPARE these experiments in foreign lands with the situation in the United States. Even here with long-established prison systems more or less rigidly fixed in their main features, new adventures have been made. Especially in the Southern states has experimentation in outdoor work gone forward. The negro element in the general population of these states, together with the established mores of the relationships between the whites and blacks, has made the problem of handling the prisoner more complex than in the North. On the other hand, the belated industrialization of the South simplifies the problem somewhat. Only recently has the organized criminal gang appeared there. The professional criminal has not until lately found the South a fertile field. Until the opening of the twentieth century the Southern criminal was predominately black and by occupation a farmer. Now, however, with the growth of cities, the development of manufacturing and the increase of wealth, more whites are being sent to prison, and the professional criminal and the gangster are troubling the people of the Southern states. Somewhat isolated from the rest of the country, a number of Southern states have struck out on lines somewhat different from those followed by the Northern and Western states. These experiments are not without interest, especially in connection with the adventures of foreign countries just described.

For comparative purposes, the most outstanding feature of the Southern prison systems in the United States is the outdoor work for prisoners on farms. Only less extraordinary as penological experiments, are the various systems used in the South for working prisoners on the roads. There are other features of the Southern prison systems which might be discussed if we were endeavoring to give a comprehensive presentation of the Southern prison systems. We are only discussing new experiments.

How did the prison farm arise in the Southern states? Before the Civil War the American prison system had not penetrated to any considerable extent to the South. The historic methods of punishment of white men prevailed there for a longer time than in the North. Hanging, fines, and commitment to the county jail took care of most of the white prisoners who violated the criminal code. Since in the black belt of the South the dominant white class was a minority, and economic and social conditions were simple, based largely upon the plantation system of agriculture, there was not the same need for a state prison as in the North. The number of white criminals was small, while the negro delinquents were cared for under the slave system. However, following the Civil War, with the slaves freed from their former masters, an entirely different problem arose. The first attempt to solve the problem of the punishment of the free negro who had fallen into the hands of the criminal law was the now infamous lease system. Negro criminals upon conviction were leased to railroads, turpentine camps, and similar activities at so much per head, thus relieving the public authorities of the actual care of these delinquents.[1]

Abuses so flagrant arose out of the lease system that they finally excited the attention of Southern law-makers and led to the abolition of this system of caring for the delinquent by the state. As a consequence the lease system in the Southern states had to be supplanted by some other method of caring for these prisoners. Since land in the South is cheap and most of the delinquents came from the plantations and farms, and since

---

[1] McKelway, "Three Prison Systems of the Southern States of America," in Henderson, *Penal and Reformatory Institutions*, New York, 1910, pp. 68–88; Heller, "Development of the System of Convict Labor in the United States," *Journal of Criminal Law and Criminology*, July, 1914, pp. 241–269.

the climate of the South is favorable to work upon the land all the year round, it was natural that the Southern states, instead of building great industrial institutions, should experiment with prison farms and with road camps, the latter especially, since the wide use of the automobile created a demand for good roads.

With the abolition of the lease system by law in a number of the Southern states the development of prison farms and of road work was rapid.[2]

PRISON FARMS IN THREE SOUTHERN STATES

While the development of prison farms has not been confined to the South, the widest use of farms for the care of prisoners has developed there. Other states than the three which will be discussed have prison farms both North and South. Of thirty-three Northern states from which reports have been received, seven only do not have farms or gardens. These thirty-three Northern states have farms amounting to 37,682 acres. In the prisons of these states in 1925 were incarcerated 34,100 prisoners. Of this number, however, only 2239 worked on the farms. Thus there was an average of seventeen acres provided for each man working on them. Only 6 2/3 per cent of the inmates of these prisons of the thirty-three states worked on the farms.[3]

On the other hand, in the three Southern states of Mississippi, Alabama, and Florida, the number of acres in prison farms and the percentage of the prisoners employed on the farms were as follows:

		Acres	Prisoners on Farms	
(1926)	Alabama	10,450	450	(Recently added a large farm near Mobile)
(1928)	Florida	18,000	800(?)	
(1929)	Mississippi	28,910	2,000(?)	1700 at Parchman

[2] For Mississippi, see Governor Noel's Message, 1913, in *Prison Labor in Governors' Messages*, Prison Labor Leaflet No. 8, National Committee on Prison Labor, New York, 1913, p. 36; for Florida, see Governor Trammel's, *Ibid.*, pp. 17 and 18.

[3] *Handbook of American Prisons*, 1926, National Society of Penal Information, New York, 1926. The above data were taken from various parts of this report.

From these statements it is clear that a much larger proportion of the prisoners in the Southern institutions work on the farms than in the Northern states, and that the acreage to each prisoner is larger except in Mississippi.

A number of the other Southern states lay emphasis also on farms for prisoners. Among them are North Carolina, Georgia, Texas, Louisiana, and Arkansas. The importance of farm work varies from state to state, and the number of prisoners employed upon the farms, as compared with those engaged in other industries, likewise varies. In general, however, I think it can be said that a larger proportion of the prisoners in the Southern states are engaged in farm work than in the Northern states. Fewer industries are used for the employment of prisoners in the South than in the North.

The Southern states also emphasize road building and maintenance for state convicts. The use of state prisoners upon the roads grew out of the precedent of their use by the counties on the building and maintenance of county roads by county prisoners. Such has been the practice in a great many Southern states for a long time. Generally with these two forms of outdoor work for convicts, it is safe to say that the majority of the convicts in the Southern states are engaged either in farming or road work.

CHARACTERISTIC FEATURES OF THREE SOUTHERN PRISON SYSTEMS

In order that a concrete picture of the activities of Southern prisons may be presented I have chosen those of Mississippi, Florida, and Alabama, first because of their extensive use of outdoor work for convicts, and second because of their differing features. While states can be found which have slightly different features from any of these three, I think it can be said that the prison systems of these three states typify the prison systems of the South. Each has features differing from each of the others; collectively they have those features which may be considered as experiments to be found in the various parts of the South.

Prisoners Picking Cotton

STATE PRISON FARM, PARCHMAN, MISSISSIPPI

One of the Fourteen Camps

Prisoners at Work

STATE PRISON FARM, PARCHMAN, MISSISSIPPI

Mississippi. In Mississippi practically all prisoners are engaged in farming. The only industries other than farming are a lime plant and a sawmill. However, it should be said that on Mississippi's prison farms are blacksmith shops and machine shops where necessary repair work can be carried out. In other words, practically all of the industries in Mississippi in connection with the prison farms are supplementary to the process of farming except the lime plant and the sawmill.

The main body of the farm land used for the prisoners is at Parchman. Here are 16,000 acres in one body. Another smaller farm is located at Lambert near Parchman, there is one at O'Keefe, and also one at Oakley. There have been other farms in the past scattered about the state. These have either been sold or have been taken over by other departments of the state. A recent superintendent recommended that all others except that at Parchman be disposed of and that further land be bought adjoining the land at Parchman to provide for all the state prisoners at this one place. This recommendation was made in the interest of economy of time and effort.[4]

The large farm at Parchman is known as the Sunflower Farm. The 16,000 acres in this farm are divided into twelve camps for men and one for women. In addition, there is a hospital on this land to care for all the prisoners from all the state farms. Each camp is allotted a certain number of acres of land, has its own buildings either of frame or of brick construction for the housing of the prisoners, farm animals, etc. Each camp is a separate unit with a sergeant in command subject only to the superintendent of the penitentiary and the supervision of the Board of Trustees. The buildings which house the convicts in each camp are called cages. They are long, one-story buildings, sometimes with a basement, divided usually into two parts, one for the prisoners who are not trusties, and the other for the trusties. The large number of camps on this area of land enables the superintendent to provide some

---

[4] *Biennial Report of the Board of Trustees, Superintendents, and Other Officers of the Mississippi State Penitentiary from July 1, 1925, to June 30, 1927, p. 27.*

sort of classification among the prisoners, although I saw no evidence when there that very much attention is paid to that. Primarily the purpose seems to be to provide a small enough economic unit to work most effectively and to supply comparison between the different camps in economic productivity. Without question this is a very superior arrangement to that found in most of the prison farms of the South. There is no reason why this provision for numerous camps might not be utilized much more than it is for the classification of different sorts of prisoners such as we find in New York state and especially in England and France. If the old principle of segregation of hardened criminals from new offenders is important, then here is an opportunity to carry it out in the prison farm. A financial account is kept of the productivity and expenses of each of these camps.

The women's camp is separate from the men's and has attached to it land enough to provide opportunity for the cultivation of gardens. The women also make clothes for the institution. When I was there in the summer of 1929 all but one of the women were black.

The hospital is a substantial one-story brick building with separate wards for the white and colored men, and a separate ward for colored women. The hospital is used also as a receiving station for the institution where all incoming inmates are given a physical examination, the Bertillon measurements, and have their finger prints taken. Complaint is made that the hospital is too small for present needs. While there are physicians at the other farms, any one in need of hospital care is brought to Parchman. The work is done about the institution by the convicts. A doctor and a dentist are constantly on duty.

All the camps except the hospital have barbed-wire fences about them with guards stationed at opposite corners.

A peculiar feature of the Mississippi prisons is that the guarding of the convicts is done by trusty prisoners.* When a gang

---

* To some extent this same system is employed in Florida. See Garrett and MacCormick, *Handbook of American Prisons and Reformatories,* 1929, p. 226.

goes to the field to work the man who holds the gun over them is a trusty. The driver who oversees the gang in the field is a free white man but has no gun. This feature has been severely criticised by members of the American Prison Association and others. The prison officials believe it is a good plan and saves the state a great deal of money. To my question as to what was the effect upon the other prisoners of having a fellow prisoner guard them with a gun, the reply was "Good." There is no parole system in Mississippi. Therefore the only chance of a man getting out before the expiration of his time is a commutation of sentence or a pardon by the governor. Hence as an incentive to these trusties to do their duty if a prisoner under their guard attempts to escape, the trusty is given a commutation or a pardon if he shoots the prisoner when he tries to get away. The officers hold that the trusty guard is not likely to abuse this opportunity, because if he did he would be demoted from a trusty to the ranks, lose his privileges, and the chance of getting out before the expiration of his sentence. Furthermore, he is not allowed to shoot until the escaping prisoner is seventy-five yards away. The opposition party in the legislature of Mississippi, however, has taken up the cudgels for free guards as against this trusty system. The probabilities are that in the course of time a law may be put through forbidding the use of prisoners as guards. The officials are in favor of the present system, although they are not opposing the movement to supersede it by free guards. The whole question is mixed up in politics and probably will not be decided upon its merits. One would have to be at the institution very much longer than I was to observe this experiment in order to arrive at a sound conclusion as to the merits or demerits of the system. Since about a third of the prisoners are lifers and since there is no parole system, it is apparent that a larger proportion of the prisoners in this prison might be of a hopeless and desperate frame of mind than would be the case in the North where a lesser proportion are in for life, and where there is a chance, by good behavior, to secure earlier release.

Of the twelve camps for men on this Parchman farm, two

are for white and the rest are for colored. White camps, however, are run on the same system as the others. The guards are trusties and the drivers in the fields are free men.

The king pin, of course, in this system is the character of the sergeant in charge of each camp. I became well acquainted with only two of these, and they impressed me as high-class men.

A special feature which the system in Mississippi provides is the segregation on the farm at Oakley of all white prisoners under twenty-three years of age. This farm consists of 2700 acres, having, when I was there, September 2, 1929, 77 boys. The cage or dormitory is a wooden building separated into two compartments, one for the trusties and the other for those who cannot be trusted. At the back of the cage is the dining room and back of that the kitchen. The day I was there they had for their noon meal beans with a chunk of fat pork, corn bread, and buttermilk. They may have had butter, but I saw none although I was told they had butter all the time.

At Oakley the fence around the buildings is not of such a formidable nature as those around the buildings at Parchman. There were four guardhouses with a guard in each about the buildings, say at a distance of ten rods. It was told that most of these boys have come from the industrial School. This statement, however, I did not check up. At Oakley, as at the other farms, the length of the working day varies with the season. During the summer they rise at four A.M., and work until eleven or eleven-thirty. Then they have three hours of rest at noon. After that they work until dark.

While at Parchman great emphasis is placed upon the raising of cotton, at Oakley there were only 50 acres in cotton and 500 in corn. This difference is due to the difference in the character of the land. They also raise sufficient sorghum cane to provide their own molasses. The day I was there they were grinding and boiling sorghum cane. The sergeant in charge at the time I was there was a man educated in the agricultural college in Mississippi.

Mississippi still retains the strap as a means of punishment.

Under the law not more than fifteen strokes may be administered to a man in any one day and this must be only on the advice of the doctor. I was told by the officials that in actual practice usually not more than five strokes are necessary to produce the desired results. They also use loss of privileges and forfeiture of "good time," as methods of discipline.

Naturally the question arises as to whether this system pays. For the biennium, 1925 to 1927, the Mississippi penitentiary made a net profit of $229,973.94.[5]

With its curious mixture of antiquated methods and new experiments, the Mississippi penitentiary provides food for thoughtful consideration on: (1) The possibility of taking care of all prisoners without the expense of incarcerating them in vast walls of stone; (2) by working them at outdoor work where they get sunlight and fresh air, instead of in shops and factories; (3) in scattering the prisoners around in numerous units providing opportunity for classification of the inmates; (4) by making such arrangements through the competition of these separate camps that the economic efficiency of each of the sergeants is made apparent by easy comparison; (5) in making the prison pay not only its own expenses but a return to the treasury on the investment of the state's money.

There is no question that escapes are more frequent from such an institution than from a high-walled, closely guarded institution. However, it is astonishing how low is the number of escapes, considering the fact that these men work in gangs in the field of from twelve to thirty with only one gun over them. It is probable that the freer life, the less strenuous discipline, and fairly decent conditions under which they exist lessen very much the incitement to escape. Certainly the health conditions in Mississippi are very much superior to those of institutions where the prisoners are more closely confined.

On the other hand, there are many features in the Mississippi prison which raise questions. There are no separate cells, the prisoners are housed in dormitories, the only segregation being

[5] *Biennial Report of the Board of Trustees, Superintendents, and Other Officers of the Mississippi State Penitentiary, July 1, 1925, to June 30, 1927,* pp. 24, 25.

that of the trusties from the non-trusties. Whipping which has been abolished in most of the Southern prisons, is still permitted. The officials here replied to me in much the same terms concerning the use of the strap as did the officials of Egypt and the Philippines concerning the use of leg irons.

Their argument is that one must take into consideration the psychology of the negro in considering the effects of a whipping. "But," I asked, "do you not also strap the white men?" They admitted that occasionally they did so, but less frequently.

There is no wage paid to any of these men. They have obsolutely no means of earning money either for themselves or for their families. It would seem, in view of the amount of money which is turned back into the treasury as profit from the institution, that some provision might be made to pay them a slight wage. However, an official objected to my suggestion concerning this with the statement that if they paid wages to these negroes, or rather to their families, many a negro woman who was the wife of a worthless negro would scheme to get him into prison, for only thus could she ever get any money from him. I am not sure, however, that the situation would be worse than it is under the present arrangement. Furthermore, the argument would have less cogency if a parole or after-care system was provided whereby these men on release could be made to work.

Florida. The prison system of Florida differs from that of Mississippi and Alabama in a number of respects. It differs from that of Mississippi in that the land of the state farm, with the exception of that attached to the dairy, is all in one body. In this farm are 18,000 acres. Four thousand of it are under cultivation. Fifteen thousand of the 18,000 acres are fenced. In 1928 on this farm were 1,000 head of Jersey, Angus, and grade cattle, 700 head of Poland China and grade hogs, 6500 laying hens, 100 head of horses and mules. In that year 6500 bushels of corn were gathered in cribs; 7200 bales of hay were put up; 12,000 bushels of sweet potatoes were raised; 7500 crates of vegetables were sold; 200 barrels of 35 gallons each of syrup was made; 2 silos each containing 180 tons were filled; 550 hogs were butchered.

Prisoners upon admission to the state prison, or state farm, are examined by the physician, their records taken, and then on the basis of the physician's examination they are divided into two groups. Class A comprises those who are sufficiently able-bodied to work upon the roads. All females and those not able-bodied enough to work upon the roads are placed in Class B. Under the Commissioner of Agriculture there are two departments dealing with prisoners, one the Highway Department and the other the Prison Department. All those prisoners certified by the physician as in Class A are then notified to the Highway Department of the Commissioner of Agriculture and the State Board of Institutions, are delivered at the prison to the Highway Department, and are placed at work upon the roads by that department. Thereafter, unless they are returned to the prison, they are not under the charge of the superintendent of the prison. When I visited the prison in 1929 there were about 1600 men at the farm. All of these were kept in one place instead of being scattered around over the estate as in Mississippi. In addition I was told that about 1500 men are worked on the roads by the Highway Department.

Furthermore, Florida's state farm differs from Mississippi's in that it has a number of factories. It runs a sawmill, a shirt factory, a shoe shop, a knitting mill, and an auto license tag factory. Raiford also has its own tannery where it makes the leather for its shoe and harness shop, the farm produces more than sufficient to supply the needs of the prison, great quantities of beans are dried, other garden and farm products are canned. In these industries and on the farm are worked all the women and the men who are not in good enough condition to go on the road, and fifty of the A Class men who are by law required to be kept at the farm. The women are kept in buildings in a separate yard and are worked in a separate shop.

A few years ago the legislature of Florida provided the money for a fine set of new buildings at Raiford. New cell houses were constructed, a license tag shop, an auditorium, and a dining room of reinforced concrete. Most features of the new cell house and dining room are excellent. Large windows fill the sides of the cell house. The dining room is divided for the separation of the colored and white at table. The cells are large and adequately equipped with all the necessary appliances. Bathing facilities are numerous and up to modern standards. There is, however, one criticism that may be made of the cells. Entrance to the cell is through a rather small cross-barred door, which shuts out a great deal of light. These small doors do not interfere seriously with the ventilation, because modern ventilating is installed in the building which provides for a constant current of air through the cells.

The Dairy Department located at Ellerbee near the main prison has 460 acres of land, 200 of which are under intensive cultivation, and another 200 devoted to rough pasturing. The remaining 60 acres are in improved pasturage. Jersey cattle are used in the dairy. The value of the cattle, on November 30, 1928, was $11,520. The surplus milk and cream not needed at the state farm is sold in Jacksonville. The dairy for the two years 1927–1928 made a profit of $17,492.78. The building and equipment at the dairy are valued at over $33,000.

Another important activity at the farm is the Poultry Department. In 1928 the inventory of the department showed a value of nearly $16,000. The department made a net profit of $20,217.68 in those two years. Buildings to the value of $11,480 are used by the Poultry Department.

The factory activities, while not numerous, provide work for a large number of inmates and contribute materially to the maintenance of the prison. The shoe factory makes shoes for the farm inmates, repairs harness, does saddle work, and many other kinds of leather work. The State Road Department obtains all its shoes from this factory. Also large orders come from the industrial schools for boys and girls, and the state hospital at Chattahoochee. The farm colony at

Field Hands Entering the Dining Hall

STATE PRISON, RAIFORD, FLORIDA

Prisoners Working on Roads

Prisoners and Work Horses Returning Home to Dinner

STATE PRISON. RAIFORD, FLORIDA

Gainesville obtains part of its supplies from this factory. In addition to the numerous cash sales and repair jobs that were handled, the shoe factory contributed to the state industry fund during 1927 and 1928 the sum of $43,948.84.

The shirt factory is a contract factory. In it are employed about 400 prisoners. For 1927 and 1928 it made a net profit of $147,502.38. In February, 1928, there was set up a factory for the manufacture of athletic underwear, employing about 150 prisoners. This also, I believe, is a contract factory. During the eleven months that it ran in 1928 it produced a profit of $18,543.06.

Auto license tags for the State are manufactured in a part of the new concrete building. This plant earned a total of $92,614.99 during the two years of the biennium.[6]

A tubercular ward and a hospital are maintained for the inmates who need them.

In Florida there is no parole system, therefore the only methods of release from the institutions are the expiration of sentence, conditional pardon, commutation of sentence, and pardon. Consequently, a very much larger number of prisoners are pardoned every year than in our Northern states which have parole. Perhaps also by reason of this situation and also by reason of the comparative freedom of the inmates a large number of escapes takes place each year. The number of recaptures, however, is large and the number of escapes is no larger than one would expect with the comparative freedom allowed the inmates.

In the Florida prison, as in all these three Southern prisons, the old rule of silence is gone. There is a cheerful air about the prisoners, they talk and sing and laugh as freely as men engaged in activities outside the prison. A commissary is provided where they may buy extras, although no wage system is provided by which they may earn anything while in the prison. One result of this was seen as I visited the prison when one of the prisoners approached me for the price of a

[6] *20th Biennial Report of the Prison Division of the Department of Agriculture of the State of Florida for the years 1927 and 1928*, pp. 21–24.

package of cigarettes.   They are allowed only fifteen cents a week for tobacco.

Since 1923 the law of Florida has provided that any corporal punishment or any cruel and inhuman punishment or any punishment by which the flesh of the body is broken, bruised, or lacerated may not be visited upon any convict or any prisoner at any time or place.   The only methods used now to punish the prisoners at Raiford or in the road camps, county or state, are a reduction of good time, deprivation of privileges, and solitary confinement on bread and water.   Since January 1, 1924, all contracts between counties and private concerns for the employment of convicts have been abolished.   Thus the scandalous "lease system" in Florida has disappeared.

Since 1915 Florida has had a law providing for what we call "good time."   For good conduct, so many days off each month of the sentence are deducted, the number deducted increasing with each year of a sentence.[7]   When solitary confinement is inflicted, the prisoner stays in the dark cell twenty-five days with ten days out before he is put back in again.   Chains are also used in a few cases.   However, while I was there I was told only four men were in chains, and they were used on them only because they were working at large.   They had tried to escape.

The management of the prison seems to be excellent.   The superintendent has been in charge for a long time and seems to be on good terms with both his employees and the prisoners. The morale was excellent.   It rained the afternoon I was there, consequently the men after dinner at noon were lined up preparatory to going to work, when it was announced that only those who worked under cover should go to work. The rest of them had a half day off.   They were not put in their cells but were allowed the freedom of the large yard in the center of the building.

Florida laws do not allow prisoners to be worked more than ten hours a day, nor more than sixty hours a week.   These hours must include the time from leaving the building to the

[7] *Ibid.,* pp. 60–78.

time they get back. Therefore the prisoners, working at some distance from the prison, do not work at the outside more than nine hours.

On the whole the prison farm at Raiford, with its industries, makes a rather favorable impression upon a student of prisons. It lacks, however, the classificatory possibilities of the system in Mississippi.

Alabama. The third Southern prison employing large numbers of convicts on farms and roads, to which the study is directed, is Alabama. In most of the features of her economic and social life Alabama resembles Mississippi more than Florida. She has a large negro population, most of her people are employed in agriculture rather than industry, and her agriculture is devoted largely to cotton.

The place of the prison system in Alabama in the state organization is somewhat different from that in either Mississippi or Florida. In Mississippi the state penitentiary is under a Board of Trustees appointed by the Governor. In Florida the prison is under the Department of Agriculture, while in Alabama the prison is under the State Board of Administration. The Board is composed of three members, the President, an Associate Member, and the Governor of the state. The President has charge of the Executive Department of the Board while the Associate has charge of the Convict Department. The Governor is an ex-officio member of the Board. Moreover, this Board purchases all materials and supplies for the various departments of the state government except the eleemosynary institutions and the educational institutions. Formerly the purchasing for these institutions also was done by the State Board of Administration. This was discontinued in 1923. The State Highway Department is a separate organization from the Board of Administration, but has very close relationships to the Board through the fact that the latter does the purchasing for it and also because the Board of Administration contracts with the State Highway Department for the employment of convicts upon the road. Interestingly the Alabama Reform School for juvenile negro law-breakers, the State Training School for girls, and the Alabama Boys Industrial School are counted as eleemosynary rather than correctional institutions.

The State Board of Administration is in direct control of the various prisons through the Associate Member. All the employees of the Department are employed by the Board. In 1926 there were approximately 350 employees and a monthly pay-roll of approximately $45,000. A full-time physician-inspector has control of the medical and sanitary work of the prison. There is a full-time licensed dentist, and there are seven all-time resident physicians. In 1926 there were two inspectors for the four mines then operated by the state, and one inspector of county convicts. There was also a manager of cotton mills, and two transfer agents engaged in bringing from various counties new commitments and handling the transfers from prison to prison necessary from time to time for the good of the service. There were, furthermore, three chaplains, one chief engineer, an inspector of equipment and property, and a parole and an identification officer.[8]

Formerly there were eight prisons in the system. Four of these prisons were owned by the state and four at four different coal mines were leased by the state. The working of prisoners in coal mines in Alabama, however, has been discontinued, the leases have been given up, and the prisoners have been distributed among the other prisons. At the present time there are five different units. The main institution, which is the receiving station of the prison system, is located at Kilby about four miles outside of Montgomery. This prison has 2500 acres of land attached to it. The buildings at Kilby are new and modern. They can comfortably house about 900 convicts. They were erected in 1922 and 1923 at a cost of approximately $900,000. They are within a wall enclosure 20 feet high, enclosing 27 acres. Within this area are located a modern hospital building, which cost $75,000, a

---

[8] *Quadrennial Report, State Board of Administration*, October 1, 1922, to September 30, 1926, pp. 7–9, 34.

modern powerhouse costing $50,000, and the main prison building costing as noted above, nearly a million dollars.

The main building contains cells on its five floors. The main floor has individual cells, the other four floors have cells so constructed that five individuals may live in each one. However, they may economically be rearranged for individual cells if so desired. These cells are fireproof throughout and each of them is equipped with private toilet and lavatory. The kitchen and dining room are in this building with a new and up-to-date equipment. Here also is a modern steam laundry, large and commodious shower baths with hot and cold water, accommodating more than fifty at a time, a thoroughly equipped dental parlor, the bureau of identification, spacious waiting rooms, a library, schoolrooms, offices for the accounting department, and private offices for the officials. Around the outside of the wall is a grove of fine oak trees in which are located thirty or more bungalows and cottages, modern in every respect, forming a village or community for the officials and employees. Moreover a hotel is operated in the village for those employees who do not have families. Recently there was added to this village a commodious community house for the sole use of the employees and their families. Furthermore, within the enclosure is a 10,000 spindle cotton mill which cost $750,000. In this are employed 225 convicts, producing 105,000 yards weekly of the highest grade colored chambray. This began operations in April, 1923. Not only are these buildings up to date in every respect, but the machinery and equipment are of standard quality. Furthermore, within the yard is located a shirt factory, the building of the same type of construction as the cotton mill building, which cost approximately $100,000. In this shirt factory work 350 convicts, making men's blue work shirts at the rate of about 12,000 dozen shirts per month. This shirt factory takes about two-thirds of the cotton produced in the cotton mill. One-third is sold upon the open market. Outside the walls at a distance of about half a mile is a modern and sanitary 100-cow-capacity dairy, which cost $85,000. Here is produced milk and butter of A grade from pure bred and selected grade cows. A large part of the lands surrounding the institution is devoted to pasture for dairy cattle, pure bred hogs, and a herd of beef cattle. Approximately 1500 acres of the land are devoted to gardens, and farm crops on a paying basis, producing food for the inmates and for the farm animals besides a substantial surplus of cotton. The entire plant at Kilby represents an investment of about two and a quarter million dollars. I have seen very few prisons which are more modern in their physical appointments than this one at Kilby.

Another unit of the Alabama prison system which I did not visit is located at Speigner about twenty-two miles outside of Montgomery on a reservation of approximately 4000 acres of good farm land. I am informed that the buildings here are new modern wooden buildings occupied early in 1923, enclosed within a spacious and substantial wood and steel enclosure to accommodate comfortably approximately 600 inmates. This institution is conducted on very much the same lines as Kilby Prison. Here there is a cotton mill where 150 prisoners are employed in the production of 85,000 yards weekly of colored chambrays, which are sold on the open market. Here also is a dye house erected at a cost of approximately $100,000, built and equipped along modern lines. Furthermore, at this institution is a state-owned hydro-electric power plant with a dam impounding water covering approximately 900 acres which generates electricity for lighting the institution and grounds, and at certain seasons contributes the power used in operating the cotton mill. Here also a large farm is in operation producing food-stuffs and cotton. This unit, including the lands, cotton mills, dam, prison buildings, etc., is estimated to be worth approximately $1,000,000.

A third unit of the system is the old Wetumpka Prison, located about eighteen miles northeast of the state capital on approximately 900 acres of land. This was the original prison in Alabama, erected about 1857. Before Kilby was built it was the central receiving and distributing prison. While the buildings are old, they have been extensively repaired, completely renovated, and equipped in modern fashion, as far as possible, for the housing of women prisoners, and aged and infirm male prisoners. Outside the wall of this prison is located a state tuberculosis hospital for prisoners. This accommodates an average of 70 patients. It is located upon a hill just a short distance from the prison, and has a fine outlook. While all the buildings are of wood, they seem to provide adequate care for the tuberculous patients, although the prison authorities say that it is too small and that the equipment is not up to date. A small garden and farm are in operation at this prison, employing the able-bodied and some of the convalescent cases of tubercular male prisoners. The institution is estimated to be worth about $75,000.

On inspection, Wetumpka Prison seems to be old and somewhat out of date. Many of the rooms are dark and the whole institution stands out in quite glaring contrast to the new and modern buildings at Kilby. The only industry conducted here is a shirt factory in which the women and some of the men work, of course, in separate departments.

The fourth unit in the prison system of Alabama is known as Prison Number Four, located about eight miles north of Montgomery, on river bottom lands of approximately 3000 acres. Here are plain wooden buildings serving as dormitories, dining room, and kitchen inside a barbed-wire fence. I visited this institution on a Sunday, which happened to be one of the two visiting days per month allowed in the prison system of Alabama. Here as in all the Southern prisons I visited, the great majority of the convicts are negroes. Their relatives and friends were visiting with them freely. Prison Number Four is devoted entirely to farming and almost exclusively to corn. It produces approximately 40,000 bushels per annum and about 200 bales of cotton. It has its own water and sewerage system, the water coming from artesian wells drilled to a sufficient depth to insure a good supply of water. This institution with its improvements is estimated to be worth $125,000.

These four units represent an investment by the state of Alabama of approximately three and a half million dollars. In addition to this amount about two hundred and fifty thousand dollars are invested in equipment, live stock, etc.

Formerly the prison leased four coal mines in which it worked about 1100 prisoners. Recently, however, these leases were terminated, all prisoners were taken out of the coal mines, a new farm was bought between Montgomery and Mobile, and the prisoners from the coal mines were distributed among the five units of the prison system. I was not able to visit the new farm, but was assured by the prison officials that it was one of the best farms they had and that certain new developments were taking place there of which they expected good results.

Alabama, like Florida, takes care of a considerable number of her convicts by working them on the road. However, the system is somewhat different in Alabama from that in Florida. While in Florida the convicts, who are found upon physical examination to be strong and in good health, are turned over directly to the Highway Division of the State Department of Agriculture, under which are both the prisons and the highways, in Alabama the Prison Department makes a contract with the State Highway Department to do specific pieces of road work at a lump sum per piece. The control of them, therefore, is kept by the convict department, whereas in Florida, the responsibility for housing and otherwise caring for the convicts is in the hands of the Highway Department.

From the financial point of view the Alabama system seems to be the most profitable one of these three states. Annually it has a profit above maintenance and court costs of $900,000. That item of court costs is interesting because here is the only state I know of where the cost of trying and convicting the prisoner is taken out of the profits of the prison system.

The attention given to the health of the prisoner is rather unusual. The hospital at Kilby Prison is the best. There is a resident physician at each of these prison units, a hospital in each, equipped to take care of most of the health needs of the prisoners. However, major operations are transferred to the Kilby Prison, where better facilities exist.

Radios and moving picture machines have been purchased and placed in the prisons and entertainment is furnished free to all prisoners whose classification merits it. Prisoners also are allowed to prepare programs for their own amusement and are encouraged to engage in all manner of recreation. The day I visited Kilby many of the prisoners were out in the yard where a baseball game was going on played by the inmates. Twilight schools are established at the prisons which the inmates are encouraged to attend. The inmates inside the prison at Kilby, and that was true also at Number Four and Wetumpka, were not confined in their cells on the Sunday I was there, but were in the corridors or out in the yard, as they chose.

Furthermore, there are no stripes in the Alabama prison system, as there are in both Mississippi and Florida. The men were dressed in light tan-colored trousers and white shirts with neckties.

While no compensation is paid to the prisoners for performing their regular tasks, a weekly allowance of fifteen cents for tobacco is made and prisoners are permitted to earn money over and above their normal day's task. I am informed that about fifty per cent of those who complete their tasks before the end of the day prefer to rest. The other fifty per cent, however, earn approximately $100,000 per annum.

In addition to the industries mentioned above, 150 prisoners are employed in the finishing lumber plant with an annual output of 25,000,000 feet finished lumber of an estimated market value of $625,000.

Summarizing the employment of the prisoners in the Alabama system, in 1926, 1150 were employed in coal mines, 150 in the lumber plant, 375 in two cotton mills at Kilby and at Speigner, 400 in the three garment factories, and 450 are on farms and gardens. Since that time, owing to the discontinuance of the coal mines and the buying of the new farm between Montgomery and Mobile, doubtless the distribution is somewhat different.[9]

There is one other interesting feature in Alabama not found in the other two systems. County misdemeanants may be sent to the state prison system instead of being kept in the county jail. Practically all of these are taken care of in Prison Number Four, which, as we saw above, is a farm project. Upon inquiry I found that the prison officials do not like this plan of sending the county convicts to the state institutions. The superintendent of Prison Number Four told me that they are usually short-time prisoners and little can be done with them and yet work must be provided for them. He looks upon them as a nuisance.

In Alabama the strap is still used as a method of discipline. They use also the dark cell on bread and water, the loss of "good time," and of other privileges. The officials are very much in favor of the whip, as a method of discipline, although they say that for certain cases the dark cell is better.

COMPARISON OF THESE THREE SYSTEMS

In these three prison systems we see three different varieties of methods used in a number of respects. The Mississippi system is entirely a farming system. Florida's and Alabama's are a mixed system of farming and industry. Again they are different in the matter of concentrating all their prisoners in one place or scattering them about. Mississippi and Alabama have their prisoners scattered in different institutions under one control. Raiford, Florida, has all of hers concentrated in one place. While Florida and Alabama work a good proportion of their prisoners upon the roads, Mississippi employs very few of hers in that way. Again, while both Florida and Alabama have the mixed system of farming and industry, Florida's industries are concentrated in one spot, while Alabama's are scattered about among three of the five institutions. Mississippi employs no prisoners on contracts with private industry, while both Florida and Alabama have contracts on which they

[9] *Op. cit.*, pp. 34–45.

Main Building

Factory

Dairy

STATE PRISON, KILBY, ALABAMA

Dormitory and Dining Hall

Grinding Sorghum Cane

Dormitory for First Offenders

PRISON FARM, OAKLEY, MISSISSIPPI

employ a certain percentage of their prisoners.   Furthermore, both Florida and Alabama have large sums of money invested in buildings and industrial equipment.   Mississippi's investment is chiefly in lands.   In both Florida and Alabama the guards are paid free officials, while in Mississippi the field guards are trusty convicts.   Moreover, while all three of these Southern prisons are financially successful, Mississippi's and Alabama's more than pay their way.   Florida receives some appropriation from the state for the maintenance of the prison. All three of these prisons use a considerable number of prisoners in farming operations.   In all three, the prisoners who work outside the prison yard work under the gun, although the gun was not so much in evidence in Florida as in Alabama and Mississippi.

COMPARISON WITH NORTHERN PRISON SYSTEMS

Let us consider the main points of difference between these Southern prison systems and the Northern.   One should keep in mind, of course, in such comparison that the South is predominately agricultural, while the North is very much more industrial.   It also must be borne in mind that in the South the negro problem is very much more prominent than in the North.   While there are other differences in the general economic and social situation between the two sections of the country, these, perhaps, are the outstanding factors which should be remembered.

In none of these three Southern prison systems is there the so-called "silent system."   The prisoners converse in any of these Southern prisons as they please.   They talk and laugh and sing very much as they would on the outside.   The negroes especially are garrulous and given to singing.   Moreover, the contrast between the silence and depression in the Northern prisons and even in the white departments of the Southern prisons is most striking.   This fact impressed itself upon me the day I visited the state prison of Alabama at Kilby.   The men about the corridors and out in the yard were no different from any group of men I have seen together in free society.

They were talking together, some were playing games such as checkers, cards, etc., in the cells and in the corridors. In the Mississippi institution there was not quite as much freedom, inasmuch as those who were not trusties were locked in their own dormitories the Sunday I was there. Nevertheless they were free to talk together as they pleased.

Another outstanding contrast between these Southern prisons and a number of our Northern prisons is the greater proportion of the men who work in out-of-door pursuits. In this connection it must be remembered that the climate in the South allows outdoor work a much greater portion of the year than in the North. Furthermore, since the South is largely an agricultural area, there is a smaller number of men from the cities.

However, it must be remembered that the contrast here is not striking on the matter of vocational training, since that is not an outstanding object in the work required of prisoners either in the North or in the South. The main purpose of labor is to keep the men occupied, improve discipline, and to secure economic output.

To a Northerner, one of the most striking things is the use of prison trusties as guards in Mississippi. I am told that the same system obtains in Louisiana and Arkansas.[10] Something like it is to be seen in certain officers in the settlements for criminal tribes in India and the police in Bilibid Prison at Manila, and in the Iwahig Penal Colony in the Philippine Islands. However, in these Oriental prisons no weapons are placed in the hands of these trusties, whereas in Mississippi these trusties are the guards who hold the gun on the men while they are at work in the fields and also act as guards in the camps. In Mr. Thames's discussion before the American Prison Association at Jackson, Mississippi, in 1925, this feature of their system attracted a good deal of attention. The novelty of the plan strikes a Northerner rather forcibly. Prison of-

---

[10] Thames, *Address Before the American Prison Association*, Jackson, Miss., November 7–14, 1925, before the Wardens' Association of that organization. To a limited extent inmate guards are used also in Florida.

ficials in Mississippi, however, with whom I talked, find no difficulty with it. They think it works well and saves the state a great deal of expense. It is a question, of course, as to whether that is not the main reason why they favor it. The legality of it was questioned by some of the delegates at the aforementioned Prison Association meeting, but Mr. Thames replied that no legal authority in Mississippi has raised that question. I raised with Mississippi officials the question as to whether a prisoner would be as likely to keep another from escaping as a free guard. The reply was that they were much more likely to do so, since if they did not do their best to prevent escapes they would lose their status as trusties, which status carries with it certain important privileges. Then I asked whether, if inducements were given to lead these trusties to shoot their fellow-prisoners trying to escape, it might not lead to shooting when shooting was not absolutely necessary. The officials replied that in practice it does not work out that way. While pardon is recommended for a prisoner guard who shoots another prisoner who is trying to escape, the official said he would not be recommended if he shot when it was unnecessary. The practice seems obnoxious to us Northerners, yet one of the problems which the administrators of Northern prisons have is to break up the solidarity of the prison population as against the prison officials. A *priori* the system of prisoner guards would seem to break up this prison solidarity. The system of stool pigeons in the prisons of the North is intended to do the same thing. However, the problem of the solidarity of the prison population against the prison officials must be solved in a quite different way from the use of prisoner guards or stool pigeons. Prisoner police are used both in India and the Philippines. These men have no weapons, but are charged with the responsibility of keeping order and preventing escapes or outbreaks. From my observation of both I am inclined to feel that the system of prison police made up of prisoners themselves is a very much better way of controlling the inmates than the use of prisoner guards or of stool pigeons. Furthermore, experience in a number of our Northern prisons and in the prisons of England has shown that inmate solidarity is not a great menace if there is a feeling among the men that the officials are really interested in them and are just to their demands.

The strap in Alabama and Mississippi is held by the authorities to be the best form of discipline in some cases. Florida abolished this form of punishment in reaction to the flogging to death of a North Dakota boy a few years ago. This method of punishment has been outlawed in most of the Northern states. It is still retained in England. While a Northerner who is not familiar with the psychology of the situation produced by the intermixture of the two races in the South ought to be cautious in judging the practice, nevertheless our feeling in the North against it as a method of discipline is based upon the conviction that corporal punishment is very liable to abuses in the hands of the ordinary prison official and that, furthermore, it is debasing both to the administrator and to the inmate. The fact that most prison officials are rather ordinary gives weight to the first objection and has led to certain precautionary measures wherever it has been retained, such, for example, as that it may be administered only by the superintendent or with his distinct approval or after approval by the board in charge of the prisons. The other objection to it goes deeper. It rests upon the theory that the purpose of the prison is to preserve as far as possible the prisoner's sense of self-respect and the value of his own personality rather than to destroy it. It is held by these theorists that corporal punishment destroys the prisoner's self-esteem, debases him from his status in the social organization through the feeling of disgrace which follows a whipping. It is customary to look upon floggings as only for immature persons. It is not administered to grown men in free society. Therefore, it violates the mores of the group and consequently is unsocial in its results.

On the other hand, the prison officials with whom I talked defended it on the basis that for certain types of prisoners a flogging changes the attitude of a man at once. It is economical in that it is over with in a few minutes and the man can go back to work.   Whereas, if he is put in a dark cell on bread and water, it is bad for the prisoner physically and deprives the state of his labor for a considerable length of time. They claim that the strapping does not degrade him from his social status any more than incarceration in a dark cell on bread and water.   The debate on both sides has been carried on up to the present, without reference to any scientific study of the actual results of the various methods of discipline.   What is needed at the present time is a careful study of the matter with all the scientific aids available in order actually to ascertain the comparative results of the various methods from every point of view.

Alabama's prison is the only one of the three I visited which enables the prisoner to earn something for himself.   No means are provided in either Mississippi or Florida, I was told, for the men to earn a cent while they are in prison.   The South is behind the North in that respect.

There is no question that the North is comparatively backward in the use of prisoners on outdoor work.   While a number of the Northern states use prisoners on the roads, the proportionate number compared with those of the South is small.   That same statement is true in regard to the use of prisoners in farm work.   There is no question that these experiments in the South on road work and on farm work is worthy of careful study by our Northern prison authorities.

It has been urged by authorities in the North that the working of convicts on the road is obnoxious to free people who see them at work there.   It is a question whether this objection has any validity provided the prisoners were dressed in ordinary working clothes rather than stripes.   It has also been argued that to work prisoners on the road is uneconomical. No careful study of this matter has been made as yet so far as I know except in North Carolina.   That only applies to the economical use of county chain gangs in road construction and maintenance.   The conclusion of this study is as follows: "In conclusion, it is evident that many convict road camps in the past fifteen years *have* constructed roads economically and with few exceptions this has been done most successfully under the honor system. At the present time the wider use of road machinery makes it extremely doubtful whether unskilled convicts who must be worked in a compact group under guard can any longer be profitably employed in road building. As for road maintenance, the evidence is conclusive that the chain gang is entirely unsuited for such work. From the economic point of view it is highly essential that the counties devise some better method of segregating and correcting the able-bodied offenders."[11] This study pertains to county convict gangs. No careful study has been made of the comparative economies of working state convicts upon the building and maintenance of roads with contract work, or with a public department where free men are employed. It is worthy, however, of careful study, inasmuch as all over the world it is a serious problem and especially in the countries where industries are carried on in the prison and labor is highly organized, where the contract system has been attacked and state use has proved to be inadequate to keep the prisoners at work. Furthermore, in view of the fact that the Hawes-Cooper Act becomes operative in 1934, making it impossible for a state to sell its prison-made goods in another state which has a law against contract labor in prison or against the sale of prison-made goods, our prison authorities must be taking thought as to how they will employ their prisoners at productive and healthful work, if the prisons are not to become houses of idleness and demoralization.

Alabama is the only one of these Southern states that I studied which also takes charge of county prisoners. This plan has the advantage of giving unified control over all the convicts in the state, both state and county. However, I found that the state officers in the prisons do not like to have these county convicts there. In Alabama most of them are kept at Prison Number Four. In the North, Indiana and

[11] Steiner and Brown, *The North Carolina Chain Gang*, Chapel Hill, 1927, Chapter vii. A recent letter from the Highway Department of Florida states that it is a question whether convict road work is cheaper than that done by free labor.

Massachusetts have state farms for their county prisoners, although the two systems differ somewhat. The difficulty in Alabama as in the North is that the terms are so short that economical use of the prisoners is somewhat difficult.

Of these three prisons in the South, only one has an indeterminate sentence—Alabama. For the quadrennium, October 1, 1922, to September 30, 1926, out of 4603 prisoners sentenced, 3740 were given indeterminate sentences and 863 determinate sentences. A number of the Northern states have the indeterminate sentence, some of them in very limited form and others with much wider limits.

The financial success of the Southern prisons is one of the outstanding characteristics, if one may judge from these three states. This fact is probably due to the large use of convicts in contract labor, which previous studies have shown is one of the most profitable methods of employing prisoners, to the large use of them in road work, and to their use in farming on a large scale. In the South as in the North there is constant conflict between financial success of the institution and vocational training. As a matter of fact, practically everywhere, not only in this country but throughout the world, emphasis on vocational training is mostly talk. Financial productivity receives the main emphasis.

If one may judge by these three Southern prisons, the South is very backward in the use of probation and parole. This fact accounts at least in part for the large numbers in the prisons of these states. So long as negroes constitute a large part of the prisoners and so long as there is a small number of social agencies in the South upon whom falls the burden of supporting the dependents of prisoners, and so long as the prisons are so profitable, one can easily see there is every reason for the South to be backward in the use of methods which will treat men in other ways than sending them to prison or to get them out of prison on parole as soon as possible. Whether the South can apply probation and parole to her trifling negro men who are now sent to prison can be determined only by trying them. If a man can be kept at work on the outside without danger to society, he is likely to be much more useful economically, and the social ties by which he is bound are more likely to be kept intact, than if he is sent to prison. Every study of probation and parole in the North has shown the superior economic efficiency of these measures to the prison. If probation and parole can be wisely and discreetly applied on the basis of a study of the individual case, it has been found that large numbers of people formerly sent to prison may be left at large, or after a short period in the prison they may be let out without danger to society and with great benefit to the individual prisoner. A Northerner should be slow to assert that it can be done in the South. Perhaps he may respectfully suggest that the South try it. Nevertheless Northern experience has shown that unless these delinquents are in the hands of competent probation and parole officers, they would better be kept in prison.

Another striking feature of these Southern prison systems is the large number of escapes. This, of course, is due to the outdoor work, where the opportunities of escape are so much greater. The authorities there tell me that the escapes are chiefly by trusties. They are given very much more latitude than ordinary prisoners and consequently they run away. Mr. Thames reported in 1925 that in Mississippi the escapes constituted between six and seven per cent of the entire number of prisoners in the institution.[12] The Southern outdoor work also accounts for the number of men killed in trying to escape. In each of the published reports of these Southern states, there is a list of these.

Another outstanding difference between the North and the South in the treatment of prisoners is the wider use of stripes in the South. Of these three prisons I studied, Alabama is the only one which does not use stripes, except as a means of punishment. The argument in the South for their use is that by reason of the fact that so many of the men are outside and are liable to escape, the stripes make escape more impossible. However, it is interesting that I was just recently told about a man who walked away from one of the state prison farms

[12] *Op. cit.*, p. 8.

in Wisconsin and who was recaptured because his shirt had his prison number printed upon it.   Experience has demonstrated rather conclusively that stripes have very little value and are attended by some serious inconveniences.   They tend to destroy a man's sense of social worth by being a badge of infamy, when the effort of the prisons should be devoted to restoring or inspiring a sense of personal worth.

Perhaps the outstanding contrast between the prisons in the North and in the South is the fact that in the prisons in the South, if one may judge by these three, there is no idleness.   In the North, as is well known, many of our prisons cannot provide work for all the inmates.   I am told that in some of the prisons of New York as many as two-thirds of the men are idle.   When I visited the New Jersey prison at Trenton two years ago I found that half the men were idle.   Three or four years ago when I visited the western Pennsylvania prison near Pittsburgh about a third of the men were idle. There is no question that from the standpoint of the prisoners the greatest curse in a prison is idleness.   The South has shown us some constructive ways in which men may be kept at work.   The road camps and the large farming operations are outstanding experiments that challenge the attention of prison authorities of the North.

COMPARISON WITH ORIENTAL AND OLD WORLD EXPERIMENTS

In previous chapters we have noticed that in the Indian settlements for the criminal tribes and in the Philippine prison system, outdoor work was a kind of preparatory stage before release.   In the Indian settlements the criminals are gradually sent out from the reformatory settlement to the agricultural settlement where they have comparative liberty before they are released.   In the Philippines we noticed that all prisoners were committed to Bilibid or the San Ramon Prison and then were collected from these two prisons for colonization in Iwahig.   The great penal colony in Iwahig is intended as a kind of a proving ground for release.   On the other hand, in none of the Southern states studied is outdoor work a kind of preparatory stage for release. It is just one method of working the convicts. India and the Philippines, whether consciously or not, have copied the "progressive stage" system invented by Sir Joshua Jebb in England and Crofton in Ireland, in the early development of the prison systems of those two countries. The adventure, however, of such a system in India and the Philippines is on so much larger scale than it ever attained in England or Ireland that it takes on the nature of a new experiment. Apparently neither in the North nor in the South is road work for convicts or work on farms conceived of as a preparatory stage for release. Physical and financial considerations determine what men shall be put at road work and what men shall go on the farms, and which shall work in factories in the South.

Alike in the Southern states and in the Orient, flogging and chains are defended as methods of punishment on the basis of the psychology of the blacks. The ordinary disciplinary punishment for the blacks do not have a good effect. Doubtless the theory at the bottom of this in the minds of the prison authorities is that with the white-black superiority and inferiority status, what is punishment to a white man is not to a black man. It is also held to be justified by the feeling that the black man is not amenable to the same social motive as the white man who occupies a superior social status. That relationship of the inferiority of the natives to the superiority of the whites obtains in the Orient especially in the Philippines and in India. The infliction of brutal punishment always accompanies the state of society in which there is this status of superiority and inferiority. It is largely a question of how different methods of discipline affect one's sense of personal worth and social status which has not yet been carefully studied.

In none of the Southern institutions do we find any attempt made to keep families with the prisoners as in India and in the Philippines. Conditions in the Southern institutions are such that that experiment could be tried out with the negroes. With the large areas of land available there is no reason why the experiment could not be tried of bringing prisoners' families to the institution and forming a village or camp in which they live as they do in the settlements of India and in the Iwahig penal colony in the Philippines. There a man learns to work in his family setting. At present in America, if one learns to work in prison, it is not with the ordinary family relationships about him. In the South, marital conditions are somewhat different from those in the North. In the North a large part of the prisoners are unmarried men; in the South almost half of them are married, at least in the only state in which I could find statistics—Mississippi.

Furthermore, in contrast with the system in India and the Philippines, no effort is made to keep alive the economic motive by making the prisoner support himself and his family. It might be well to experiment in the Southern states, especially with the negroes on this matter. Place certain of the negroes with their families upon pieces of land, charge them for what they get, and give them credit for what they produce, thus keeping the ordinary economic and social relationships and at the same time putting pressure upon the man to work, advising him and his family how to save, thus teaching him the elements not only of good agriculture, but of sound economics. Without question, on the basis of the evidence in India and the Philippines, such a plan would very greatly decrease the present number of escapes. Mississippi, Louisiana, and Arkansas are like India and the Philippines in that they make use of trusties for the control of the convicts. However, they differ from the Indian and the Philippine practices in that they allow the trusty guards guns and charge them with the responsibility of keeping the other convicts from escaping. The Indian and the Philippine practices are upon a much sounder psychological basis. There they do not put guns in the hands of prisoners to guard other prisoners, but they place responsibility upon them to keep order among the prisoners and furthermore develop in the Philippines responsibility for the conduct of the inmates by organizing a court to try offenders. The court is made up of convicts. To most of our prison officials in this country that looks too idealistic. One wonders whether the failure to try it is not due to the fact that it is much more trouble than the more primitive and more direct methods of punishment.

Mississippi much resembles the penal colony at Witzwil, Switzerland, in that farming is the main industry. In Mississippi, as in Witzwil, the industries carried on are accessory to farm operations. The difference between the situation in Mississippi and in Switzerland is that in the former you handle the problem of different races and a different character of crops. Mississippi has no honor camp such as that near Witzwil, Switzerland, in the Kiley Alps, where trusty prisoners go with the cattle each summer and stay there without guard. Certain of the road camps in the South are on the honor basis and resemble that experiment in Switzerland in this respect.

One other difference stands out between the Southern prison system and the Indian plan for the criminal tribes. The main objective so far as one can judge in the Southern prisons as in the Northern in this country, and to a lesser extent even in the Philippines, is to make the prison as nearly self-supporting as possible. In India the chief objective seems to be to teach the Indian predatory criminal to learn to live in normal social relationships, and how to make a living without crime. In other words, the Indian plan is for the purpose of teaching these criminals, criminals by the very mores of their social group, to learn a new set of economic standards and new principles of social living in accordance with those established in the rest of society. In other words, the reformatory purpose is very much more prominent in India than in this country. To the extent that the Philippine system keeps the family unit intact and the economic motive dominant in each man's treatment, the same is true there. One wonders if a similar understanding of group psychology, if properly applied, especially of the negro in the South, of the unskilled laborers, and of the mental deficients in the prison population in the North, might not bring about the same results with these classes. In theory it is pretty generally agreed by prison officials as well as by penologists that unless prison treatment turns a man out with a new set of attitudes and habits toward labor, toward efficient management of his financial affairs and toward social relationships, no matter how profitable it is to the state, it is a failure, yet in actual practice we act as though the main purpose of imprisonment is punishment so far as the prisoner is concerned and financial productivity so far as the state is concerned. We destroy the economic motives which dominate a man in ordinary society by providing for the prisoner's usual necessities. The only motive for labor is the fear of punishment. Why not substitute for the fear of punishment economic and social motives?

BIBLIOGRAPHY

Biennial Report of the State's Prison, North Carolina, 1927–1928.

Biennial Report of the Board of Trustees, etc., of the Mississippi State Penitentiary, 1925–1927.

Biennial Report of the Department of Institutions of Tennessee, 1926–1928.

Bulletin of the North Carolina State Board of Charities and Public Welfare, Vol. 6, No. 1, January–March, 1923.

Cox, Wm. B., "Convict Labor in the South," *Proceedings, Annual Congress of the American Prison Association, 1928,* pp. 207–214.

Garrett and MacCormick, *Handbook of American Prisons, 1929,* National Society of Penal Information, Inc., New York, 1929.

"Life in a Prison De Luxe in Louisiana," *Literary Digest,* April 21, 1923, pp. 50–52.

McKelway, A. J., "Three Prison Systems of the Southern States of America," in Henderson, *Penal and Reformatory Institutions,* 1910, p. 68.

Quadrennial Report, State Board of Administration (of Alabama), *1922–1923.*

Report of the State Prison Inspector of Alabama, 1927–1928.

Steiner and Brown, *The North Carolina Chain Gang,* Chapel Hill, 1927.

Twentieth Biennial Report of the Prison Division of the Department of Agriculture of the State of Florida, 1927–1928.

Twentieth Annual Report of the Prison Commission of Georgia, 1916–1917.

The Texas Committee of Prisons and Prison Labor, *The Texas Prison Survey*, Vol. I, 1924.

Tannenbaum, Frank, "Southern Prisons," *The Century Magazine*, July, 1923, pp. 387–398.

Thames, J. F., Address before the American Prison Association, Jackson, Miss., 1925.

Winslow, Chas. H., *The Rights of the Prisoner to Vocational Training, Prison Leaflets*, No. 55, National Committee on Prisons and Prison Labor, New York, 1919.

CHAPTER X

CONCLUSION

You have followed me around the world in this adventure of penological discovery. You have seen through my eyes how the Japanese, emerging only sixty years ago from feudalism, awaking to the currents of Western thought for the first time, have attempted to meet the rising tide of crime due to the impact of a strange and new civilization upon an old. You have watched the Filipino, released only thirty years ago from the lazy despotism of Spain, and then experiencing the impress of vigorous, impetuous United States, sure of itself and its culture, intolerant of the cultures of the head-hunter and the Spanishized Filipino, attempt a striking experiment in colonizing his erring brothers, in preparation for full freedom. You have seen the Sinhalese under British leadership attempting to adapt the English prison system to that mixed multitude attracted from the shores of the Indian Ocean to that natural paradise. You have watched Indians, proud in the consciousness of past greatness, again under British leadership attack the problem of the criminal tribes, that strange institutionalization of criminality. You have seen Switzerland, that political experiment station of Europe, try the high adventure of re-training criminals for useful life by putting them upon land once waste, in order to redeem it and in doing it find redemption for the criminals themselves. You have watched Belgium, in trying to solve the problem of her beggars, find a solution for her criminal ne'er-do-wells and her delinquent youth. You have, with me, looked into the prison system of England and have seen there the most elaborate system of classification of prisoners to prevent prison contamination and to apply individualization of treatment ever tried on

293

earth. You have also seen her Borstal treatment of young
offenders and her Preventive Detention experiment for habituals. And, finally, you have seen how some of our own
Southern states are experimenting with prisoners on the land.

What tragedies of human personality this panorama has revealed! What depths of human despair lie beneath the prison
garb of these thousands of human beings shut away from their
fellows! What agonies of torment have swept over the souls
of thousands of women and children, of fathers and mothers
who have been left behind by the prisoner!

Neglected childhood stares at us from beneath many of
these criminal brows. Slave morality in Indian, Filipino, and
Negro criminal—a morality taught by centuries of oppres-
sion—cries accusingly at us from silent lips. Others are the
victims of the maladjustments incident to the impact of one
civilization upon a vastly different one. Still others are the
products of inherent incapacity and unhappy circumstance.
But all, how unutterably saddening! What a challenge to
civilization is the criminal of every land!

How slow we have been to apply science to this problem,
we who have built on science our material civilization! For
the most part in our relations to the criminal we have been
the bond slaves of uncritical tradition. In what prison of the
world is science, even the little science available for prison
officials, used as thoroughly to determine the treatment to be
given a criminal for his correction as is applied in the prison
shops to produce economic goods? True, in some states the
prisoners are given medical and psychological examinations,
good as far as they go. Crime, however, is a function not
merely of either physiological or psychical native endowment, but of personality reactions to social stimuli.

How many prisons have a good social history of many of
their inmates? How much use is made by prison officials of
the medical, psychological, and psychiatric information, in-
complete as it generally is, now in their files? How differently
does the hard-boiled prison official treat the man with an I. Q.
of 65 from the one with an I. Q. of 100 or 120? Or the

prisoner emotionally unstable from the hard, calculating, but subservient professional?   If he makes any difference in his mass treatment, does he not favor the "good" prisoner who has learned from many experiences to conform to prison regulations in order the earlier to be admitted to parole or by means of "good time" to shorten his sentence?   Those burning eyes, that restless pacing of the cell, the outburst of passion which smashes a machine or attacks a fellow-prisoner or a guard to most prison officials means nothing but inborn "cussedness." On the other hand, that apathy, that listless, indifferent, hang-dog attitude which no official "cussing" can dissipate, means nothing to him but native "stubbornness."   The deep tragedy of it all he does not sense.   The moral depths of disturbance on the one hand and the slowly dying spiritual flame under the strokes of fate on the other are unknown to him.   They are as though they did not exist.   These men are not as others; they are a class apart.   No wonder such a prison official can say, as one said to me recently, "These fellows!   I would not believe 95 per cent of them if they swore to a statement on a stack of Bibles a mile high!"   Apparently it never occurred to him to ask himself seriously why men in prison lie to prison officials, why prisoners are restless, grumble at the food, try to escape, attempt to beat the rule of silence, refuse to work, malinger, are vicious and make all kinds of trouble for their jailers.   Are they all, or most of them, some strange species of human being?   Or are they the product partly of our social system, especially of our prison system, and partly of their own inborn tendencies?

What monuments to stupidity are these institutions we have built—stupidity not so much of inmates as of free citizens! What a mockery of science are our prison discipline, our massing of social iniquity in prisons, the good and the bad together in one stupendous *pot-pourri*.   How silly of us to think that we can prepare men for social life by reversing the ordinary processes of socialization—silence for the only animal with speech; repressive regimentation of men who are in prison because they need to learn how to exercise their activities in constructive ways; outward conformity to rules which repress all efforts at constructive expression; work without the operation of economic motives; motivation by fear of punishment rather than by hope of reward or appeal to their higher motives; cringing rather than growth in manliness; rewards secured by betrayal of a fellow rather than the development of a larger loyalty!

The correction of delinquents is a problem in education. How often is it so conceived? How often are the officials skilled educators? Prisons and reformatories are not usually classed as educational institutions. They are not usually governed by the state department concerned with the schools. They are places of punishment.

The inmates and prison officials reflect that conception in speaking of the period spent within such institutions as "doing time," "paying the price," "squaring the account." That concept is written in the law—so much punishment for such a crime. Yet, inconsistently, we describe them as penal and correctional institutions. As if we could fix in advance the amount of time it will take to correct a bad attitude! Worse yet, as if the effectiveness of correction or re-education depends upon the severity and harshness of treatment, or as if the way to get a man to change his attitude is to *force* him to do the things contrary both to nature and social conduct on the outside! Education does aim at discipline, but at self-discipline by appeals to one's latent capacities and by exciting interest in achievements socially valued. By repression in the prison we develop a deadening slave conformity from fear of punishment. Why not develop active interest in self-improvement? We develop an attitude of resistance to the officers. Why not stimulate co-operation? We educate for rebellion against authority. Why not for social purposes in a free society? Scarcely any take account of the great advances in psychology and social organization for the reconditioning of human actions. One would never guess from visiting most of our so-called correctional institutions that anything had been discovered by modern psychology. A conditioned response is an unknown tongue to most of our prison authorities. The play of mass stimulation upon the individual is recognized in the attempt to keep the new and young criminal from the hardened, but not at all in reconditioning the warped personality to a new social outlook upon life and to the formation of new habits.

If a few degenerate and hardened criminals can corrupt a whole prison of comparatively uncorrupted delinquents who arrive in the prison by a slip, and who are not set in the ways of confirmed criminals, why cannot prison authorities manage things so that the great mass of inmates who desire the better things of life control the degenerate and hardened? How often men can be found in our prisons who react against the impurity which floats about prison cells like a degrading atmosphere, who feel so alone because they cannot at once sink themselves into the slime of iniquity generated by the corrupt among the prison population. Of what use is classification in a prison, if it does not make possible the organization of the clean, the aspiring, the ennobling elements left in men's characters for further development? If circumstances brought these men here, why cannot circumstances be so ordered in the thoroughly controlled situation in a prison that men develop into manhood instead of degenerate into beasts? Certainly nowhere else are men's lives so subject to social control as here. The tragedy is that they are negatively rather than constructively controlled. The predominating attitude of officials is negative and repressive. They are not allowed to talk with these men except to direct them to perform certain acts laid down by the rules. They cannot be friends to the prisoners. Why? Because the guards are of such low caliber that they cannot be trusted to become friends with the prisoner for fear that the latter will "work" the former. The guards are conceived as officials who have just three duties—keep the men at work, keep them in order within the prison, and prevent their escape. Why talk about reforming the prisoners with such men? No. We do not look upon prisons as educational institutions. They are places of punishment.

However, perhaps it is too much to expect that prison authorities will look at the matter in such radically different ways so long as the general public still thirsts for the blood of the killer and the rapist, and, worse yet, still thinks that all criminals deserve punishment rather than treatment. Perhaps we have as good prison officials as we deserve. Is it not likely that our prisons are really a reflection of public sentiment? Can we not see as in a mirror the actual state of public intelligence on this matter in the ways in which our prisons are run? Do they not reflect our ignorance of, and our lack of intelligent interest in, the criminal? Are not these institutions, with all their failures, their cruelties, their repressions, monuments to our stupidity? And what monuments! About 50 per cent of the men incarcerated in them return again and again. Suppose that our educational institutions flunked out half or even a quarter of the students enrolled in them. Would we be satisfied with the schools and colleges? Yet right along, year after year, half of the men whom we send to our correctional institutions flunk the course. Can we be enthusiastic about institutions which produce such results? Can we with good grace call them "correctional institutions"? Is it the material which enters them? Or is it the methods used? Or is it both? These are questions which should be frankly faced.

Such strictures upon our prison systems made by idealists are not without value. They call to our attention how easily we fall into traditional ways of treating the offender. They challenge our complacency. If we are prison officials or members of boards controlling the penal and correctional institutions, they probably stir our anger. We feel that they are not wholly true. We have made progress. However slowly we have followed the progress of science, we have introduced some measures born of the marriage of science with practical prison management. That prison authorities are concerned about the matter is indicated by the experiments that are going on in

various parts of the world in the treatment of prisoners.   Let
us summarize, then, the adventures which we have passed in
review.   While these experiments are not based upon careful
study, they do represent an empirical attempt to vary the
conditions surrounding prisoners in the hope that better
results may be obtained.

Classification.   Almost everywhere where Western civilization has become established, attempts at classification of the
prisoners have been made.   The most outstanding experiments
in this line are to be found in Japan, Ceylon, Belgium, and
England.   The chief purpose back of these classifications seems
to be the prevention of contamination, a traditional theory that
goes back to the early days of prisons in the United States.
Too little attention has been given to the matter of classification as a means for the individualization of treatment.   If all
the difficult prisoners were removed to one or more institutions,
the discipline now imposed upon all might be reserved for
these more difficult individuals.   Belgium, perhaps, is the only
country which has organized its prison system with this purpose in view.   The classification, as we have seen, in Belgium
is made upon the basis of a study of the individual.   There is no
evidence, however, that Belgium has found this a means
whereby less rigorous discipline may be imposed upon those
who are not difficult to handle.   In the Philippines and in
some of our prisons having prison farms the lessened severity
of the discipline for the men upon the farms is to be seen.
A few of our prison wardens see clearly that if they could remove the more tractable inmates from those who must be more
rigidly disciplined, that the more tractable ones could be subject to a very much less severe repression and given a greater
degree of liberty.

Self-Government.   Nowhere is the scheme of self-government suggested by Osborne carried out to a very great degree.
It has been modified in this country in the institutions where
it was tried.   Probably it is impractical so long as the hardened
prisoner is kept with the more amenable individual.   Today
the world around, perhaps the greatest degree of self-govern-

ment practical in a mixed community is to be found in the Philippines and Ceylon. Even in these countries it is most extensively used in certain selected classes. For example, in the Philippines, the Filipino Scouts and the colonists at Iwahig have the greatest degree of liberty and self-government. Nevertheless, the inmate police officials who assist in the government of the prison, both in Bilibid and in the Iwahig Colony, represent a degree of self-government to be found rarely throughout the prisons of the world. In Ceylon the group of men in the Welikada Prison who are organized as Boy Scouts are given a degree of self-government which is to be found elsewhere only in the Filipino Scouts. The development of the court composed of inmates in Bilibid and in the Iwahig Penal Colony is a very promising experiment in self-government. These are adventures in the government of men confined within prison walls or under penal conditions of the greatest promise; there is no reason why these experiments should not be tried out elsewhere.

After-care. We have talked much about after-care, but most of our governments have given very little attention to its practical application. At the present time, after-care by private agencies is developed in Japan, Ceylon, England, and India. These are tentative experiments which, so far as we can judge from the results, are of the very greatest promise. Is there any reason why the government itself should not undertake this important work? Certainly if society is interested in seeing that these men who are discharged from prison find an honorable place in society after discharge, it would seem that this is an important measure which should be seriously followed out by those authorities charged with the care of criminals. In America scarcely anything is done, the man is dismissed at the gate of the prison with nothing but a suit of clothes, and either a ticket to his home destination or a small sum of money to face the world. On the other hand, in the countries where parole exists, an attempt is made to place the man in a job before he is paroled. Why should not that principle be extended to the discharged man?

The Progressive Stage System. The device of progressive stages toward release invented by Sir Joshua Jebb and Maconochie so long ago has made very little progress since. Today it is to be found in the Philippines, in Switzerland, and in India. In the Philippines the Iwahig penal colony is a step in that direction. As we have seen, certain men are selected from Bilibid after careful training there, and intensive study of the individual, to be placed in this colony without walls, with few guards, and with a large degree of self-government. Here they learn to control themselves and adapt their conduct to the condition of free citizens. In Switzerland, the colony of Witzwil is itself a step toward freedom. The building of cottages in which these men may live after they are discharged before they go out into the world is a further step, although it does not apply to a great many of the men released. Again, in India we have seen that in the reformatory settlements for the criminal tribes, men, according to their conduct, are released from the most closely guarded condition gradually by steps in freedom until they are discharged. In the reformatory settlements they gradually work their way out by good conduct to the comparative freedom of life outside the fence. Furthermore, one may be transferred from the reformatory settlement either to an industrial settlement or to an agricultural settlement. Since these last two types of settlements are very much more lenient in the discipline of the inmates than the reformatory settlement, they again represent a progressive stage toward release. From one point of view, the placing of prisoners outside the prison walls upon farms and the use of the trusty system in some of our American prisons are steps in the same direction. However, a large part of the prisoners in our American prisons never have a chance at this stage of comparative freedom. They go directly, on their discharge, from within the prison walls to free life on the outside. The parole system also represents a progressive stage system in a sense. From every point of view this is a most desirable device. Nevertheless, for many of the men an intermediate stage is desirable where they are more closely restricted than is possible upon parole. Doubtless if in all of our prisons we had an intermediate stage of comparative freedom, yet under the watchful eyes of the officials of the prison, many more of the paroled men would do better than they do at the present time.

Prison Labor. One of the most difficult problems which prison authorities have had to solve is that of prison labor. The difficulty lies in the fact that not only must the prisoners be kept as busy as possible, but they must be engaged in labor which does not compete unduly or unfairly with free labor. Furthermore, if possible, it must be a kind of work which will train the man for a job on the outside. And again, so far as possible, it must be labor which will return a good profit to the prison. Now, with all these objectives in view, the problem is very difficult. Often the desire for profitable employment within the prison is directly opposed to the ideal of training for a job. Moreover, the desire for profit does not always go on all fours with the ideal of not competing unfairly with free labor. Hence the task of adjusting these various ideals to one another is one of the most difficult problems in connection with the administration of prisons. Usually what happens is that one or two of these objectives will be pursued to the neglect of the other. Perhaps the one which is primary in the minds of the prison officials is that all inmates should be kept employed. From this point of view the prison systems of the Philippines, of Japan, of Ceylon, of Switzerland, and of our Southern states are outstanding. At the opposite extreme are some of our American state prisons, where from a third to a half or more of the inmates are idle. In the attempt to get away from competition of free labor, some of our legislators have laid down conditions which practically result in a large proportion of the prisoners being idle. Such a policy results in the increased difficulty of discipline, adds to the personal demoralization of the prisoners, places a greater burden for the support of the prisons upon the tax-payers, prevents teaching these men a trade, and violates every other principle of prison labor. Careful study of the matter has shown that unless prison labor is carefully managed, a prison industry may, by unfair competition, drive out of existence free labor in certain industries. A study of the matter by the United States Bureau of Labor a number of years ago showed that the making of hollow-ware in prisons and the making of cooperage ware drove out of existence the free manufacturers of these articles. What is needed at the present time is a careful study of the whole matter so as to ascertain what lines of industry in free society are likely to be injured by prison industry. Furthermore, the demand that the prison shall pay as much as possible of its way often militates against the ideal of training men for a trade. Frequently the industries in our prisons which are profitable are not proper trades in which the man can engage on the outside. For example, while knitted wear does not compete, so far as I can find, seriously with free labor, nevertheless, most of the men who are following this trade in the prison can find no employment on the outside because it is a trade which in free society employs chiefly women and girls. In England, the sewing of mail sacks, a state-use system of prison labor, while it does not compete with men in free society, is absolutely useless as a trade when the man is discharged. In none of the countries studied has this matter of prison labor been carefully worked out. All of them are going at it in more or less of a haphazard way, and without any thorough knowledge of the whole situation. While the state-use system has been recommended by union labor, no single state in the world, so far as I know, has worked out the matter yet in such a way as to make state use a practical proposal.

Profitable Employment upon the Land. Possibly because there has been less organized opposition on the part of farmers to the raising of agricultural products, the prison authorities have found in this field less opposition than in any other. Hence, the enormous growth in the last few years of the size of prison farms in this country and the development of farm colonies for prisoners in the Philippines, in India, in Switzerland, in Belgium, and in the Southern states of the United States. The Iwahig penal colony in the Philippines is largely an agricultural colony. What industries it possesses are chiefly incidental. Again, the prison farms in the Southern United States are a good illustration. In India, the Criminal Tribes Settlements are either agricultural in their nature or the inmates work in industries as any free citizen. Up to date there has been no serious objection to this plan in that country. A few of the reformatory settlements have industries of their own and sell the products in the open market. The number of these, however, is small, and the amount of the product is negligible. Again, in Switzerland, the Witzwil penal colony is primarily an agricultural colony. Its products compete with the products of free farmers in the open market. Nevertheless, so far there has been no objection to this procedure. The same situation exists in Belgium, except that in the shops at Merxplas are produced articles which compete in the open market either through contractors or by the prisons selling the product with the products of free labor. In the Southern prison farms the products of the land and of the factories compete with the products of free labor either through the contractor or through the prisons selling the products upon the open market. So far as the manufacture of cotton goods, shoes, and clothing are concerned, the amount is so small and manufacturing in the South so undeveloped as yet, that there has been no serious objection. With the growing class consciousness, however, of the farmers, it remains to be seen how soon serious objection to prison-produced farm products will arise. In all of these problems of prison production, what is needed at the present time is careful study of the entire situation to ascertain the proportion of goods put upon the market by prison industries, what part this amount plays in the entire output, whether they are marketed in an unfair way, and what is the effect upon the price level of all goods in the respective fields. There is also needed continuous experimentation on the basis of these facts in order that a system of prison labor so diversified as to fit the training needs of the institution, and so profitable as to contribute to the upkeep of the institution that the present objections and those that may arise in the future may be obviated.

Selection of Prison Officials. Some of these experiments which we have studied in different countries of the world show serious attempts to select prison officials for their capacity in discharging the duties committed to them. In this respect our survey has shown that Japan, India, Switzerland, and England take greater care than the other countries we studied. In India and England all of them are under civil service. Civil service in these two countries has become so well established that no one would think of questioning it. In Japan and Switzerland, while it is done somewhat differently, the ideals of efficiency are such that great emphasis is placed upon the capacity of the men chosen to head these penal institutions. Here are examples that may well be taken to heart by the governing authorities of our American states. There is evidence that in some of our states wardens and other prison officials are not selected to pay political debts. In most of our states, however, that can not be truly said. Consequently, prison officials change with each change in the state administration. This is a matter to which more serious attention might well be given in our American states.

Training of Prison Officials. Japan stands out as the one country we have studied which devotes itself seriously to the training of prison officials. The two sets of courses which she assiduously pursues and which she forces all of her prison officials to take, are of the very greatest significance. In this matter she has set an example for the entire world. England and a few other countries have made a tentative beginning of the training of prison officials but have not gone very far in the matter. For the rest of the world, practically nothing is done. In most states of the United States the salaries of the prison guards are so low that very poor material must, of course, be obtained. Whatever training they get is got upon the job. This combination of the lack of proper training and the haphazard method of selecting officials produces its results in the rapid turnover among the prison guards and in the mechanical and repressive attitude which they manifest. One would suppose that so difficult is this task, especially if we hold in view the ideal that these prison officials are to prepare these men to go out into life again, that one wonders why we do not require at least as careful inspection of their qualifications as we do of elementary school-teachers. Apparently, according to our notion, almost anybody who has a good physique is eligible to become a prison guard. Why should not these prison officials be selected for their arduous duties according to standards that take into account the difficult tasks they have to perform? Why should we not give them the training which will prepare them somewhat for the difficult task of endeavoring to reform distorted personalities?

Keeping Intact the Economic and Social Ties. From the beginning of the prison system in the United States up until recently the ideal seemed to be to cut every tie which bound the man to the economic and social organization in free society when once he was sent to prison. His labor was forfeit to the state. In the early Pennsylvania system he was allowed to see no one and to hear from no one except the warden and the chaplain. From the time that he was incarcerated until he was released, no word was allowed to reach him concerning the condition of his family. He had no share in the products of his labor. He was housed, fed, clothed, warmed, ministered to if sick, without any reference to his economic production. He was denied every opportunity for the exercise of social qualities. Even speech was denied him. This rule of silence continues in many of our prisons at the present time, both here and abroad. In later times he has been allowed to receive a few letters a month. He is permitted a visit once in so often provided his conduct has been good. The theory at the bottom of this was that men had become delinquent in the ordinary human association. They would change him from a criminal to a useful citizen by cutting off all these contacts, and by denying him the exercise of his human propensities in these lines. If the theory had actually worked, no one could object to it. Yet the history of the past hundred years in prison management has shown that that theory is essentially unsound. Cut off from human contacts and human interests, what was left to these men but to turn in upon themselves? What could we expect but that such men should lose their reason, degenerate morally, become perverted, lose ambition, and become mentally and socially demoralized? Strange that it never occurred to our prison authorities that what these men needed was training in social life and in economic independence. If they had failed economically, why should they not receive training in economic relationships, rather than be denied every opportunity for the exercise of themselves in economic adjustment? Why not make the prison community a social organization for the training of these men in human relationships when confessedly that was where they had failed? Prison authorities have been strangely blind to such fundamental considerations. However, step by step, in the interest of discipline primarily, many of these rigid requirements have been relaxed. Visits are permitted as a reward for good conduct. Letters may be written; in certain institutions studies may be pursued; library privileges are granted; and recently a movement has begun to provide the opportunity for a prison wage for these men. Even today, however, less than half of our prisons in this country allow men to earn anything. The few visits which these men are permitted to receive are but slight mitigations of the severity of denying them all their contacts with friends and family. The endeavor to force these men to live in a social vacuum results in all kinds of evil activities. Man is a social animal; his social impulses will not be denied. If he cannot keep intact the ties which bind him on the outside, he is forced back to a community of spirit with those within. Hence, the convict solidarity which results in so many evils now complained of by the prison authorities. They have reaped what they have sown and wonder why.

In only two countries in the world are the social ties of a man with his family kept intact, in the Philippines and in India. In the Philippines this is a special privilege for about 90 men out of 2000 in the colony at Iwahig. They are permitted to take their families with them and to live there with them in normal social relationships. Their children go to the same schools as those attended by the children of the officers. The convict and his family live in their own hut on a piece of land granted them by the government.   They make their own family arrangements.   On the other hand, in India, if a man has a family, as the result of experience with the settlement, the family is brought into the settlement with him.   The experiment has shown that escapes are very much lessened by this plan; through the children a reorganization of the man's outlook on life may be accomplished, and the whole family may be trained to a new outlook.

Moreover, in the Iwahig Philippine colony and in the Indian settlement for the criminal tribes, economically each man is on his own feet.   He must make his own living for himself and his family.   His standard of living, as on the outside, depends upon his own efforts.   He is assisted and trained in doing that task, but the motives which moved him on the outside are not destroyed.   The economic motive is kept intact in the Philippines even for the men who do not have their families. After the first six months they must make their own living. What that living shall be depends upon their own efforts. The results show that these experiments in training men for the ordinary relationships of life in free society are very much worth while.   We wonder that it has taken us a hundred years to learn it and that the discovery has been made in lands like the Philippines and India.

As I watched the negroes on those farms in the South, I wondered why some such arrangement could not be made there.   I see no reason why with careful thought and attention to this matter, that many of these negroes with families could not be located in villages on this land and the family treated as a unit.   Long ago we have learned in family social work that the only way to consider the family is as a unit.   The child does not live in a social vacuum; it lives in social relationships. The man must be considered in view of his whole family situation.   Why should not that principle apply to prisoners so far as possible?

Indefinite Sentences.   Nowhere more than in penal treatment can we see the enormous force of tradition, and nowhere is there a better illustration of Bagehot's concept of "Cake of Custom." Coming down from our classical penology was the theory that such and such a crime should be punished by such a definite length of imprisonment. Both Beccaria and Bentham insisted that crime should be classified and punishment likewise classified to meet the crime. It was assumed that by some God-given prerogative a legislature could set down in the statutes just the amount of punishment that was necessary to expiate a given crime, without reference to the differences between individuals. It was assumed that each individual would suffer exactly the same. Did ever more sad psychology obtain such century-long adherence? Practically everywhere, with some modifications due to the Neo-Classical School, such a penal theory still remains. True, we have modified the original rigidity of the scheme by giving to the judge the possibility of sentencing between the minimum and the maximum. However, we have still kept the maximum, and in most states that does not extend to life. The absolutely indefinite sentence is nowhere to be found. The limited indefinite sentence is to be found in England, Ceylon, and the United States, and to a less degree in some of the other countries. Gradually we are coming to the state of mind that can see that it is impossible for us beforehand to have that omniscience to enable us to say how long a man should be kept in prison before he is returned to free society. Perhaps some day we shall come to the place where we shall commit a man to a penal and correctional institution until such time as certain authorities decide he is fit to return to society. We do that now with the insane and with the feeble-minded. Why are we more fearful to do it with the criminal? Every criminal authority will tell you that each year hundreds of men are discharged at the expiration of their sentences when every indication is that they are not ready to go out, and that they will inevitably return. The statistics on recidivism are indications of the unwisdom of allowing many of these men their freedom.

In England and Ceylon attempts have been made to correct this situation by means of the so-called preventive detention. As we have seen, for men who have been convicted four times for non-bailable offenses, there is provided an additional sentence of from five to ten years in an institution for preventive detention in order thus to protect society from their depredations. The working of preventive detention, however, only suggests that further steps should be taken. England's experience has shown without a doubt that most of these men sentenced to preventive detention should never be let out again, or if so, only after they have shown unmistakable signs of reformation.

In this study we gave no attention to the question of criminal procedure in the various countries. In no one of them, however, did we find any attempt to restrict the function of the court to ascertaining the guilt or innocence of the party accused of crime. The result, however, of all of these experiments in criminal procedure based upon the Classical and Neo-Classical penal theories, leads to certain questions which must be faced. There is no reason any longer why the legislature should have the sole power to determine how long a man should be put apart from his fellows. Actual administration by the legislature has long ago been given up in economic matters. In our most progressive states, Industrial Commissions, Railroad Commissions, Tax Commissions have been set up by the legislature to take over the administrative duties once exercised by the legislature, because of the conviction that no legislature was wise enough to determine beforehand, by statute, the regulation of all the multiple details which come up in connection with our industrial life. Hence, the legislature has confined itself to the function of declaring the purposes, the policies, in broad terms, which the state will follow out with reference to the control of these matters. It has then placed the administration of these matters, in accordance with those broad policies worked out by the legislature, in the hands of commissions, giving them abundant authority to regulate the details which no human foresight could anticipate. Why should not the same theory prevail in connection with the punishment of the criminal? What human being, or group of human beings, has the wisdom to know beforehand just what treatment is necessary to accord to the prisoner, protect society, and to return him to society a useful man? Therefore, almost ten years ago, I proposed that the whole theory back of our criminal law should be changed. It should be the function of the court to determine only the guilt or innocence of the man charged with crime. Even in doing that many changes are necessary, as England has already found. The legislature would then set out the broad policy that the purpose of depriving a man charged with crime of his liberty is to protect society and to give that man such treatment as will return him to freedom a socialized individual. Then let the legislature set up a commission for penal treatment or correctional treatment into whose hands are committed these men found guilty by the court. This commission should then have the authority to determine, on the basis of a careful study of the man and his entire history, into what kind of an institution he should be placed. If the evidence shows that he is insane, then into an institution for the criminal insane he should be placed, and kept there, as he is today, until he is fit to return without danger. If he is a hardened criminal, then he should be placed in another institution in which, on the basis of a careful study of his individual characteristics and his past history, a treatment would be given him the purpose of which would be to change his point of view, his outlook upon life, and his whole attitude toward himself and his fellows. If he is an individual who has just made a mistake, this commission could then see that he is placed either on probation or in some institution where he is given training for a time in the hope of returning him to society a more useful citizen. Those men who are irreformable would be kept in safety and society would be protected. On the other hand, those who are not dangerous individuals would, after proper reconditioning, be given their freedom because there is no danger from them. In this way many of the evils of keeping a man in an institution too long simply because the law provides for such a sentence would be done away with, and the institution would have a chance to do its maximum work on the lessened number of individuals which would be entrusted to its care.

INDEX

313

ployees, 179; rules for prisoners of, 180; education in, 182; diversity of agriculture in, 185; finances of, 187.

Switzerland, origin and development of correctional idea in, 166; penal system of, 165 ff.

System, Prison, of Japan, 6; of Ceylon, 66, 70, 102; of England, 218; of England and Wales, present, 218; Progressive Stage, 300; of the Philippines, 62; in some Southern states of the United States, 257; comparison of Southern with Northern, 279; comparison of Southern with Oriental and Old World experiments, 287.

Thames, Mr., 280, 286.
Trachselwald Reformatory, 168.
Training of prison officials, 99, 305.
Tribes of India, Criminal, 105; numbers in, 106; characteristic crimes of, 108; wandering and settled, 106; first attempts to deal with, 110.
Tribesmen, physical, mental and social condition of, 107.
Tucker, Booth, 123.
Types of settlement provided, 115.

United States, some Southern prison systems in, 257; comparison of Southern with Northern prison systems, 279.

Vagrants, colony for at Merxplas, 201; history of colony for, 201; organiza-

tion of colony for, 203; purpose of colony for, 203; classification in, 205; labor and salary in colony for, 204.
Vandervelde, Mr., 192.
Victorio, Director, 47, 49, 53, 51, 54, 57.
Vilain XIV, Count, 190.
Visapur Settlement in India, 120.

Wages of employees of Swiss Correctional Colony, 179.
Walker, Mr., 104.
Wandering and settled tribes of India, 106.
Welikada Prison, 70, 75, 76, 92, 93, 94, 100, 102.
Wetumpka Prison Farm, 274.
Witzwil, the Swiss Correctional Colony, 165; description of, 168, 169; extent and character of the land, 169; products raised on the land, 169; cost of, 170; employees and inmates of, 171; discipline of institution, 174; guards of, 177; foremen of, 178; wages of employees of, 179; rules for prisoners of, 180; education in, 182; industries of, 182.
Women prisoners of Ceylon, 75.
Wood, Governor-General, 57.
Wright, Luke, 57.

Young English prisoners, separate institutions for, 233.

Zamboanga, 61.

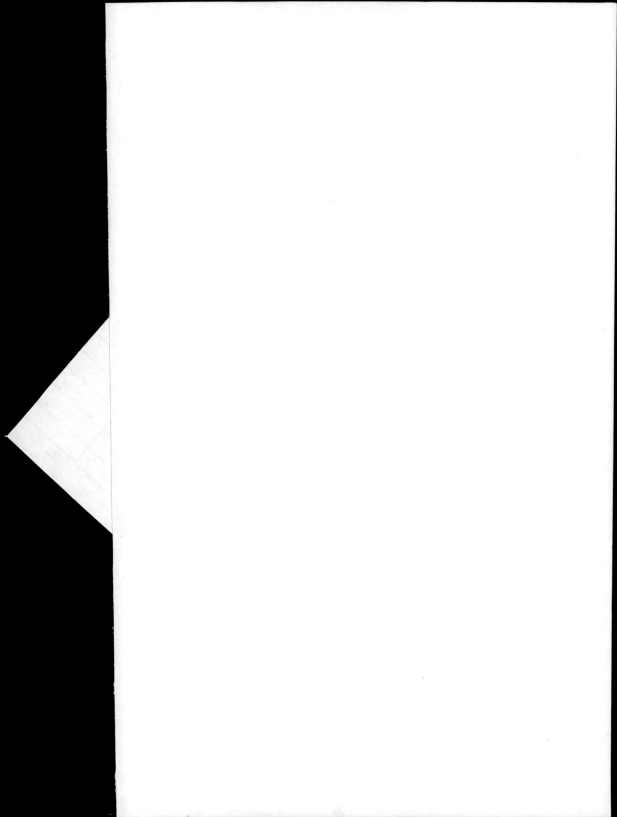

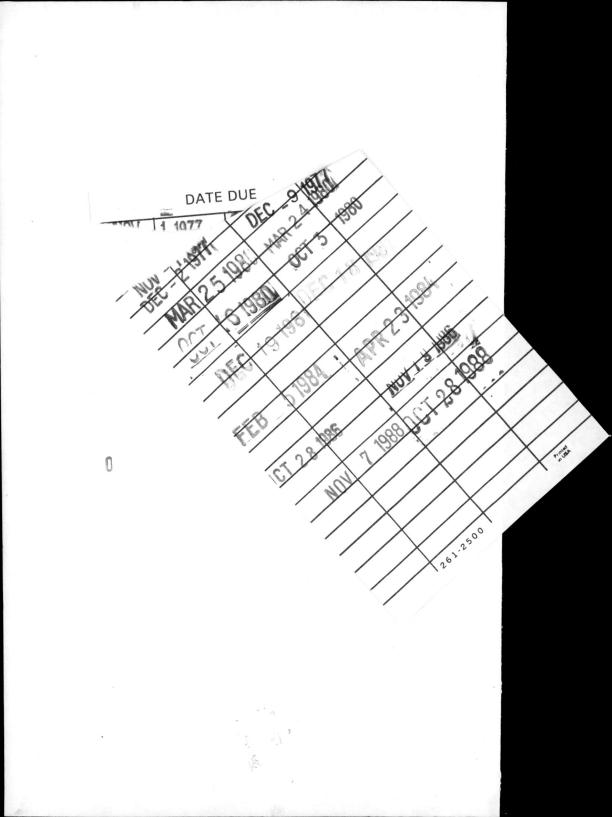

0